The Art and Craft Book

Compiled by Henry Pluckrose

 Evans Brothers Limited London

Published by
Evans Brothers Limited, Montague House,
Russell Square, London, W.C.1.

© Evans Brothers Limited 1969
First published 1969

Printed in Great Britain by
Fletcher & Son Ltd.,
Norwich
237 35141 2   PR 2058

Contents

Introduction

This book is, in effect, an anthology made from some recent issues of *Art and Craft in Education*. To select from the vast range of material which was available was not easy—and the reader might well wonder why his favourite craft has not been featured. Thus the inveterate tatter or weaver, colour block expert or screen printer might well put this volume down in disgust—indeed I would advise him not to read on for this book is not for him.

Rather it is for the non-expert—the mother who, faced with six long weeks of summer holidays, cries out for some ideas on how to occupy John and Mary before the blessed tranquility of school time returns, or who needs help to fill those wearying days of convalescence after some childhood illness when Peter is well enough to be difficult and tiresome at home but not yet fit enough for school. It is at times like these that paper bags, drinking straws, match boxes and fabric scraps come into their own—a sort of manna from heaven for the mother who is prepared for a little mess in return for a modicum of peace.

But I feel this selection will also appeal to hard-pressed teachers, those who were trained for Juniors yet find themselves with reception class infants or those whose first love is English but find that teaching also involves for them Art with 3B and 2D on Monday and Wednesday afternoons. Now I could be altruistic and philosophical about this (and quite dishonest!) and suggest that teachers are never depressed by such a situation and are all brimful of ideas on such varied topics as art, craft, creative writing, free movement, music and modern maths. But from personal experience I know this is not so.

Progress in the field of education is now so rapid that it is virtually impossible for us to keep abreast of every modern development—and this is particularly true in the realm of art materials where new paints and modelling materials are continually being marketed. As the editor of *Art and Craft in Education* I receive weekly requests for mundane details of such things as synthetic modelling clays (page 161), cold water dyes (page 140) acrylic paints (page 61) and display techniques (page 41) as well as for information on open plan schools or the philosophy underlying particular educational developments. These latter requests, are not as common as the former, but the very fact that they are made at all suggests that to a certain extent we must provide for these more specific interests in the magazine and in this anthology.

Thus I would suggest that here is a book which has much to offer to a wide variety of people. Those of us who work with children will find it rich in ideas and ideals; those who want to understand a little better what Patricia does in school that makes her come home each evening splattered with paint and clay will at least be able to face her teacher on equal terms; those engaged in youth work (from cub and brownie to sophisticated youth clubber) are here provided for with plans for group work and corporate projects, and for the parent suggestions of all the things which might be attempted to give Fred or Janet something better to do at home than simply sit and watch television.

Picasso when asked what was a work of art, is said to have replied 'What isn't?' The four year old daubing paint or using egg boxes, the seven year old experimenting with cut paper shapes, the mum decorating a cake, Grandma making mats from rope and raffia, all are contributing something of themselves to the activity, even though the results may not be world shattering.

Art is doing,

Try some.

Henry Pluckrose
July 1969

Henry Pluckrose is the editor of *Art and Craft in Education* and has therefore been responsible for the selection of the pieces included in this volume. Although he is concerned with writing and the world of books (he has written over a dozen hard backs and technical pamphlets) he is essentially a teacher, working full time in a London school.

Making Dolls and Puppets With wire

Doll making is a popular activity with children of all ages and requires little expensive material or complicated equipment.

This small wire doll lends itself to a variety of uses; it can be a plaything, a mascot, a puppet, a model for costume display, an actor in a model theatre. As the foundation is wire it can be bent into any shape as required so it will perch or sit easily. When standing, a piece of cardboard given two loops of bead elastic for the feet will be necessary. Once the framework is finished the dressing of it is as for any doll and the clothes can be stitched on unless a change is required.

Suitable wire is garden wire which can be bought in coils very cheaply and is covered with plastic. This is the right thickness for bending with the fingers and will not rust. It cuts with secateurs or old scissors. To make a doll 7 in. high cut two pieces, one 9 in. long for arms, the other 22 in. Fold the long piece in two and twist a round about the size of a penny for a head. Make 4 twists for the neck, then insert the arm wire and continue twisting for 2 in. of the body. Divide for the legs and at each end of the wire make a loop about an inch long for feet and twist up the ends. Loop the hands in the same way.

Now cover the wire frame with skin-coloured felt. This has to be done piecemeal but the joins will not show under the clothes. Draw round the wire head allowing $\frac{1}{8}$ in. all round for sewing. Pad the head centre with cotton wool and seam round the edges as invisibly as possible. The face can be embroidered on or suggested with crayon and a ball point pen. Both arms can be covered together. Again allow $\frac{1}{8}$ in. all round but cut double with the fold coming over the arm top. Nick the felt at the body twist to fold over neatly. The legs must be cut separately, also the feet and body portion. To give an impression of shoes add a piece of black felt when completed, either sticking or stitching it on. The feet can be then bent at right angles.

Hair can be made from double knitting wool which is a good thickness. Cut the required length and stick on with glue into any style. Any bits and pieces of felt, silk, cotton or woollen material make the clothes. Do not stitch on too tightly as play must be allowed for the doll to go into action. This is the kind of doll that gets a mate for the second is easier to make than the first and a family is soon born.

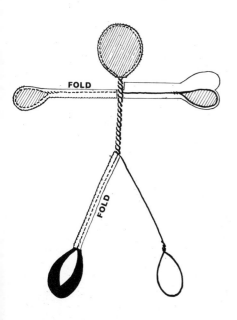

With String

Materials:
String

Scraps of felt or cloth for hands and feet

2 pieces of cloth about 7 in. x 7½ in. for dress or trousers

1 cotton reel for head.

Cut: 1 length of string 2 ft. 4 in. for legs
1 length of string 1 ft. 3 in. for arms
1 length of string 9 in. or more for hair.

Cut: from pattern 2 in. felt for feet
                 4 in. felt for hands.

Cut: from pattern 2 in. cloth for dress or trousers.

Instructions:
Glue the felt feet on to the two ends of the piece of string 2 ft. 4 in. and the hands on the piece 1 ft. 3 in.

Make a reef knot by looping method with the two pieces of string.

The short piece of string for hair is put through the loop of the reef knot (see drawing of string body).

The cotton reel is then painted and the hair pulled through, glued, and the strands of string are separated to look like hair.

The dress or trousers should be glued where indicated on pattern and placed on the body.

The dolls or puppets are so light that a piece of cotton or wool can make them dance if placed at the back of the dress.

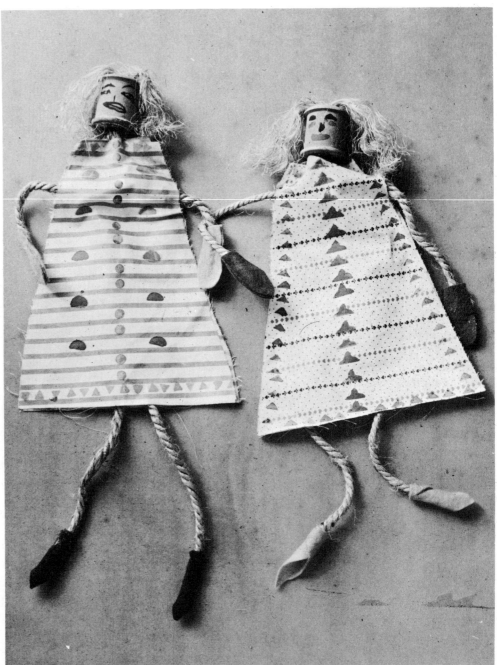

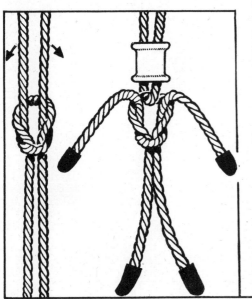

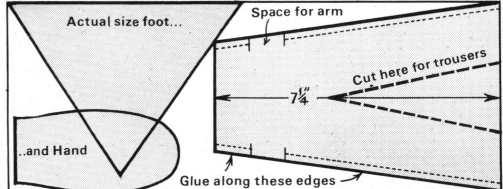

Actual size foot...

...and Hand

Space for arm

Cut here for trousers

7¼"

Glue along these edges

With Polystyrene and Wire

Mardel, a high grade Polystyrene marketed by **Margros Limited,** that is now available for use in schools, enables pupils to make and work at various crafts of which the following is an example.

These are simple lay figures made with Mardel, thin wire (20 gauge) and white adhesive tape.

Fig. 1 (p. 12) shows the proportion of block shapes cut from Mardel to form the figure.

Parts A, B, C and D are made 2 in. thick by joining two pieces of thick Mardel with Marvin Painting Medium (notice B and D are of exact proportions, D being cut down the centre to form the upper parts of the legs tapering to 1 in. square at the knee; part E is made with 1 in. thick Mardel tapering to ½ in. square at the ankle.

Figure 2 gives the side view showing the cutting at the front to form the chest and the shaping of the head and back. It also shows how the wire is looped around the back of the head and twisted double to the base of the torso where it is divided half way to right and left and fastened down with tape at right angles to the base of the torso. See Figs. 3 and 4. Care should be taken to make the wire armature quite long enough for its purpose. Any extra length can easily be cut with scissors at the finishing stages.

For the proportions of the model in this diagram, about 40 in. length of wire would be ample. This is doubled to form a loop for the head, then twisted tightly until it reaches the base of the spine. To insert the wire in position, both parts of the body are placed front downwards and cut about ½ in. inwards

right down the centre. This forms a sort of backbone when the double wire is inserted leaving enough length for the neck. The head having been shaped properly is then placed inside the loop, until the wire encircles the top and comes down to be pressed under the jaw.

The looped wire can then be made tighter by turning the head many times until the wire for the neck is tightly twisted. This also enables the short column for the neck to be placed into position after cutting it through to the centre.

This can then be made more secure by squeezing it tightly and wrapping adhesive tape around it.

The wire for the arms is now attached by encircling it around the base of the neck, pulling it tightly on either side

and fixing it down at the shoulders with tape as in Fig. 3. Care should be taken at this stage to ensure that the wire on either side comes down to knee length or more as it has to be looped to give the arms their right proportion and to enable the hands to be attached with adhesive tape as in Fig. 3.

All the various parts of the model are rubbed down to shape on a sheet of medium rough glass paper fixed to a board. This will prove a much easier method than holding a piece of material in one hand and a piece of glass paper in the other.

The parts for the legs and arms should be rubbed from end to end at the corners in an oblique position until these elongated cubes become cylindrical in shape, tapering at the wrists and ankles.

The chest, head and back parts of the body, after being cut to shape, are best rubbed on the glass paper in the opposite direction, i.e. to and fro. After the arms and legs are smoothed to shape, the wire is attached by cutting each part with a razor blade or sharp knife to the exact centre, so that when the wire is inserted it will appear to emerge from the centre at each end. Each cylinder is then encircled with a piece of adhesive tape closing tightly at each end. Before finally fixing the adhesive tape to wrists and ankles the complete limbs are slid into position at the shoulders and torso. The wire is then looped to attach the hands and feet. Care should be taken to make these loops identical pairs, and to have about an extra inch of wire left to insert with the main piece before applying the final piece of adhesive tape (Fig. 3 and 4). Hands and feet can then be cut and shaped and attached to the looped wire, Fig. 3.

The lay figure being now complete, cotton wool can be added where any padding may seem necessary and muslin strips wrapped tightly round any parts of the figure to enable any sewing or needlework to be done with regard to the appropriate costumes that may be chosen.

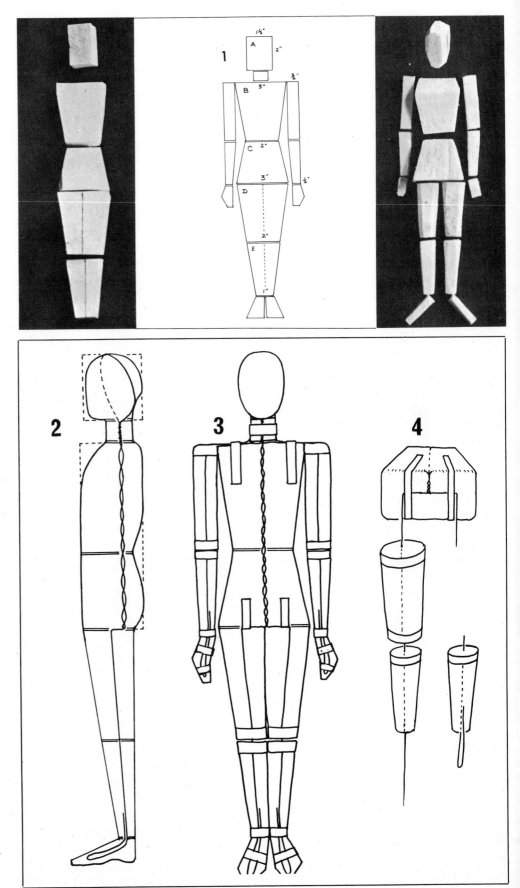

Puppets from Junk

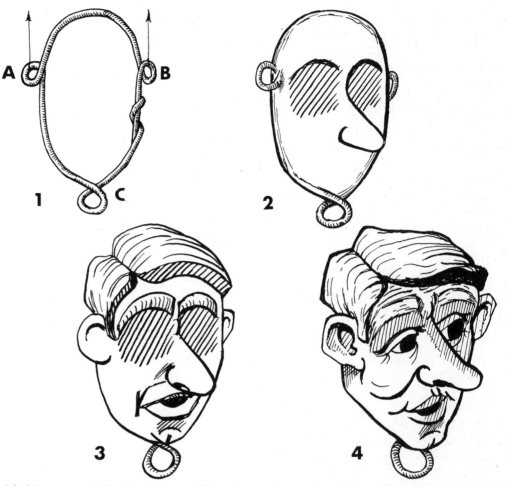

A puppet head

1. Take a length of wire and twist it to the shape shown in Fig. 1. The head strings are attached later to the two loops at A and B. The loop C is the neck joint. Take a ball of clay (garden clay will suffice) and model the features of the puppet. The clay should fit inside the wire frame.

2. Press in the eye-sockets, using the thumbs. Pull out the shape for the nose. Make sure to over-emphasize the features.

3. Firmly apply rolls of clay for the eyebrows and upper and lower lips. Add further rolls of clay for the hair and ears.

4. Finish the details with a modelling tool, pencil, or piece of wood.

Cover the clay puppet head with several layers of small pieces of paper, using flour paste or cellulose adhesive. Now paint the head using poster paints, which can be varnished, or use oil or emulsion paint. Remember that the two head strings have to be fitted later—so leave a small part of the wire at A and B showing.

A puppet body

Bend the wire to the required shape for the shoulders and arms. In Fig. 5, the body is of wire only and is covered with strips of paper. In Fig. 6, the body consists of two cardboard boxes joined together by pasting newspaper over them. The shoulder wire is pushed through the boxes. The feet can be made of papier mâché, clay covered with paper, or blocks of wood. The hands are made of wire covered with papier mâché, or cardboard. Strips of paper are pasted and rolled around the arms and legs to give them a sufficient thickness. Remember to keep the joints free from any paper.

Puppet hands

Wire hands are easily covered with strips of paper and painted (Figs. 7a and 7b).

Hands made of cardboard can be joined to the arm by means of a paper clip, or a piece of bent wire, Fig. 8.

Puppet feet

The wire feet are covered with papier mâché, or modelled in clay and then covered with paper. Alternatively, a wooden block can be used, though it is advisable to weight the feet of the puppet by nailing on a thin strip of lead, Figs. 9a, 9b and 9c.

A simple cardboard puppet

For 7 and 8 year olds a puppet may be constructed from strong cardboard and paper clips. A template could be used if desired for the card shapes of the limbs. A simple head shape may be made from card, too. The construction can be seen from Fig. 11; paper clips or string being used to join the limbs. This simple puppet would serve as an admirable introduction to the realm of puppetry for the young child. There is no difficult modelling or wire bending to do.

The head should be painted with poster paints and simple clothes made for the puppet. Six strings are sufficient: two from the head, two from the hands and two from the knees. In Fig. 11, a simple puppet control is shown. The two strings attached to the knees are fixed to the movable arm. The control is held in the left hand and the movable arm C is held in the right. When the arm C is moved forwards, the puppet walks. There is a hole in the centre of the arm C and this fits over a screw or nail, so that the arm is supported on the main control when not in use.

A puppet from wood

A simple puppet may be made from blocks of wood for the body and suitable lengths of dowel rods for the limbs. Screw hooks are used throughout. Fig. 12.

Individual clothing for the puppets should be made, each puppet representing a different character: clown, tramp, policeman, pirate, etc. Certain puppets, spacemen, circus strongmen and boxers are best left as a wooden painted body.

Punch and Judy (Fox Photos)

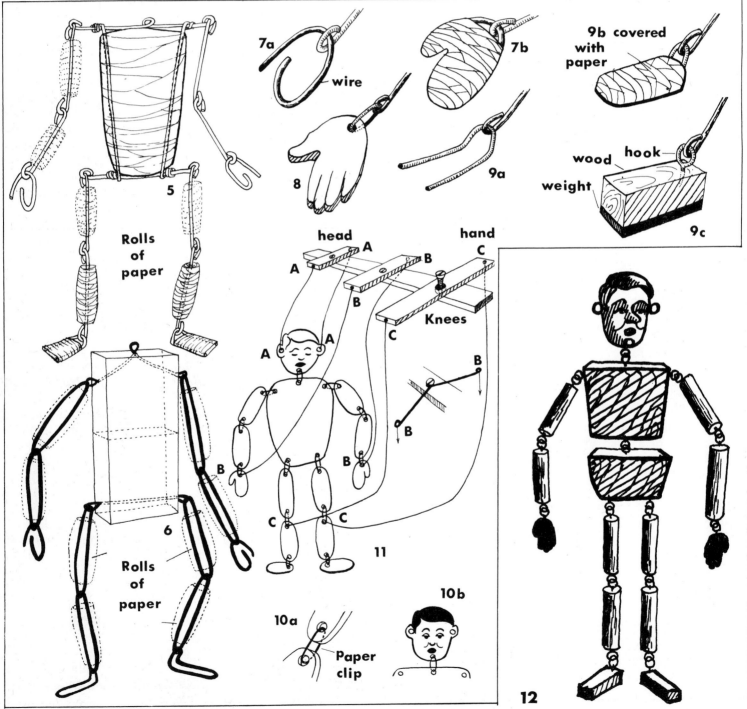

7a   wire

7b

9b covered with paper

8

9a

wood   hook

weight

9c

Rolls of paper

5

head   hand

A   A   B   C

A   B

       C   Knees

A   A

B

B   B

B   B

C   C

11

B

6

Rolls of paper

10a   Paper clip

10b

12

14

Constructing a puppet from wire and cloth

Pieces of scrap wire can be used to construct a frame, which is easily clothed and completed with accessories.

This is a simple method to construct a marionette and is especially suitable for 11–14 year olds. Firstly, a head should be constructed with a wire framework (see Fig. 1). Cover the framework with strips of newspaper. Actually, any type of papier mâché head would be suitable, provided that the head incorporates a bent piece of wire attached to the body (see Fig. 1). The shoulders are made by bending a thick piece of wire to the shape shown in Fig. 2. This joint is used throughout the construction of the puppet. A piece of cloth, sewn together to form a movable joint (Fig. 3), is used to join the limbs and movable parts. The hands and feet are constructed of a framework of wire and any pliable material (Plasticine, clay, etc.) is placed inside. It is then covered with paper mâché (see Figs. 4 and 5). The complete figure is shown in Fig. 6.

Constructing a puppet from wire

Take a length of iron wire and twist it to the shape shown in Fig. 7 so that a loop is formed at each end. This is the basic wire shape needed to construct the puppet. Vary the lengths of the wire shapes according to the required size of the puppet.

Loop the shapes together to form the puppet (Fig. 8). Join the two cross-pieces at A and B with thin, pliable copper wire. The head, hands and feet can be constructed in any way; but a loop is needed to join them to the puppet body. The control strings are attached at C, D and E. A further string may be placed at F if the puppet is required to bend.

Constructing a puppet from rolled paper

This method is best for clowns, tramps, etc.—indeed any figure which does not need to stand up erect.

Roll up newspaper until it is shaped to the required limb (Fig. 9). Put two holes at either end and slot the string through. Tie up to the next limb (Fig. 10). The body and limbs are constructed alike, and can be reinforced with string (Fig. 11). The hands and feet are made similar to the limbs; but are slightly smaller and fatter. All the joints are the same. The complete puppet is shown in Fig. 12. The clothes can be made loosely fitting. This will give more character to the puppets.

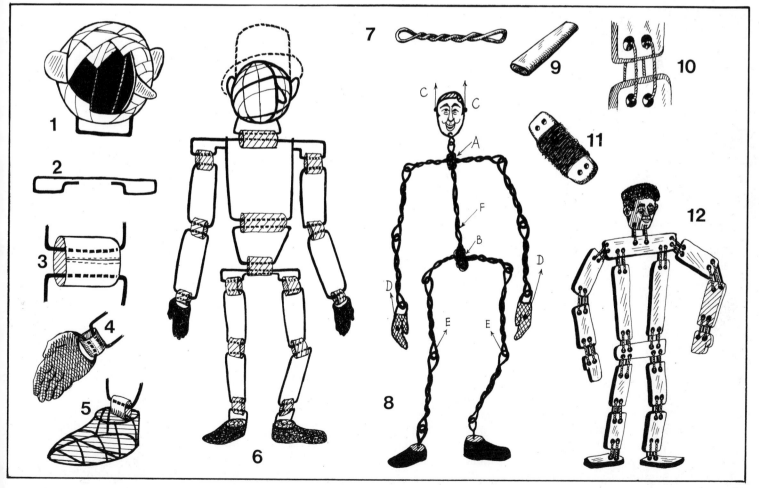

Papier mâché

Papier mâché in its various forms is very useful for puppet heads, hands and feet. Its application is almost unlimited. The usual method of preparation is to place torn paper into a bowl; flour paste and water can be added and mixed to give a plastic mass which is readily moulded into the required shape; this sets quite hard. With the addition of sawdust and wood shavings, the result is a thicker modelling composition.

The torn paper can be saturated with glue size and the resultant pulp strengthened with sawdust and wood shavings in the same way as the previous composition. The foregoing preparatory methods enable the puppet's features to be modelled as in modelling with clay.

Modelling a puppet head from papier mâché composition

The puppet head is an important and basic essential for the creation of a good puppet; so it is opportune to describe some basic methods. The methods are simple and require very little equipment, so are especially suited to children's needs. The puppet head is a suitable introduction for the children into the realm of puppetry.

Firstly, a tube is required for the base (Fig. 1). This is easily made from thick paper (preferably of two or three pieces pasted together), using flour paste. The tube is then wrapped around the index finger to ensure a good fit. The modelling composition is put on to the top part of the tube, to form a base for the head (Fig. 2). Figs. 3 to 6 show the stages of modelling a puppet head from papier mâché composition. It is modelled in the same way as the clay puppet head. The features should be made quite large and exaggerated. The glove puppet head may be joined to a cloth body with tape or thick embroidery silk. The hands of the glove puppet are made from stout cardboard, painted and sewn into position. This type of simple glove puppet may be made successfully by almost any age group.

Modelling a puppet head from strips of paper

Wind a tube of stiff paper for the base (Fig. 7). This is held firmly together with a strip of paper or thin wire wound approximately 1 in. from the base of the tube (Fig. 8). Strips of newspaper are then pasted around the tube to ensure its rigidity. Fig. 9 shows the building-up process, using the strips of paper. Several layers of paper (sugar paper is admirable for this purpose) are wound around the tube until the thickness is approximately 2 in. in diameter. The thickness will naturally depend upon the length of the tube and the type of puppet face required (a thin face would obviously require less layers of paper than a fat face). Let the children decide the thickness of the puppet face. If the paper is applied loosely and is slightly twisted when sticking to the tube, then less paper will be required to build up the thickness. Fig. 10 shows the layers after several applications.

From this basic core it is a simple matter to build up the required features. It is convenient to start with the nose. For this, stick together three or four layers of sugar paper (or paper of equivalent thickness) and tear it to the shape shown in Fig. 11. Bend this into a U-shape, paste, and stick it on to the core (see Fig. 12). Paste newspaper strips over the edges of the "nose" to keep it in place. Fold a piece of paper several times until it is the shape shown in Fig. 13. Bend this slightly, paste, and apply to the core in the position of the eyebrows, upper and lower lips. Small pieces of newspaper can then be pasted over the edges (see Fig. 14) to hold the features in place. When the nose, eyebrows, and lips have been pasted on to the core, further strips of newspaper or sugar paper can be pasted on to the features until they are built up to the required thickness. Detail may also be added by pasting small pieces of newspaper on to the puppet head until an appropriate effect is achieved. Turn head sideways and with a suitable tool pierce a small hole through the side of the head (Fig. 15). Slot a length of wire (thin copper wire or galvanised iron "flower" wire is suitable) through the hole, and bend the ends of the wire to a rough outline of an ear (see Fig. 16). Cut a piece of cardboard to the shape of an ear, place this in position on the wire outline and wrap thin, long strips of pasted newspaper around the ear (Fig. 17). The ear will dry quite hard and firm. The wire will stop the ear from falling off under normal conditions of usage. Hair, straw, bristles from old brushes, coconut matting, string, wool, can all be used with good effect as hair for the puppet. If these scrap materials are not used then the hair will have to be painted, using poster colours. When the head is ready for painting, check the tube inside the head. If this is loose, pour in thin flour paste, or glue with casein glue. Leave this to set hard. When the puppet head is dry, use thick poster paint to cover the newsprint, then paint in the details of the eyes, nose, mouth and ears. If a shiny surface is desired, the puppet head, when thoroughly dry, can be varnished. Varnishing with gum gives a semi-matt finish.

A solid paper head

Each pupil needs several newspapers. The newspapers are rolled into a rough ball. This is then tied with string or raffia to hold it into shape (see Fig. 18). Flour paste is poured over the paper ball, then it is wrapped into a parcel, using large sheets of paper. This procedure is repeated until the head is of the required size. The features are pressed into shape using the thumbs (see Fig. 19).

Firstly, using the thumbs, press two holes, one on either side of the face. The mouth is constructed similarly (Fig. 20). The nose can be pulled out from the face, or, a roll of newspaper can be stuck into place for the nose. The ears can be pulled out from the sides of the head, or, like the nose, a roll of newspaper can be stuck into a hole on either side of the head, in the position of the ear. Flour paste should be used liberally during the various

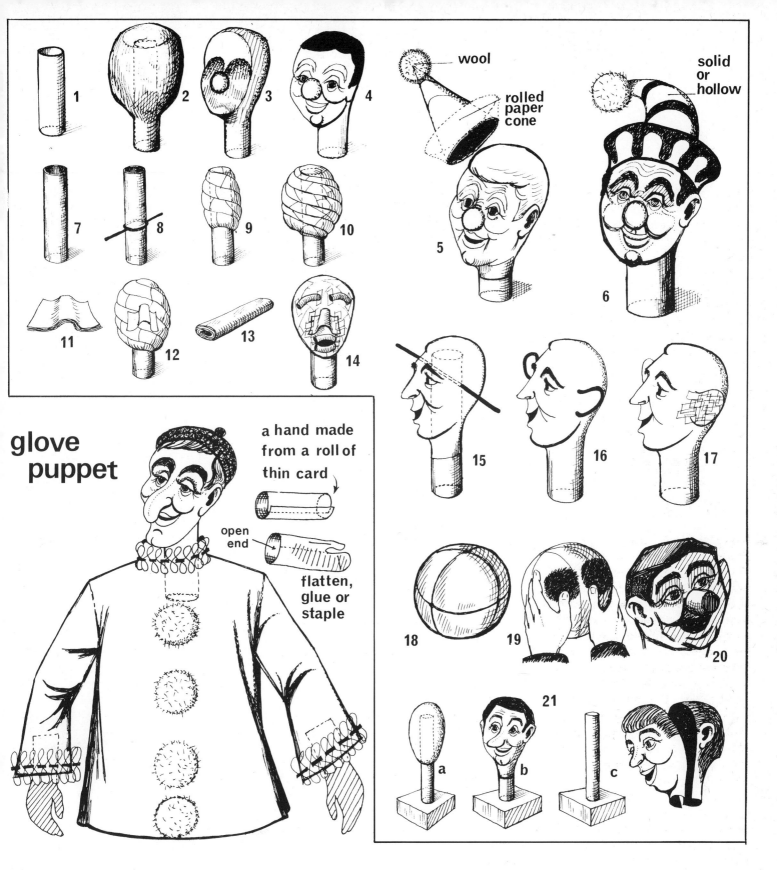

glove puppet

a hand made from a roll of thin card

open end

flatten, glue or staple

wool

rolled paper cone

solid or hollow

stages. When the features are complete the head is allowed to dry. The newspaper face will be found to be completely hard and can be finished with poster paint and varnished if desired.

Heads made in this way may be made life-size quite easily. However, great detail cannot be achieved with this method unless pieces of paper are stuck on to the features to build up the more subtle details.

A papier mâché puppet head using Plasticine or modelling clay

Mould a ball of clay or Plasticine around the wooden support (Fig. 21). Then using several rolls of clay, model the features and complete the finer details with a modelling tool. Remember to over-emphasize the features as shadows and more character is given to the head.

The clay model head is then covered with several layers of small pieces of paper saturated in flour paste. Allow the paper to dry hard. Cut the head in half, remove the clay or Plasticine and rejoin with pieces of paper pasted across the join. Paint and varnish in the usual way. Whilst this is the conventional way to make hollow puppet heads —it is much quicker when making marionettes to use wire and clay covered with paper (as shown on p. 15), making the head solid.

Figures with Wire and Tissue

Since tissue is a soft material some sort of armature or base is essential before it can be used for model making. Young children (5-8) will find it excellent for mask making using a scrap of manilla board or a paper plate as the base. The tissue may be glued in "wads" on to the card base, in screwed up twists or simply in single overlapping sheets. Best results are obtained when using a cellulose adhesive (like Polycell or Klix).

Older children will be able to use armatures made from thin wire. Eighteen gauge galvanised wire, sold by most ironmongers is the most suitable material, although pipe cleaners are adequate for the 7-9 year old age range.

Tissue on wire is essentially a small scale modelling technique and it is best to point this out to the children before they begin to work. This is best done by precutting the wire into 6 in. to 12 in. lengths. This is then twisted into models. I find that action studies of people is the most satisfactory way of introducing the technique. Before the wire is given body with the tissue, trim off any sharp edges with pliers.

The most difficult part of the modelling process is to get the first layer of tissue to stick to the wire. Watching children at work I noticed that the most successful method was to prepare some tissue by tearing it into strips—about 6 in. to 8 in. long and 1 in. wide. The wire shape was then plunged into the paste and a dry tissue strip wrapped around it. This was repeated several times until the whole of the wire shape had some paper covering. This made an excellent base for further layers of tissue —especially if left to dry before the model was built up in any detail.

The unusual characteristic of tissue paper models is that no painting is required because the paper is coloured already. Thus the tissue must be selected with care. One group of children I worked with preferred to leave parts of their model as wire twists. Feet were hard to fashion and wire loops for heads did not detract from the overall effect of the design (see photograph).

The boxing ring

Ten year old working with wire and tissue

Thoughtful display will do much to enhance the models. "The boxing ring" (made by a ten year old) illustrates this clearly. Additional details can also be added, fashioned from tiny scraps of wood, cane, fabric and metal foil.

Editor's note
Tissue papers in an excellent range of colours are obtainable from Reeves and Sons, Lincoln Road, Enfield.

Faces from Paper, Vegetables and Junk

The three young sons of the Count Begouen stood before the figure of a man—he had a long beard, the eyes of an owl, the antlers of a stag, the ears of a wolf, the claws of a lion and the tail of a horse. They had stumbled upon a Palaeolithic cave "picture" of a shaman or sorcerer wearing a ritual mask.

The sorcerer, in the depth and gloom of a pre-historic cave some 20,000 years ago, must have looked a frightening creature, half-lit by the flickering torches which cast his shadow, now small, now huge, upon the walls and floor. Did he hope to frighten the awed spectators, or the gods, who watched with invisible eyes?

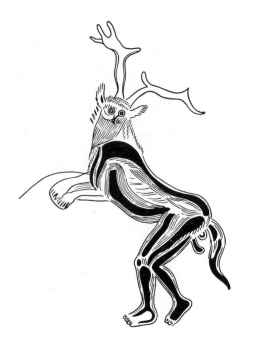

"The Sorcerer" from Prehistoric Religion by courtesy of Thames and Hudson Ltd

Men have obviously worn masks for many thousands of years, for religious purposes, to frighten their enemies and to amuse their friends. Chinese actors wear masks to this day and it could be argued that circus clowns do too, for their real faces are very effectively disguised behind thick grease-paint, bulbous noses, stringy hair and huge ears.

Masks are not always worn, of course; often they are set up outside dwellings to ward off evil spirits—and not always dwellings. Our churches bristle with ghastly gargoyles whose only function is to frighten away supernatural creatures.

Perhaps we all have inherent in us a desire to dress up, to hide behind a mask and to "be" something else—certainly children love to make and wear masks and when Guy Fawkes' night draws near, it is a good time to interest them in masks and mask-making. How far you pursue this subject depends upon the age and capabilities of the children in your class. (Listed below is some information which may be of use when planning your lesson.)

No doubt most children will be helping to make a guy to burn on their bonfire. They may be persuaded to dress it with a mask made in school, instead of using one of those mass-produced ones bought over the counter.

Empty boxes and packets, rolls of corrugated paper, tins, fruit and egg trays all make good bases. The features can be built up with smaller boxes, egg box sections, Plasticine, clay, etc. Packets and boxes which have a waxed finish will be difficult to paint—these may be covered with layers of paper and glue before painting, or with gummed coloured paper.

Figurehead of a Viking Ship. British Museum

Hair can be made from wool, straw, raffia, wood shavings or paper. You will need a good glue—something like Copydex—and the children must be well protected, as this sort of glue is very difficult to remove from clothes. Grapefruit and melon skins, marrows, turnips and big potatoes all make interesting masks, with features either cut out or painted on to the surface. Paper bags, filled with screwed up newspaper, may also be used.

While talking about bags, may I include a few words of warning—beware the plastic bag! Once a child has been foolish enough to put one over his face, one breath is enough to "mould" the bag on to his nose or mouth and he will suffocate in a few seconds.

Carrier bags make excellent masks, being both strong and roomy. Tubes or cones of card, corrugated paper, cartridge paper, brown wrapping paper, two or three thicknesses of newspaper or foil all make good mask bases. For the very young, you will probably have to cut out the eyes in the right place and adjust the mask so that it fits properly.

Bibliography: Paper Faces. Michael Grater. Mills and Boon.

A variety of vegetable masks

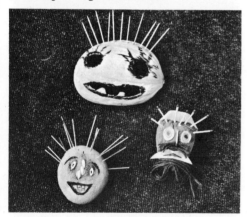

Cocktail sticks, spaghetti, matches, wool, etc., may all be used as hair

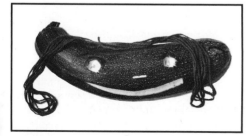

African Sculpture Ladislas Segy Dover Publications

Corrugated cardboard

Hats with brims of card and crowns of boxes, or drinking cups, could be added

Fruit tray

Squeezy bottle

Egg box lid

Paper bag

When features have been added to a pre-packed fruit container, cover with coloured transparent paper before putting on ears

People of the Past

Relics from the distant past always have a very special fascination. This applies especially to metal engraving which usually seems to be almost untouched by the ravages of time. For anyone interested in the past or attracted by fine craftsmanship, monumental brasses have an immediate appeal.

Brasses are a type of memorial dating from the early 13th century. They take the form of metal plates, engraved with the figure of the deceased person they commemorate, and correspond to effigies. They were set in slabs of stone placed over tombs and are to be found in many of the old parish churches of England, large and small.

Costume

Nowhere is the attractive costume and armour of the mediaeval period better displayed. Armour particularly shows up to advantage on brasses. Mediaeval warriors, solemn and formidable, encased in plates of metal, stand beside their dutiful wives. Occasionally, they hold hands but generally they stand in an austere attitude of prayer.

A fine example of a knight and his wife (1400) can be seen in Little Shelford, Cambridgeshire. The feet of the knights rest on proud lions, symbolic of their prowess as fighters, or on sleek hounds with which they hunted.

The development of armour may be traced very clearly on brasses. The earliest knights, like Sir Robert de Bures (1302), or Sir J. Darbenon (1277), are dressed in chainmail armour, but the early 14th century saw the introduction of plate armour to reinforce vulnerable parts of the chainmail, which, being constructed only of rings of metal, could not always stand up to the strain of warfare. The really superb monument of Sir John de Creke, shows this part plate, part mail armour. During the period 1350–1420, however, mail gradually gave way to plate armour whose weight must have made infantry combat impossible. Then, during the reign of the Tudors armour was less important, and although men like William Prelatte (1462), who lies in Cirencester Church, would have been expected to lead the local levy of men-at-arms to battle on behalf of the king, the Tudor monarchs brought peace and prosperity, so that armour was worn only for show or in the jousts. After the 16th century a knight is shown in a decorated heraldic tabard or tunic, and in the 17th century armour is even rarer.

Other distinctive types of costume seen to good effect on brasses include those of merchants, ladies, bishops, archbishops, and priests. The rich area of the Cotswolds contains very many fine brasses of merchants, especially at Cirencester, Northleach and Chipping Campden—merchants who made their fortunes in the exceedingly prosperous wool trade, and donated large sums of money to the building of churches in the hope of saving their mercantile souls. In these churches they were buried and had their memorials erected. Their brasses show them with their feet resting on sacks of wool, clearly demonstrating the source of their wealth. Their dress is always sober and simple, since of course the colourful, fashionable costume of the day (which can be seen in contemporary manuscripts) was hardly appropriate to monuments of the dead. Such a merchant is shown (left).

Nevertheless, the large splendid brasses of priests testify to the immense wealth of the mediaeval church. An extremely fine one shows a priest in his lavishly embroidered cope and other vestments (the embroidery takes the form of figures of the saints) whilst over his head can be seen an ornamental pinnacled canopy.

Female costume too is well represented in considerable variety. Large ornamental head-dresses are common and so are long graceful robes. At the feet of these ladies, a puppy with bells tied to its neck is often portrayed —in sharp contrast to the fierce hounds at the feet of their lords. Most women appear with their husbands and a stupendously large family of children.

A very curious type of brass which comes into fashion in the 16th century is the shroud and skeleton brass. An excellent example is that of Ralph Hammersley. He is in the act of being consumed by hideous long worms. Often these frightful monuments were laid during the lifetime of the person they commemorated. They were intended to be a salutary reminder of the doom which awaited mortal men.

Development and Construction

It is interesting to trace the development of these monuments. The earliest brasses belong to the late 13th century; the latest to the second half of the 17th century. Huge numbers were unfortunately destroyed at the Reformation, when monasteries and other church property were plundered. The metal of which brasses were made, was a singularly durable alloy of zinc which was expensive and difficult to manufacture.

The earliest brasses are certainly the finest, the engraving being bold and simple yet sensitive. But the brasses of this period show a somewhat stereotyped uniformity, with sombre or mournful facial expression—the corners of the mouth being turned down, for instance—and not until the 16th century is some attempt made at portraiture. Then each brass tends to have a more individual appearance, though the quality of engraving deteriorates, and the old, graceful simplicity is abandoned in favour of realistic shading. And whereas at their first introduction brasses were obviously an extravagant luxury for the very rich, in this later period the social cross-section they represent is much wider.

Brass-Rubbing

Brasses, then, are both artistically very pleasing and historically rich in information. They can do something to make a distant and very different age a concrete reality. What is more, there is an excellent method of copying them for collecting or household display. This method, known as brass-rubbing, has become widely popular in the last few years. It is relatively cheap and easy to learn. The basic materials required are "heel ball", or cobblers' wax—a black substance like crayon, only not so hard—and large sheets of paper, which should be either detail paper of good quality or shelf paper. The paper is spread over the brass and made secure with weights at the corners if necessary, then rubbed over with the "heel-ball" so that the engraved lines show through as pale or white in a background of black. This of course is like the popular children's game of rubbing the image of a penny on to paper with a pencil. Hints and more detailed instructions may be found in many handbooks: but possibly the best cheap handbook available on brasses is "Monumental Brasses" by H. W. Macklin, published by George Allen and Unwin. Anyone interested in the subject should consult this; it contains the best list of brasses in England in print. Brass-rubbing should not be attempted without consulting this or a similar handbook with more detailed instructions. Brasses are ancient and valuable, and may be damaged by use of the wrong materials. If, for instance, hand crayon is used instead of heel ball the brass may be scratched. It is, of course, essential to obtain permission from the vicar or rector of the church before embarking on a rubbing. Churches with very fine or ancient brasses may make a substantial charge in order to deter the casual amateur from rubbing, or to help finance upkeep of the church.

Left. The wife of William Prelatte (1462)

Above. Lady Cobham (1374) to be found in Lingfield, Surrey

Knights and Ladies

Materials needed

To make the egg-box knight you will need a strong glue such as Evo-Stick or Bostick, several egg-boxes and a small cardboard box approximately 2½ in. by 3½ in. and ¾ in. deep. Egg-boxes come in various styles and in the construction described here a common ½ doz. type is used; but armour is remarkably easily and effectively simulated from all sorts of egg-boxes and the imaginative pupil should be able to adapt and elaborate the basic idea.

The parts are cut from the egg-boxes with a sharp pair of scissors and should be assembled as they are cut. First two cups are trimmed and stuck together to form the helmet. A third cup is then cut in two round the form, the upper part providing the neck and the lower which is cut open, a visor (see fig. 1). Once these are fixed in place, the head is stuck on to the upper end of the box.

Breast plate and skirt are built up on both sides of the box with vertically halved cups.

The limbs are made from the cups by cutting a suitably shaped section up one side of the cup, round the indentation on the top and down the other side. The indentation forms the joint and the angle at which the strips are cut will determine the gesture of the arms. In this case it is better not to trim the bottom of the cups as the extra pieces of material are convenient for attaching the limbs to the body and for fixing the hands and feet. These latter are cut as desired from odd scraps. A section of a cup over each shoulder completes the knight.

In the construction of the charger, the plain parts of the egg-box are used. The section shown in fig. 2 is cut to form the horse's head and is trimmed to half depth and attached to a corresponding part. It will be found that in order to match these two parts, they will have to be cut from separate boxes. However, if two knights are to be made to form a jousting pair, another horse's head can be made from the remaining sections. Nostrils and eyes are cut from the tops of the cups and the ears from scraps. A complete half box is used for the body and the legs are shaped from the sides of two more boxes, making use of both the top and side planes. The tail also makes full use of the form of the box.

The knight can now be mounted on the charger and weaponry, plumes and a trapper can be added if desired.

Egg-boxes have a crisp, neat appearance and painting is not necessary. Being rough-textured, they are in fact difficult to paint. If colour is insisted on, it should be mixed to an intense but thin consistency and used rather in the manner of a dye, soaking into the awkward corners. Probably a more satisfactory means of elaboration is decoration with string glued in patterns, as shown in illustration. Alternatively the new acrylic paints may be used. Although expensive they will give additional support to the model as they are excellent adhesives.

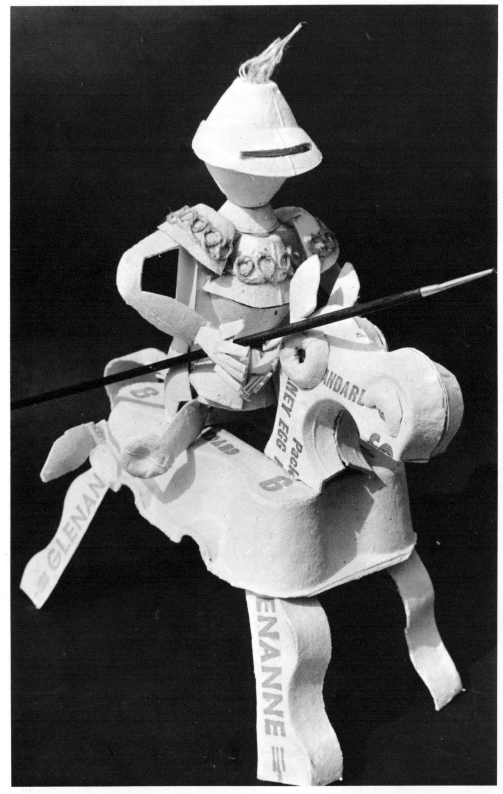

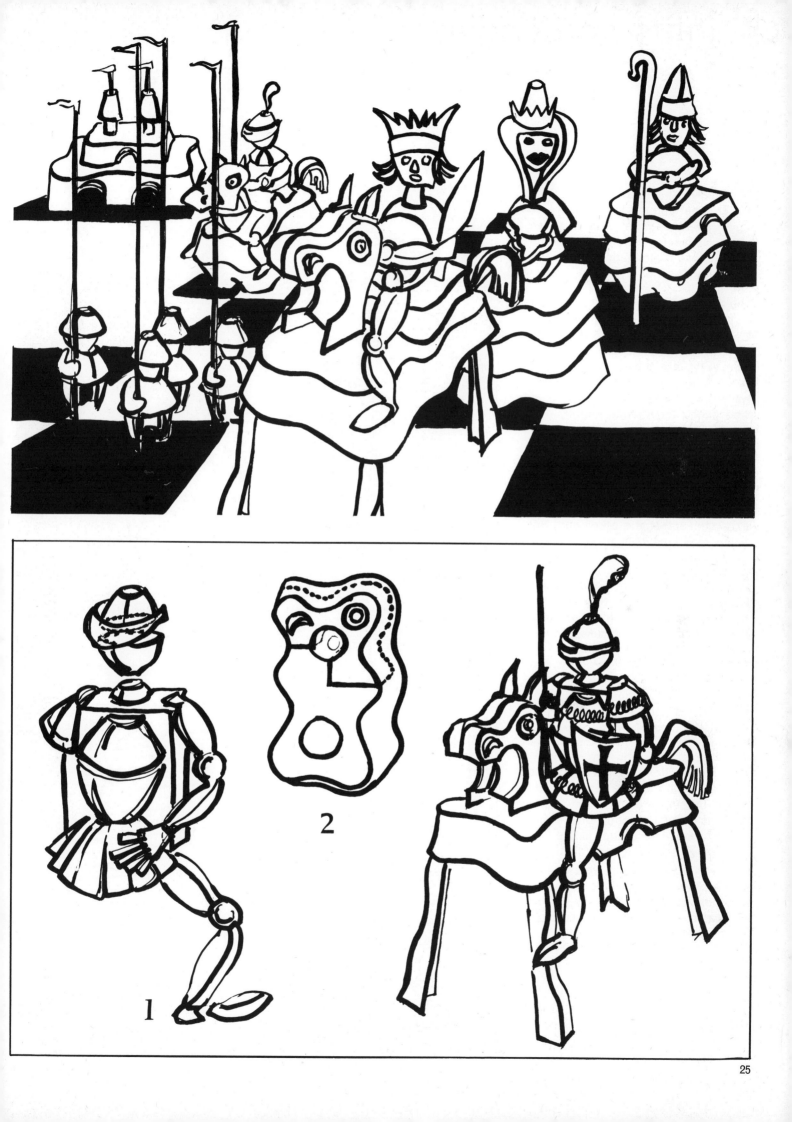

2

1

Paper Faces

Mask making need not be restricted to late October and the few days preceding Guy Fawkes night. It is an activity which will fascinate children of all ages and can lead to dramatic play—both at home and at school.

The chief materials required are sheets of fairly firm card measuring $12\frac{1}{2}$ in. by 10 in. These are measured up as shown and the shaded areas are cut away. Slits are then made along the lines on the 10 in. edges to the points marked X. The ends of the two Cs are then pulled together to slightly overlap. The B strips are then pulled into place over these, and As similarly overlap. All are then capped by strip D and pierced by a compass point to enable a brass fastener to hold them all together. Similarly the same process is carried out at the other end, thus giving a suitable basic mask shape.

Decoration is very much a matter of personal choice and artistic ability. There are few problems from this point on if the teacher tells the class to be very imaginative and to use the wide choice of materials available. The latter should include coloured card, metal foil, small boxes, raffia, beads, straws, and all manner of odds and ends. Bostik No. 1 and staples are usually the best methods of securing these.

Two helpful points should be made however. First the eyes can be located by pointing to the same whilst wearing the mask. Secondly one of the most useful forms of decoration is that made by making a card fringe (illustrated)

However in this type of work children of ten or more need little further instruction other than how to produce the basic shape. Inventiveness and enthusiasm will do the rest.

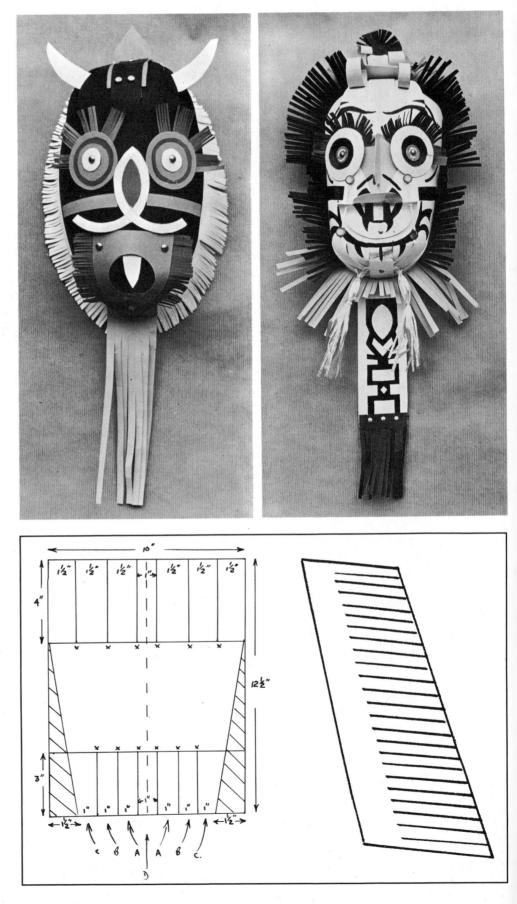

Jointed Figures

Constructing a puppet from scrap wood, using cloth joints

This is probably the cheapest and quickest method of puppet making, and is suitable for most age groups. The rough pieces of wood are joined together with cloth joints as shown below. Ordinary tacks may be used to join the cloth to the wood. Naturally, the children enjoy the hammering! The clothed puppet looks effective.

Animals and imaginative birds, fishes and reptiles may all be made using scrap materials—in a similar way to the ordinary puppet. Imaginative creatures lend themselves particularly well to the creative approach. Here are some ideas upon which to base further experiments with scrap materials.

Various puppet joints

Combinations of wood, rubber, leather, sheet-metal, springs, cardboard tubes, etc., may all be used to create good puppets. An experimental attitude to puppetry should be adopted, and the various details shown here will serve as a general guide.

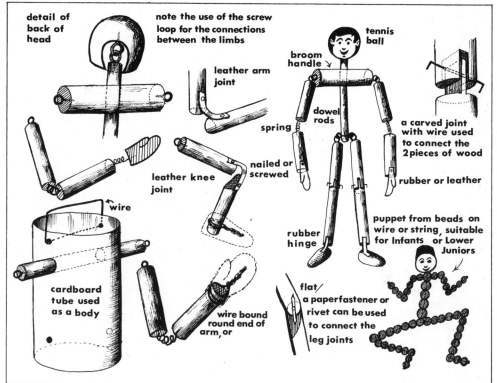

detail of back of head

note the use of the screw loop for the connections between the limbs

leather arm joint

tennis ball

broom handle

dowel rods

spring

nailed or screwed

leather knee joint

wire

cardboard tube used as a body

wire bound round end of arm, or

rubber hinge

a carved joint with wire used to connect the 2 pieces of wood

rubber or leather

puppet from beads on wire or string, suitable for Infants or Lower Juniors

flat a paperfastener or rivet can be used to connect the leg joints

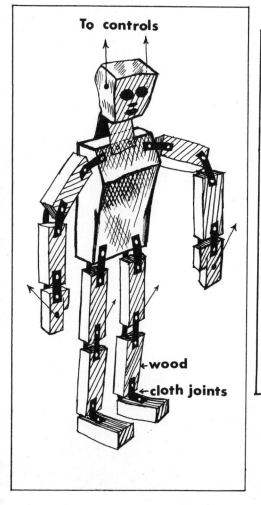

To controls

←wood

←cloth joints

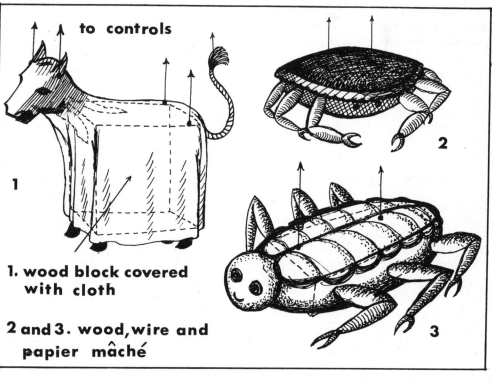

to controls

1

1. wood block covered with cloth

2 and 3. wood, wire and papier mâché

2

3

Puppet animals

Using blocks of wood, many interesting creatures may also be made. Children should be encouraged to use their imagination when making puppet animals. The results will be more artistic, lively and interesting. Animal controls should be kept as simple as possible, using only the minimum number of strings.

Dimensional Modelling Arc Welding

Arc welding

This is an activity which is best left to the metal work shop at school, though ambitious fathers might well decide that here is a craft which they might decide to follow at an Evening Institute before establishing a unit of their own in garage or shed.

Casting will gradually become an important part of the sculpture department but welding has been gaining in popularity in schools and colleges. Welding provides ample scope for self-expression and can be deeply satisfying. In contrast to carving wood or stone, welding builds up form and offers a technical challenge. The essence of welding is the use of heat to marry two similar metals together. This can be achieved with gas or using an electric arc. Gas welding can be awkward to use and in unskilled hands is very dangerous—needing constant supervision. On the other hand, electric arc welding can be done with simple equipment and when the student has understood the dangers, need not be so closely supervised. The electric welder works on the principle of completing an electric circuit. Two output cables, the electrode holder and earth clamp complete the circuit with the rod and piece of sculpture in the middle of the chain. This is more simple than it appears if one realises that the clamp or earth cable is attached to the "job" and the electrode with the rod in the holder can be then used on any part of the "job" that requires welding—thus it completes the circuit.

Some teachers and students have not attempted welding because of the lack of metalwork facilities—although this is a handicap when trying to cut or beat metal, it can be overcome by using a gas torch and anvil. Metal can be cut with a rod but compared with gas equipment it is somewhat slow.

The real danger with arc welding is "arc glare" which can lead to "arc blindness"—it usually causes headaches but in extreme form can be very distressing although not always permanent. Safety measures are essential; students should wear gloves, aprons and spats, these will protect the skin and clothes although nylon stockings seem to be particularly prone to sparks and girls should wear trousers when using the equipment! The eyes are protected by either

28

a helmet or a hand screen. The former fits over the head and leaves both hands free, while the latter requires one hand but does protect the face. Beginners seem to prefer the screen. On no account should students wear sunglasses. Both the screen and the helmet have dense dark glass windows—made of a sandwich of two pieces of clear glass with dark glass in between. This is awkward because one is unable to see the piece of work until the arc has been struck and the beginner is apt to look round the screen, and as soon as the rod touches the metal, is dazzled by the sparks which could damage the eyes. Once the student appreciates the difficulties and dangers, welding becomes fairly easy.

The arc must be "struck"—that is to say the rod is scraped along the piece of work until it arcs and then the student can see the work and start taking the rod slowly across the part he is welding. The rod is made of mild steel coated with flux—the rod core can vary with the metal that is being welded.

The welding machine is a metal box which contains a condenser controlled by a handle that varies the amperage output. This is not as complex as it may appear! Usually the front of the machine has a panel marked off in amps on one side and metal thicknesses on the other. By turning the knob the indicator is either raised or lowered depending on the type of metal that requires welding. Once the machine is set and the suitable rod selected, welding can proceed.

It will be found useful if the machine is set on a wood work bench and the front of the bench is covered with a clean steel plate. This sheet must protrude over the front edge, the earth clamp can then be fixed to the steel so the need for the clamp to be attached to the piece of sculpture is obviated. Large pieces of sculpture can be rested on the floor leaning against the edge of the table—this method eliminates lengths of cable from stretching across the work bench. The vice can also be earthed in the same way for small or awkward pieces of work.

Two other pieces of equipment are a wire brush and chipping hammer. The metal must be cleaned of all rust and dirt if it is to make a clean join and if two pieces of metal have been joined and another piece is to be added it is as well to chip off any slag to make a clean join with the next piece.

It will be seen that welding can be done by students of both sexes and with only a few pieces of equipment. The difficulties are the

element of danger and the small number of students that can be involved at a time, and the fact that they have to be screened off from the class where they cannot attract an audience. But if the students and teachers are aware of the basic rules that must be followed, they can develop their own techniques and methods. The possibilities of the craft are only limited by their talent and time.

Arc welding is used widely in industry and many utilitarian everyday objects from cars to cookers are constructed by using this process. Sheets of metal are cut, punched and welded to form the finished article. The industrial approach to teaching welding might be very useful for the technical student but when used in a sculpture department the results and disciplines can be most unfortunate. The process must be used to develop imagination and inventive skills. The accidental slip or odd weld can be developed to produce tactile qualities that would be frowned upon in industry.

For the first welding project it is best to concentrate on a few simple materials and limit the aim so that the student can come to terms with the problems of the craft. A suitable project for the first effort would be to build a low relief using quarter-inch rod and thin sheet steel. This would enable a low relief to be built up in three stages—(i) support, (ii) sheet covering, and (iii) decoration.

If a fish form were selected (Fig. A) the back structure would have to be made of quarter inch square rod. This could be cut with a hack saw and bent to the required shapes. As the pieces are made they can be arranged on the earth plate (see first article). This covers the top of the work bench and is earthed to the welding machine by the output clamp cable. When all the pieces are ready and laid out (illustration B) they should be weighted down. The student then puts on the apron, gloves and spats, turns on the machine and holds the screen in place. The rod can be scratched on the table top to get an arc and then the student can see the structure through the screen window. It is advisable at first to only tack the pieces together at the main meeting points. Once this is done the weights can be removed and the design adjusted. If all is well, welding can commence. Here the difficulty about welding a seam becomes obvious, the rod must be brushed along the seam and once the arc is struck the flux can be puddled slowly down the joint by slightly raising and lowering the rod. It will be noted that the rod burns down as the work commences so that the electrode has to be lowered down towards the sculpture. The difficulty is that the beginner often pushes the rod against the metal so that the flux falls on to the surface and the subsequent jerking and pulling upsets the arranged pieces. The rod must not be allowed to burn down too near the electrode as it will damage the plastic. When the rod is within a few inches of the holder the spring-loaded trigger is pulled. This releases the old rod and a new one can be inserted into the hole, the trigger is released and the rod is firmly held in the electrode.

When the basic frame has been made the sheet metal stage can start. The fish B has to be covered with a metal skin from the tail towards the head. The pieces should be cut with a rod and it will be found helpful if the amperage is increased so that the output of extra heat will help to cut the metal. The scale pattern C is cut out on each piece and the straight edge should be inside with the appropriate cross piece in the backing. When all the pieces are cut they should be tacked on with small spot welds using the lowest possible amperage. Too much power will burn through the sheet metal.

When the body of the fish is covered, the decorative pattern can be added. Washers, steel screws and old clock wheels can be spot welded on to the edge of the fish's back and into the mouth as teeth. It is difficult to hold these small pieces in place but if they are set in a strip of clay they can be welded on without the rod pushing them out of order. If the decorative elements can be welded from the back it will be found easier and often stronger.

The fins and tail must be welded on to the sheet steel where the frame has had extra supports put in when it was made, see illustration. These supports help to make a firm hold because each fin has to be welded into place and the heat could damage the thin steel sheet. The decorative elements can be cut out from sheet metal, made from odd scraps, or even constructed from welding rods themselves. If a decorative element can be cut and prefabricated and then welded with the main structure, then often this will overcome many of the difficulties.

If the finished sculpture looks too bare, the metal surface can be "drawn upon" by striking an arc and slowly dragging it across the surface of the steel leaving burnt lines. The rod can also be used to draw circles, squares and triangles. This technique can be overdone and the results can spoil a piece of work with fussy detail, but if it is used in limited areas it can greatly enhance the textural contrasts and lay stress on certain areas.

To finish the sculpture and make the metal uniform in colour—it can vary from silver to dull rust—the "job" can be covered with raw linseed oil and then burnt with a torch. The flame should be played over the whole surface until it changes colour. The advantage is that it will weather-proof a piece of work but the smell can be trying!

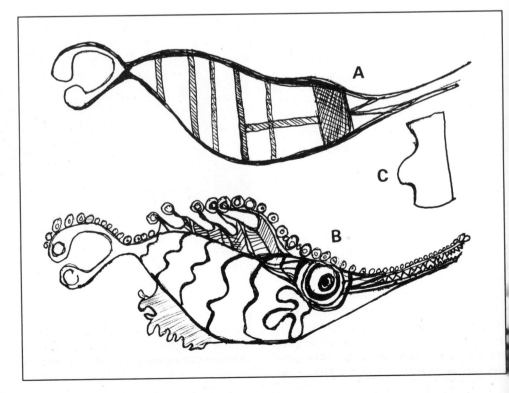

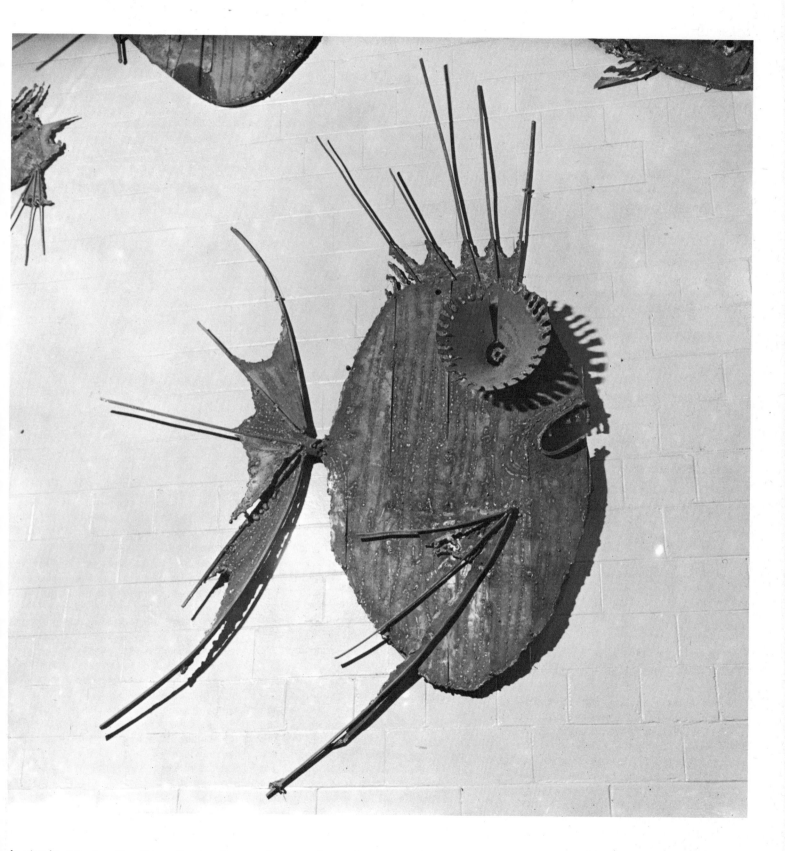

A simple exercise like this will give the student an insight into the design and technical problems and can lead to a development of the theme. Several flat pieces can be made and then joined together to form a sculpture in the round. Once the problems have been appreciated, errors and mistakes analysed, the student will be able to express himself with freedom. One such work is shown above.

Welded Shapes

So far I have concentrated on building a simple relief structure using sheet metal and rods. The process was much the same as that used in making simple domestic appliances. Another approach to arc welding is to use heavier metal and put it together using the same methods as used by the shipbuilding and girder trades. Large pieces of steel are cut and built into three dimensional structures. The difficulties of this method are that the metal must be cleaned as it can be both greasy and rusty. The other disadvantage is that the student is apt to build "junk" sculpture that avoids the need for thought and working drawings. The ideas for the piece of sculpture must be conceived first and then executed from selected metal. Without working drawings this type of sculpture can lead to very stereotyped work. The extremes of the method can vary from beaten metalwork of sulptors like Greco, and the fragmented structures of Cesar. The West African sculptors of the Yoruba with their shaped and riveted work, and the nail fetishes of the Bakongo peoples, are perhaps the best examples from the teacher's point of view as they depend on a simple and direct approach, displaying a strong artistic discipline, and in no sense has the craft led to a flamboyant decadence.

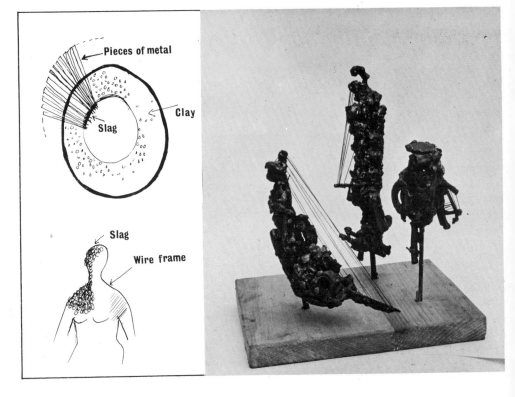

An over-elaboration and self-conscious use of medium can obscure the artist's intentions. Technique becomes an end in itself and fails as a means of communication. Clear preliminary visualisation of aim should lead, first to drawings, then a sketch model. Once the design is clearly visualised technique is relegated to almost a mechanical matter. Like Michelangelo, who said that his task was simply "the freeing of the statue from the marble", the student should express himself with freedom and not hesitate to abstract or simplify in order to overcome his problems.

The school or college with metalwork facilities can develop the beaten metal technique. The shapes can be beaten out and then "tacked" on to a metal frame. The changes of direction of form and use of light are obtained by beating the metal. The hammer textures can also be most effective. The lack of metalwork departments makes this type of work almost impossible, as the problem of annealing and heating are almost insuperable. This handicap can be overcome but it is better to approach the problem from a different angle—by building up the form using pieces of metal. A frame is needed, as with the beaten sheet work, but into the frame is built a plane of metal. The metal can even be added in layers to give recession of form and textures. The technical side is more difficult as the metal has to be held in place and then welded. The snag is the combination of rod and screen—the piece of metal and rod end cannot be seen through the dark glass of the screen and the metal can easily be knocked out of position before the arc is struck. Clay can be used as a means of support and also is easily removed at the end.

Clay can be used in many other ways. If a large hedgehog shape is required, a clay football can be made—the metal is then pushed through the clay so that all the ends touch. The ends are then welded and the clay hosed out of the finished work (see illustration). Any slag and clay mixture can be brushed away and chipped out with the slag hammer. Clay slabs can be used under pieces of metal so that parts of a job do not get tacked to the bench plate (see article on p. 28), or to parts of a piece of sculpture that has to move, e.g. a part of a mobile.

Another method of building welded sculpture on a small scale is to build up layers of slag, rather in the manner of clay modelling.

The basic shape is made of chicken wire or odd pieces of scrap. The welding rod is then used to puddle on drops of slag that can be built up and rubbed down to give flat planes.

The most sophisticated form of welded sculpture can be making mobiles. The movement, balance and engineering problems are fascinating. Lightness is the key to this type of work—the rods and light sheets of steel offer technical difficulties because of heat and making a good joint—a falling piece of metal from a mobile can be quite alarming! To get the structure balanced it is best to build the mobile on a piece of string and hang it from the shop roof. As the pieces are added to the structure, the string is pulled and balance can be checked. The decoration and textures are most important because the form will be moving and offering different planes and surfaces.

It will be noted in all forms of welded sculpture the basic frame is the essential part as it pre-forms the two functions of support and structure. If a large piece of work is to be made, the frame can be split or even fitted into sockets. But the design must always be visualised and conceived with the structure as the main element in the work.

Model Making

This section gives information on first principles for teachers and club leaders on buying materials.

We shall be writing, amongst other things, about the use of expanded Polystyrene, Wood, Newspaper and Metal, both for conventional model making and for Stage Decor, which also includes fabrics, metal casting and scaffolding.

Before reading much further, a question which the reader will inevitably ask of us is, "But how can we afford such items as Polystyrene?"

We had to answer this question at the outset, and this article is about our answer, and the ways we arrived at it. We don't claim originality for the ideas we put forward; they are an amalgam of what we have met, experienced and talked about over several years.

We decided first to establish an order of priorities. We took the materials we were using and the use we were putting them to and examined the relationship between the material and its use, and whether or not that material was particularly relevant to the concept in hand. This showed us that materials were often used uneconomically. As an example, a large proportion of our capitation was being spent purely on paper, particularly cartridge. The situations in which cartridge, and only cartridge, will do are few, and by re-thinking our use of the various types of paper we saved money. We now use expensive papers only when others will not do, and use mostly cheap sugar paper, and above all, newsprint. The latter has a much wider usability than is at first apparent, and is our staple paper item. Having applied this line of thought to paper, we extended it to cover all materials. We now ask ourselves at each requisition, "What is the cheapest material available for the job?" Having decided this, the next step is to find where to buy it. The obvious sources are the educational Art suppliers, who offer a wide, readily-available range. It may be worthwhile, however, to shop around the local firms for competitive quotations in the case of certain materials. Assuming that the ordering has been done satisfactorily, there is further room for manoeuvre in the re-use of used materials. There may also be local access to free (or at least nominally-priced) materials. By this, we mean anything from scrap papers from food packs to waste from a local factory. In a tight spot for paper, we were once helped out by a local newspaper, who sold us remnant rolls of newsprint, although for obvious reasons they do not encourage this!

This method of working from requisition to requisition was an obvious improvement on previous years, but we found that it could be improved by long term planning. We eventually settled on a four-year plan. This allows in any one year extra expenditure on a specific item at the expense of others, which in turn balances at some point in the overall cycle. It also allows the piecemeal build-up of materials for specialised activities. For example, we wished to develop etching, but could not afford the initial outlay. We therefore first acquired acid, then paraffin wax, later metal, and finally two years after the start of the build-up, straw hat varnish and ink. During this time, elementary work was still possible by using tin lids.

The "piecemeal" principle was initially decided upon for financial reasons, but in operation two other advantages emerged. Firstly, we have found that the availability of only part of the equipment needed, stimulates fresh thinking as to its uses. With only acid available in the first stage of the etching plan, any printing was obviously out, and this forced us to explore the possibilities of direct etching of pieces of metal (tin-lids) for their own decorative value. Secondly, since any specialised activity usually arises from the particular interest of one member of the Staff, a large outlay of money on a complete set of equipment can often seem wasted if that member suddenly leaves, and no one else has developed that particular interest. With our system, this situation is less likely to arise, because the availability under experimental conditions of unfamiliar materials and equipment often arouses the interest of other members of the department, encouraging them to take part.

Saving money is not an aim, it is merely a responsibility. What really matters is what happens with the materials purchased. If it is felt necessary to spend a large sum of money for a particular activity which is educationally valid, then we say "spend it"— and we hope by all the economies elsewhere, to have the money available. The object of the exercise is not to save money, but to have money when and where it is needed.

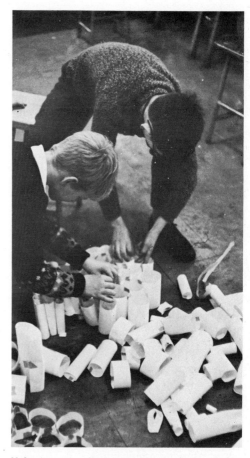

Using paper cylinders to teach awareness of space

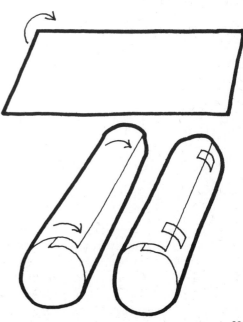

How to make a paper cylinder

Modelling with Polystyrene

Expanded Polystyrene is one of the new materials belonging to the Plastics range. It is easy to work, very light, and has a wide range of application.

It can be obtained from some Art firms (Margros, for example), and since it is used industrially for packing, can often be obtained free. However, we got our main supply from local builders merchants. Variations in price for the same article make it worthwhile shopping around, and substantial reductions can often be obtained by collecting the material oneself. Polystyrene from this source is in sheet form, up to four inches thick. We supplement this with industrial waste, our chief source being T.V. Set packing. Cubes, which are comparatively expensive, we get from Margros.

Here we can give an example of its use, which incidentally also illustrates how it can be used with greatest economy. When working on a set for Anouilh's "Antigone" we wanted to produce some Mayan Stelae, complete with carvings, to a depth of about eight inches. For these columns we used one foot cubes. Each cube was cut in half and a death mask was then cut on the outside, taking care not to cut deeper than 3 in. except in initial forming. Next the inside was cut out, leaving a hollow mask. In the same way, another hollow mask was cut from the inside piece. The piece we were then left with was too small for another mask, and was used in another part of the design.

All the cut-outs, the eye sockets for example, were done as cleanly as possible, so as to leave large pieces of usable waste. These pieces were then stuck to the surface with Marvin Medium and modelled with a hot tool to produce, for example, the bone structure of the nose. It can therefore be seen that by using cut-out waste the material can be used quite economically.

Aesthetically, the main value of Polystyrene is, we think, the ease with which it can be cut. This quickly leads the children to a real three-dimensional approach, and when they come to carve wood or plaster they do not tend to "draw" on the surface, but immediately attempt to work towards a sculptural concept of space.

Unlike some other forms of carving, it does not need any physical strength, and girls can handle it with comparative ease.

Working Polystyrene needs little special equipment. It can be cut with any hot tool. There are a number of electrical cutting tools

Above. A decorative panel in a low relief Polystyrene
Right. A pillar for "Antigone" set using Polystyrene coating

on the market; this hot-wire principle is relatively simple, and they can well be made in school. We have not used one of these, but prefer to use old hack-saw blades and thick wire, held with pliers, or more safely, mounted in a wooden handle. These we heat with a bunsen burner. The only problem here is the smell. The sensation of using one of these tools is similar to moving a hot knife through butter. Polystyrene can be sawn cold in the normal way using a sharp knife or a hacksaw blade. Because of the granular structure of the material, this is useful if a coarse textured finish is required. A hot tool is necessary, however, to obtain a smoother surface. Pieces can be joined by passing a hot blade between the surfaces, while at the same time pressing them together. We have not found this

very satisfactory, and prefer to use Marvin Medium.

It can be coloured by sticking on tissue paper, painting, wax-crayon and so on, but some paints will attack the surface. One carefully made head-dress vanished when we painted it with a special paint which was sensitive to ultra-violet light. This can be overcome by giving it a protective layer of some kind. We do not think this will be a common problem, but it is worth taking care if only to save the disappointment of a child having to re-make a piece of work.

We have already mentioned its use for stage sets, where its lightness is a great asset. It has also proved useful in smaller quantities for props, such as the head-dresses for the goddesses mentioned above.

Above. Part of the "Romeo and Juliet" set, showing use of Polystyrene in Castellations, Relief Heraldic device and mock sculpture

Right. Masks cut from Polystyrene blocks

In schools where there is a metal work department Polystyrene can be used for metal casting. The piece required is carved directly in expanded Polystyrene. The finished model is packed in a mould of either clay-bonded green sand or sodium silicate bonded sand, with the necessary gates and vents. The molten metal is poured in, and the heat of the metal vapourises the Polystyrene, the metal taking its place in the mould. There are certain similarities between this casting process and the lost wax *(cire perdue)* process.

We have obviously tended to deal with the more usual side of this material, and therefore the work mentioned was done in societies and extra-curricular activities. It has other uses in the ordinary classroom situation. We have already mentioned its possibilities as a carving material, and

linked with the more traditional materials, it can form an important part of a sculptural course. For collage work we have used small off-cuts, which can also, when cut to the required shape, be used for printing blocks. As the material will crumble under undue pressure, its use in printing is limited to "hand runs".

It is not possible, and we would not claim to be able, to present all the aspects of this material, which range from the techniques used in the car industry for making pressed tools to the filling of cavity walls for insulation. Polystyrene is, as we have said, a plastic. During the past few years a number of books and articles have been appearing on plastics. Two we have found useful are —*New Materials in Sculpture* by H. M. Piercy (Alec Tiranti) and *Plastics as an Art Form* by T. R. Newman (Pitman).

Models from Spills and Newspapers

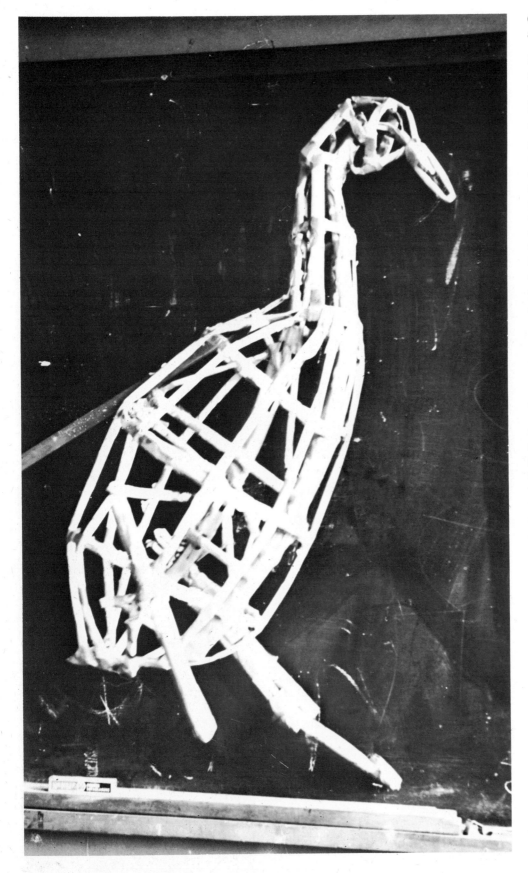

The basic skeleton of paper spills before "skinning"

Old newspapers are one of the most available and plentiful of free materials.

Papier mâché is the most well known way of using newspaper, and is familiar to all. We have had a lot of success using newspaper as a constructional medium.

The basic ingredient is the paper spill, i.e., a sheet of newspaper tightly rolled into a rigid strip and held with gumstrip. The size can vary from a few inches (a magazine page) to several feet (a double sheet of newspaper). Younger children often enjoy the discipline of spill-making, although to older ones it quickly becomes a bore. Combating this boring phase is one of the major problems of spill construction. With younger children it is best to jump in at the deep end, making the bulk of spills needed for a job all at once. Competitions for the longest spill, the shortest, the tightest, and the quickest all help to keep interest going, as does setting groups to work against each other or the clock. With the older set it is better to spend a reasonable time making a starting supply, and then make the rest as work progresses.

Small spills are a good medium to teach spatial awareness. Starting from a three-spill triangle and adding further spills joined with gumstrip, constructing up and out forces the child to think about space. It is immediately apparent to him that he has either an ordered construction in space or a jumbled pile of spills. Working on the constructions from string stretched across the room helps to give a feeling of space, and encourages the child to work in the round, and not merely from the base up, which can happen when working on a flat rigid surface.

If outdoor space is available (and weather permits!) this form of construction can be carried out on a large scale. Working on this scale has to be done in groups, and the results are sometimes spectacular, sometimes dismally disappointing (beware high winds!) but always of great interest to the constructors. Outdoor construction needs larger spills, which can be made by fitting one spill into the end of another and binding the joint with gumstrip.

Larger constructions are possible, and they give a lot of scope to group work. We believe strongly in the principle of group work; as well as its educational value in highlighting the problems of human relationships, it is also a means of producing work of a high standard. It allows combination of the best talents of each member of the group, and the less able members are able to feel the satisfaction of being associated with a successful project (or mutual consolation in failure!). Spill constructions in this type of work can take many forms. The individual spatial constructions mentioned above can be expanded on to a large scale; life-size human figures, animals, and full-headed masks can be made in this way, both for their own sakes or as "props" for a project in another subject.

The skeleton for the model is made from jointed spills. A single spill is obviously not strong enough to act as an armature, but several spills bound together have considerable strength.

In the case of a model based on life, the problem of articulation arises, and the attempts to solve it teach a lot about limbs and their movement. In the same way, making a large model of a head tells a child a lot about facial contours and proportion.

The basic construction is then covered with strips of newspaper soaked in paste, building up layer upon layer to form a skin. The resulting model is quite sturdy, belying its flimsy origins. It can then be painted or treated in any way desired.

Spill construction is a convenient and cheap way of making stage props, ranging from features of the set, such as trees, to hand props. As long as the article has not actually to take weight or bear strain, the most solid and realistic effects can be obtained. In a job which demands experimentation and constant trial and error methods before results are achieved, with consequent drain on materials, newspaper is an ideal cheap medium.

Another important drawback of spill construction is storage. Even thirty small individual spatial constructions present a problem, whereas three 10-foot high men, four 8-foot alligators, or half-a-dozen large assorted heads cause handfuls of torn-out hair. There are three solutions—store, display, or destroy. Constructions which have been made merely for the experience of what happens during construction can be justifiably destroyed immediately, since their storage serves no useful purpose. Models which have been made for a specific job can also be destroyed once they have served their purpose. The real problem is the model which six people have spent six weeks perfecting, and represents a great deal

A finished head (approximately 3 ft. square) based on spill skeleton and skinned with pasted newspaper

of skill and effort. We have found that the best way out is to display the models for a reasonable period. When the display has to be moved, a photograph provides a permanent record before it is destroyed. If the proud constructors cannot bear to see their precious giant destroyed, you can always suggest they take it home! An advantage is its lightness.

A large scale spatial construction

Models from Wood and Metal

Wood and Metal

The wood that we use consists of all types of odd pieces that have come from all types of free sources. If one intends to make use of this kind of supply it is important to build up a stock. We are always on the look out for materials that might be of use to us one day.

This means storage problems, which we meet by using a number of tea chests for small pieces and the back and top of a cupboard for larger pieces. Not only wood in the form of old furniture but fabrics, metal, card, old sheets and a whole range of items arrive from all types of people.

The only wood we buy are hardboard sheets of 8 ft. x 4 ft. for painting on and lengths of 1 in. x 1 in. and 2 in. x 1 in. for framing.

The type of wood and tools that we use are directly related to the nature of the work. By using odd pieces of wood we aim to involve the children in a direct creative approach to the work.

Given a piece of one of the traditional woods used in carving the child tries to produce a figure or other object by imposing his idea upon the wood. This idea is often more applicable to clay or plaster. Our approach is to confront the child with this supply of wood and through assemblage to get him or her to look at the pieces of wood, react to their shape and texture and work upon them. The end result may be abstract, or be evocative of some figurative form; it should however, be natural to the wood and not conflict with the form or nature of the material. Often the wood is used with metal or other types of material. The range of finishes is almost endless. Both wax and wood stains provide a whole range of finishes, as does paint. We have even used black boot polish to good effect. Alongside this work we use wood in the usual ways, for making armatures, wood cuts and framing.

The tools we use include chisels, saws, Surforms, Stanley knives and saws. We tried some of the cheaper ranges in tools but found these saved nothing over the years; if anything, it cost more. Sets of tools (that is tools bought as sets) were not ideal either, since the quality of individual tools vary, and there are often tools which are not necessary for our level of work. An example of this is sculptor's carving sets. Some tools can be made—we have managed several usable mallets, and of course many tools and items for other fields of work are unnecessary if one has wood and the tools to work it with. All our modelling tools are made from old

Assemblage of found objects
Scrap metal on wood base

rulers, paint brush handles, knives, forks, and spoons. Frames for fabric printing are another item that we can make ourselves.

Metal

Like wood we rely mainly on free sources for this material. Wire from packing cases, old tin lids, and aluminium from scrapped motorbike engines are some of these.

We do some work in assemblage which is mainly centred on the display of found objects, such as watch and record-player interiors. Until we develop soldering and other methods of joining the material further, our work will have to remain limited.

In collecting tools for this activity we have concentrated our efforts upon individual tools such as pliers, wire cutters, tinman's snips, files and the like. This was done to enable the working of metal by reasonable numbers of pupils without the borrowing of tools, which often loses friends!

Casting in lead

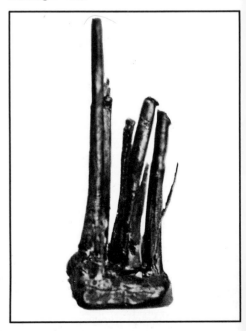

Modelling for the Stage

Drama productions

Most schools and many youth clubs embark on drama productions with tremendous verve and enthusiasm. The set, the costumes, the lighting all involve mastery of a wide range of skills and a knowledge of seemingly unrelated things such as painting a backdrop or winding a dimmer. Therein lies the usefulness of the drama club or group for it embraces such a wide range of activities that almost every child who wishes can be purposefully occupied. Let us consider this type of activity within a school framework (for ease of description) though the points made are equally relevant to club, scout group or evening institute.

Before beginning an ambitious production it is important to set up some form of organisation. This is especially so if a number of members of staff are involved. Each must know his area of responsibility and the dependence of others in the team upon his completing a job before they can begin. There is bound to be strain, so one must ensure that the situation develops methodically if the team is to cohere.

We try and visualise the end product, the play, as early as possible, and from this point decide our individual spheres of activity. Designs can then be produced of an ambitious nature, giving plenty of time for each section to plan its effort and set about finding solutions to the problems it faces. If the children are to be given the opportunity of experimenting and contributing in a creative way they must have plenty of time. If not, one of two things will happen. The children will either be used as cheap labour and do painting by numbers, or will have to use first ideas and first attempts, resulting in a shoddy end-product.

Before any decoration can be produced the structural elements of the Set must be tackled. We are lucky in that both the Metalwork and Woodwork Departments take a very active part in this. However, a capable Art Department should be able to build much of the basic structure itself if need be.

Builder's scaffolding was the basis of this balcony from "Romeo and Juliet"

A paper spill tree under construction

The thing to avoid is always to make the set in the same way. This comes from looking at the play with past sets in mind and then adapting these to the current situation. We think it best to work fresh from the problem that each play presents.

As a result of this approach we now make great use of scaffolding for producing our basic structure.

Some time ago the school presented "Romeo and Juliet". From the production point of view it was felt important to have a balcony at least 8 ft high, and for Romeo to be able to actually climb up and down. The structural problems and the cost of producing this in

The use of covered scaffolding in "The Tempest" to vary levels

stage flat which in the early designs was to carry a large heraldic device. This started as a simple shield, using card, newspaper and string. As the visual possibilities began to emerge Polystyrene was used, and the shield grew into a complex pattern of light and shade. Stage lighting heightened the effect and in the end the device became a major production point.

For the Capulets' tomb we found Polystyrene the best material for producing the castellation and sculptured figures in niches necessary for the Gothic effect desired.

For "The Tempest" the major problem was to create by means of the set the visual atmosphere of the "Isle full of noises, sounds, and sweet airs". All the obvious means of creating shrubbery and foliage seemed too conventional and solid. The material we eventually used was coloured tissue paper, built up in layers and pieces to form exotic flowers and plants. These looked delicate and mysterious and changes of lighting brought spectacular effects. The paper spill tree silhouetted against the cyclorama looked very solid and English until we faced it with fabric (orange canvas seat-covers discarded by the repairer), when it took on a completely different aspect.

A last example from "King Lear" illustrates a slightly different problem. The basic set consisted of several enormous rocks. The bareness could not be relieved by any work on the surfaces, but relief was achieved by producing large colourful banners for the various households using dyes and wax, to give richness without gaudiness.

The problem of props we tackle in the same way as set construction. Experiment, rejection, and trial and error, both of techniques and materials, usually leads to a solution. A roast swan for the feast in "Romeo and Juliet" was eventually made from Polystyrene. Prospero's magic staff was a broom-handle covered with layers of newspaper and the golden leaves which grew from the end were painted wire and card. In order to break the staff at the end of the play and not Prospero's knee, it was sawn, re-joined by means of a thin dowel, and the break re-covered by paper each night.

We feel that if decor for the school play is seen not as a separate problem to be tackled in isolation but as part of the Art Department's overall responsibility within the school, to be tackled in the day to day running of the Department, the result will reflect the complexity and breadth of the effort.

wood suggested that a better solution could be found. Scaffolding was suggested, and as well as solving this particular problem it led to an ambitious bridge and cave for the following year's "The Tempest". The use of scaffolding has provided us with a whole range of structures that cost or constructional problems would have defeated in any other medium. Faced with hardboard it produces buildings, and covered in chicken wire and rags it can become trees, banks or caves.

A large point in its favour is the ease with which it can be dismantled and re-assembled again later. It can be used either in the

conventional builders' way or as a sculptural armature.

Another method of producing structures is to use wood formers with fabric stretched over the top, similar to a traditional flat but in three dimensions with lumps and bumps. This technique, suggested by the work of some modern painters and sculptors, Richard Smith in particular, led to a solution for rocks needed for "King Lear".

Having achieved the structure, it becomes much easier to visualise the final effect. The next stage is to work on the surfaces to create this effect. For "Romeo and Juliet" the focal point of the stage was a single up-

Abstracts from Card and Plastic

Simple three-dimensional abstracts

Materials required: Base for work (cardboard, hardboard, plywood, etc.), cardboard cylinders, small boxes (matchboxes, cigarette packets, etc.), corrugated paper, cardboard off-cuts, glue, coping saws, sandpaper, paints, sprays, coloured paper.

The introduction of abstract picture making is always difficult. The children are restricted

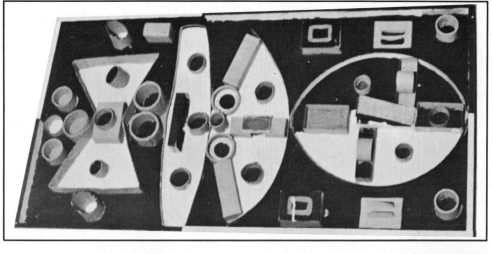

Abstract using cylinders, small boxes and cardboard strips. Painted finish

Abstract using strips of corrugated paper

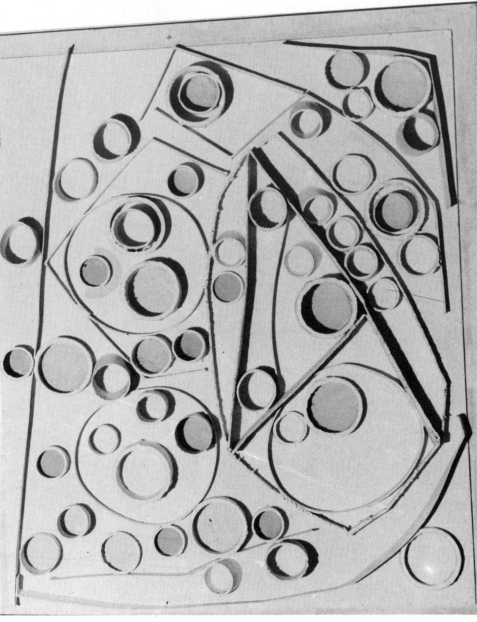

Simple cylinder and strip card abstract in low relief

at all times by the shapes available, i.e. circles, rectangles and triangles. The easy way in which we gain the third dimension, using this method, means that the children do not become too involved with the process and can concentrate on the new and different problems set by the medium and gain a visual awareness by experience.

We begin with the base; this can be of any size from 12 in. square up to 8 ft. by 4 ft.; hardboard, plywood, beaverboard or insulation board all make adequate bases. If a large base is to be used it is advisable to fix wooden strips to the back of the board to give it more rigidity. Thick cardboard can be used for smaller pictures but any base over 2 ft. square will need wooden stiffeners.

When the base is prepared place it on a flat surface—desk, bench or floor—and begin to select your cylinders and boxes to start the arrangement of the design. Preliminary direction and assistance may be desirable here and a talk on the best way to cut cylinders with a coping saw and sand the edges for smoothness will be necessary. Once begun you will find that children work away quite happily moving shapes about, arranging and re-arranging over and over again with no loss of materials. The arrangement can be made more complicated by massing the cylinders or boxes. It can be in high or low relief or any mixture of the two.

When a satisfactory arrangement has been reached each piece is carefully removed and its position on the base noted. Use a well known proprietary impact adhesive to fix each piece in place. If a large and complicated picture has been attempted deal with a small section at a time.

The next stage after gluing is painting; for this you can use emulsion, distemper, tempera or powder colour. Make sure you mix enough to cover the whole area, then carefully paint over the whole picture; this will in effect simplify and help pull the picture together into an entity. If an absorbent card has been used anywhere in the design two coats of paint may be necessary.

After painting comes the stage of assessing the work so far. Try to insist that the children keep an open mind as to the finished result: add more boxes or cylinders if necessary and with a sharp knife remove pieces which are not required. If the panel is fairly large the overall design tends to be rather "bitty" with isolated pockets of pattern which do not connect together. If this is so try introducing long strips of scrap cardboard. These can be used flat, or on

42

Some suggested shapes which can be cut from ordinary cardboard or plastic tubes. Lengths can be cut from ¼ inch to about 8 inches

edge, overlaid, or in large coils. Corrugated paper can be introduced to help fill blank areas. Try turning the whole picture over and viewing it from different angles.

When it is considered that enough has been added and the design is complete, colour can be introduced; this is probably the most crucial and most difficult phase of the work. First decide if colour is necessary or if the picture is complete with one flat wash

of colour. If a simple colour scheme is required try coloured paper cut-outs laid into or on to the boxes and cylinders. The use of a paint spray can sometimes give very pleasing results.

Generally speaking I feel that each picture demands a different finish and treatment; introduce the children to all the finishing methods you have available and let them experiment.

Abstracts for Wall Hangings

Materials required: Off-cuts of cardboard, corrugated paper, cardboard cylinders, impact adhesive, staple or tacker gun, scissors, craft knives, coping saw, hammer, tacks or panel pins, wooden strips.

The abstract screen is an extension of the method I described in my last article on three-dimensional abstracts (p. 41) using mainly scrap materials. It is not necessarily more difficult than the last method and it can be simplified for younger or less able children or made more intricate for more advanced children.

The article on p. 42 dealt with a bas relief type of abstraction with all the materials—cylinders, boxes, etc.—being built up off one main base. This method has one main advantage over the screen method in that it can be assembled and the whole image adjusted before being glued down. With abstract screen the design should either be planned on paper from the very beginning or assembled slowly, letting the design evolve spontaneously.

The first stage is the making of the frame. The kind of timber required depends on the size of the frame envisaged, as the larger the frame the thicker the timber will have to be to give it rigidity. Strengthening struts may be needed also (see diagram) but these can often be used as part of the design. For a screen 6 ft. by 4 ft. the timber used must be at least 3 in. by 1 in. planed, but for smaller screens it can be 2 in. by ½ in. planed wood. The method used to fix the corners depends on the facilities available in the school; if there is a woodwork room, have the class making their frames under the expert supervision of the woodwork master, but if this is not possible the four simple methods shown in the diagram are quite adequate.

Now it is time to decide which method of progression is to be used—the planned or the spontaneous. The children who are going to plan their designs will need a piece of scrap paper the same size as the frame, pinned to the back of it. The children who are going to build up a spontaneous design will need all their materials to hand before they begin. It is a good idea at this point to demonstrate the types of curves, circles, ellipses and spirals which it is possible to make with strips of card and let them have a period to experiment.

Constructing the screen design is quite simple. I suggest as a first step that the children break up the inner area of the wooden frame with long strips of card. One end of a strip is fixed to the inside of the

frame with a tacker or staple gun, the strip is curved into a pleasing shape and the opposite end secured (see above). The whole inside of the frame is covered in this way. The children using the planned method can work in the same way but tell them not to worry if the curves of the card do not follow exactly the plan as it is only there as a guide.

The next step is to fill in the shapes remaining and to try to draw the design together. If you find the design is too open try rolling strips of corrugated paper into solid circles or wrap them around three or four cardboard cylinders and then stick them to the design. Ordinary cardboard strips can be curved around into spirals and circles using

paper clips and glue and inserted into the open spaces. Cardboard cylinders cut into short lengths with a coping saw can be used to fill small spaces and to create texture.

Judging the exact moment when a screen is finished can be most difficult as children do tend to cram too many shapes on and the effect can be far too fussy. It is a good idea to stop the work every so often and stand back to discuss and criticise it. Try silhouetting the screen against a window so that the completeness of the design can be appreciated.

Finally comes the introduction of colour. This can be achieved in two ways. First the applying of colour to the screen itself; painting with a brush is a long and tedious job—try diluting the paint and using it through a spray, although two or three coats may be necessary. Try painting only part of the design, or if the cardboards are fairly uniform in colour, just the frame. Another method is to let in areas of coloured paper or cellophane on the background of the screen. Make sure the coloured areas follow the contours of the design and are evenly distributed. You can of course use both paint and coloured background.

Simple methods of joining corners

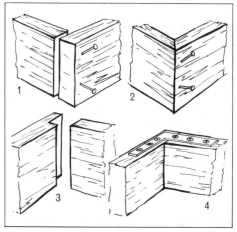

Abstracts from Wood

Wood presents us with new problems of selection and application and gives scope for a different type of abstract work.

Materials required: hammer, nails, stiff base, impact adhesive, small collection of wood tools, saws, clamps, files, chisels, sandpaper and a large selection of scrap wood.

The collection of scrap wood needs to be started a few weeks before the work begins. Our collection grew from the woodwork room in school, pupils' homes, neighbours, friends, the local timber yard, demolition dealers and any local industries dealing in wood. We were soon inundated with scrap wood—old clocks, television cases, chairs, toys—half of which were no good but from the remainder we found some very interesting pieces with which to begin our "pictures".

The first method I suggest you work in is base relief abstract pictures. Although this is very similar in execution to the abstracts described in previous articles it is far more difficult to control and requires greater skill in selection, arrangement and application. This being so I would recommend that this type of work is attempted only by small groups and by children of the older secondary range.

Having collected a good supply of wooden shapes and chosen a suitable base board—hardboard or plywood suitably supported and strengthened—you are ready to begin.

The most successful way to make a start, I have found, is to search through the wood and find a few interesting pieces which can be arranged into pleasing designs on the board. When the main shapes have been chosen new pieces can be introduced to break up the open areas and add interest. Another method is to begin by choosing pieces which suggest animals, fishes, birds and then build up a picture based on these shapes. Pictures can be built up using abstract design and using more textured and grained woods. These methods are just suggested as general guides but children should be allowed to experiment with their own ideas for the media. Fixing the wood pieces to the

1 and 2. Pictures using wood grains and colours for main interest

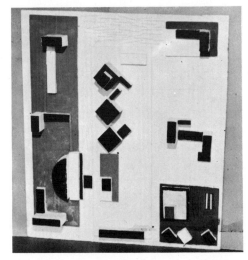

3. Picture using wooden blocks of mixed sizes. Paint emphasises the design

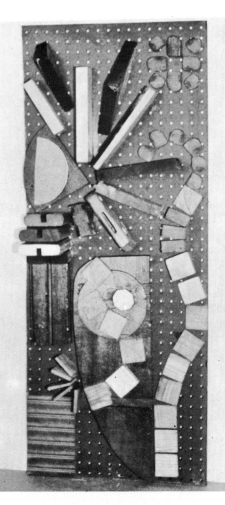

base is as mentioned earlier, using a good impact adhesive glue and carefully following manufacturers' instructions.

The finishing of the pictures depends greatly on the type of effect required in each individual picture. It can be left in natural woods with parts varnished or stained to heighten shapes or grains. Paint can be used on the design—this loses the wood colours and grains but heightens the three-dimensional effect. Colour should be used only in small quantities to emphasise a particular aspect of the design. These finishes again are only mentioned as suggestions as each picture needs to be judged on its own merits and a suitable finish accorded.

4. A face

Free Standing Abstracts from Wood

Materials required: tenon and panel saws, smoothing plane, mixed sizes of chisels— 1 in., $\frac{1}{2}$ in., $\frac{1}{4}$ in., mallets, G-clamps, Surform files or sandpapers, wood work bench or other good solid working surface.

The type of wood required is the off-cuts from building sites or timber yards. The length can be anything from 9 in. to 3 ft. and the width 2×2 in., 3×3 in., 4×3 in., or 6×2 in.

Some of the blocks will most probably have a rough finish on most sides; if so, this can be planed and smoothed down, before starting to carve.

The approach to carving the block can either be spontaneous or planned and disciplined. In the first method show the students examples of the type of cuts and shapes possible then leave them to develop their ideas freely. The second method I have found more successful: the students are limited to one or two shapes only (see diagram). The positioning on the block and the size of these cut shapes is left entirely to the student. It is a good idea to draw the shapes to be cut on the block before beginning to carve. When the main shapes have been carved away the block should be looked at from all angles; then secondary shapes, which will add interest to the design, can be decided upon. When all the carving is finished, smooth off the surfaces with sandpaper.

The final stage is the application of various stains and/or varnish. The application of colour can be considered but should be used very sparingly and only to give emphasis to parts of the design. Generally speaking, however, each piece should be judged on its own merits and the students concerned allowed freedom to personalise their own sculpture in whichever way they like.

Examples of shapes possible with saw and chisel cuts. A larger variety of shapes can be added by using a drill. See also the illustration on p. 46

As well as pure abstract shapes, stylised forms may also be attempted
Illustration 3 represents a face

Making Pictures

Blow the Paint

A

As an experiment give out some indian or coloured inks. Invite the pupils concerned to pour out a little on to a sheet of drawing paper and then with care to steadily blow it in various directions. The shapes formed by this method are often quite fantastic and such an example is shown in Fig. A. Possibilities are shown by B and C where cut out fish swim through fantastic forms taken up by weeds, and grotesque tree shapes are outlined against the moon. Similar experiments can be carried out with liquid paints. The possibilities are numerous, and once introduced all concerned will find a great deal of pleasure and satisfaction in the blowing of paint.

The majority of artists have tried doing most things with paint. Experiments with running colour have been followed by dripping, trailing, and splashing in the Tachist technique. Many of these methods have found their way into the art room, but perhaps one of the most fascinating has often been overlooked. Have your pupils ever been invited to blow paint? If not it is well worth a try.

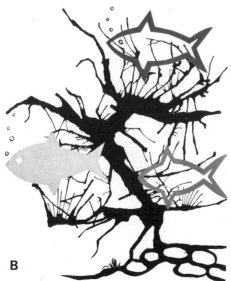

B

Smudge the Paint

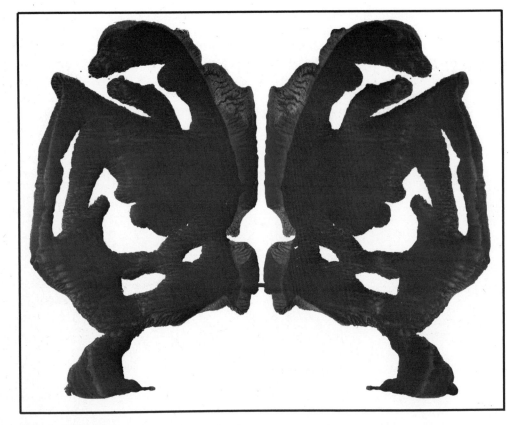

Fig. 1. The blot

Fig. 2. Adding imagination to an original blot

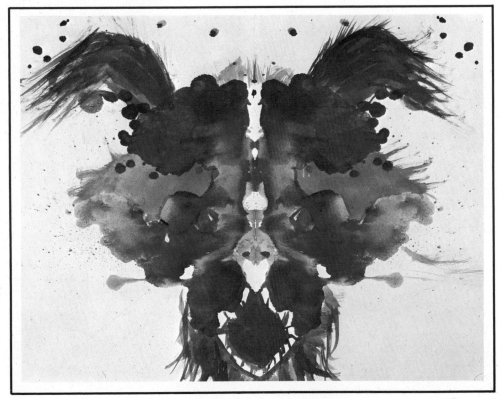

Not the least of the difficulties facing many teachers must surely be their ability to ignite the imaginative powers of children, and enable them to approach the process of image-making with less trepidation. There must be many teachers who, having embarked on a programme of free activity in the art lesson, find the experiment so fruitless (inasmuch as the incidence of the question "what shall I do?", tends to increase), that they revert to less inspired, but more productive methods of teaching.

Quite apart from the dubious activity of being "taught" how to draw, and the dreary results which inevitably follow, there are methods which, whilst allowing the degree of freedom necessary for creative work, nevertheless begin with less anarchic roots. The value of these methods is not one of pure alternative, nor of predetermined results; it is a genuine and important aspect of the child's creative development.

From experience I have learned that children are generally predisposed to problems which enable them to exercise a creative attitude to their solution. They are anxious to assert themselves as individuals, and it is in creative problems that this assertion is given room for expression.

I am at no point suggesting that this method is exclusive; it serves a more immediate and necessary function: that of giving inspiration and impetus to qualities latent in most children. Without such an impetus, children can lose all interest in art.

Given the opportunity, most children are only too willing to attempt imaginative work of all kinds. Often their efforts seem wasted. They are unable to produce the desired result, they become apathetic, or apathy is forced on them. Their genuine attempts seem predestined to fail. It is as if the child were saying, "I really want to be imaginative, but I don't know how to be".

They lack only the inspiration. With this and opportunity they might well produce as D. H. Lawrence puts it, a "golden gush of artistic expression".

The following methods give some indication of inspirational processes which could be used with children of all ages. The methods themselves could be collectively titled automatic processes, in that the initial stage is consciously uncontrolled or automatic. It is in fact this initial step which so often presents the greatest difficulties, the imagination barrier, as it were, and having been broken, the leap of inspiration is far easier to make.

The Ink Blot

Blobs of ink are dropped at random on to a sheet of paper. The paper is then folded in half and pressed together. On unfolding the paper a symmetrical image is obtained, Fig. 1, which forms the basis for a composition, Figs. 2 and 3.

It is important that the entire process is carried out quickly, otherwise the ink dries and fails to produce a corresponding image. This is particularly so when using absorbent paper, i.e., sugar or kitchen paper. Better also to use too little rather than too much ink, for whilst with small amounts the process can be repeated *ad libitum* using different colours, too much ink floods the paper and destroys the image. The emphasis on "dropping" rather than brushing the ink on the paper is to prevent the use of preconceived images, and because ink or paint brushed on tends to dry out rather too quickly.

When a large blob of ink or liquid paint is dropped on the paper it can be transformed either by tilting the paper this way and that, or by blowing it. The exercise produces the best results by employing both techniques, Fig. 4. The delicacy of this tree-like form is illustrated on the next page. The ink can be blown directly, or by using a drinking straw. The resulting image can

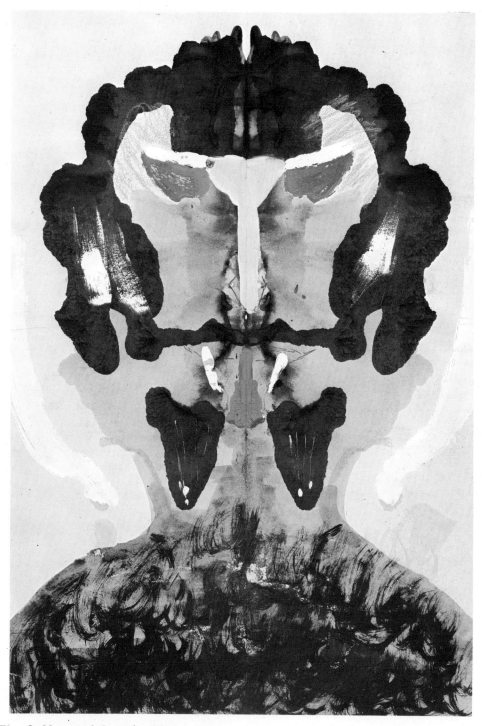

Fig. 3. Humanising the blot

then be used as a basis for imaginative composition.

Further variations of these methods are numerous, especially if we consider the uses of other materials. Painting on cellophane papers, corrugated paper, cloth, canvas, glass, etc., and painting with inks (water or oil bound), paints of varying consistency, flour paste, etc. If liquid glue was used, the resulting surface could be dusted with powder paint, rice grains, etc.

It should be emphasised that all these methods serve only to initiate the first step in a chain reaction; a reaction which culminates in an imaginative re-organisation of the primary image.

49

Fig. 4. The tree

50

Drawing with Lampblack

Materials required. A sheet of medium weight manilla board (12 in. × 15 in.), a candle, pastels or chalk, fixative, mouth spray.

The technique. Light the candle. Rotate the manilla board over the flame. The board should not touch the flame but pass 2 in. to 3 in. above it. This will pattern the surface of the board with swirls of lampblack. The strength of the pattern will obviously be determined by the length of time which the board is over the flame. This textured board can now be used in a number of ways:

(a) Draw a picture or pattern in the lamp black with the finger tips. If mistakes are made the surface should be repatterned over the candle. Finally fix the design with charcoal fixative applied with a mouth diffuser.

(b) Use the lampblacked board as the base paper for a pastel or chalk picture. Fix the lampblack. When the surface of the board is dry use it for a pastel drawing. Try to relate the subject of the picture to the texture of the board e.g. sky and sea scapes, mist and fire themes. Fix the pastel drawing before displaying or storing.

(c) A combination of the two processes described above, i.e. some parts of the picture are drawn in the lampblack, other parts coloured with pastel or chalk.

Note. This process is particularly suited to the secondary age range, especially if the children have lost interest in the more conventional methods of picture making.

Picture Making with String

For many children, the most important factor governing their ability to put down ideas in visual form, is that of inspiration. For this reason we are continually searching for new areas of experience, and for new ways of experiencing these areas. We try to make the environment of the children as varied and interesting as possible, and by doing this we ensure that each child has something to capture his interest, to stimulate his urge to discover, to analyse and to understand.

When the teacher reads a story or a poem, he is in some way contributing to this widening of experience. The story may be used as a catalyst to enable the child to identify himself with the characters in it, and to make this identification so real that the child is able to accept the situation and develop it imaginatively. Nevertheless, the act of painting which may result is a secondary process, insofar that it is a visual representation of a mental idea. The great advantage which automatic processes possess is that of making the visual representation synonymous with the idea—the art of image making is itself the source of inspiration. In other words, the image is made immediately, and does not rely on any preconceived idea or experience for its inspiration.

The following methods are all based on the use of a few simple materials, string, rollers, ink; each method being almost totally automatic, but each one resulting in an image which in itself is a source of inspiration, and which provides a starting point for imaginative re-organization.

Simply by dropping a piece of string, wool, cotton, etc., which has been previously dipped into paint or ink, on to a sheet of paper, and then removing it, provides us with a host of ideas, Fig. 1.

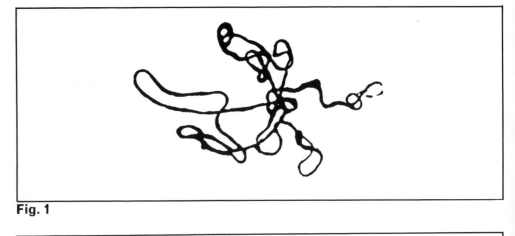

Fig. 1

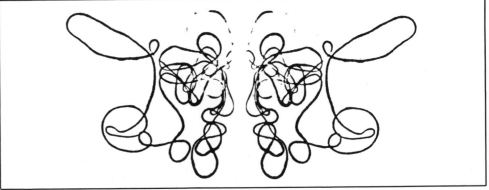

Fig. 2

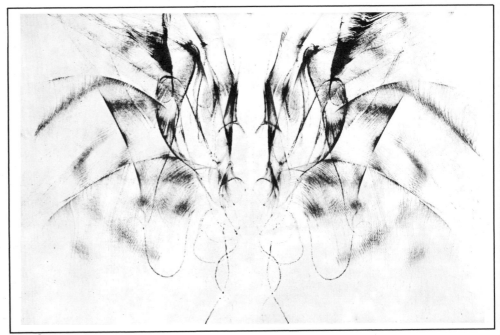

Fig. 3

If we fold the paper in half and press it down before removing the string, we are left with a symmetrical image, Fig. 2. If, whilst the string is still pressed between the folded halves of paper, we pull the string out, we obtain a further and more dramatic variation still, Fig. 3. The string can also be wrapped round

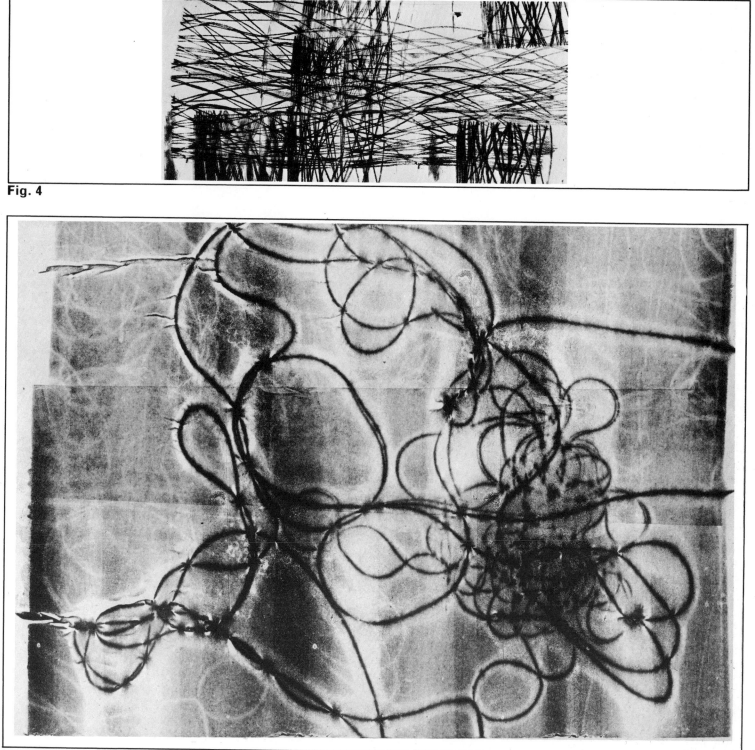

Fig. 4

Fig. 5

a cardboard tube or roller. If the string is now inked up we can roll out a repeating design, Fig. 4.

And without even inking the string at all, we can obtain an image from it by covering a random-dropped piece of string with paper and rolling over it with an inked up roller, Fig. 5.

This latter method can be repeated ad libitum, with a great variety of objects, and for a classroom activity it has the advantages of being extremely clean and simple.

53

Spatter the Paint

To participate in this activity you will require some clean sheets of white paper, a stiff-haired brush, some paints, or coloured inks, and plenty of old newspapers.

Spread out the newspapers on the floor, which will be the most convenient place to work, and on top of them place a clean sheet of paper. Next obtain some flat object, such as a leaf, and place it in the middle of the paper. Charge the brush with colour (thin powder colour or ink). Until you have become used to spatter work try not to load the brush too heavily. (Fig. 1)

The next step is illustrated in Fig. 2. Hold the brush in your left hand and with a piece of stiff card or metal object (e.g. comb, nail file) in your right hand draw it across the ends of the bristles. Make sure that you draw the card or file towards you. This will cause a spray of colour to be thrown away from you and this is aimed at the paper.

The closer you hold the brush to the paper the heavier will be the spray. When the paper and object have had a good covering of paint, carefully remove the object when you will find a white silhouette of the object you used. An example of a leaf which was treated in this manner is shown.

There are countless objects which can be treated in this way. A collection of leaves could be made, all-over designs may be created, or you could cut out various shapes from cardboard. Initials would be suitable and they could be spattered on to various backgrounds, such as the top of a sheet of writing paper; some of these are illustrated opposite. Naturally you would not want to spatter the whole sheet of paper, so in order to avoid this place an old piece of newspaper over any part of the writing paper which is not to be treated.

Beforehand make sure that the newspapers are well spread out or any objects near will also be spattered.

Charging a stiff brush with colour   **Fig. 1**

Applying colour round motif   **Fig. 2**

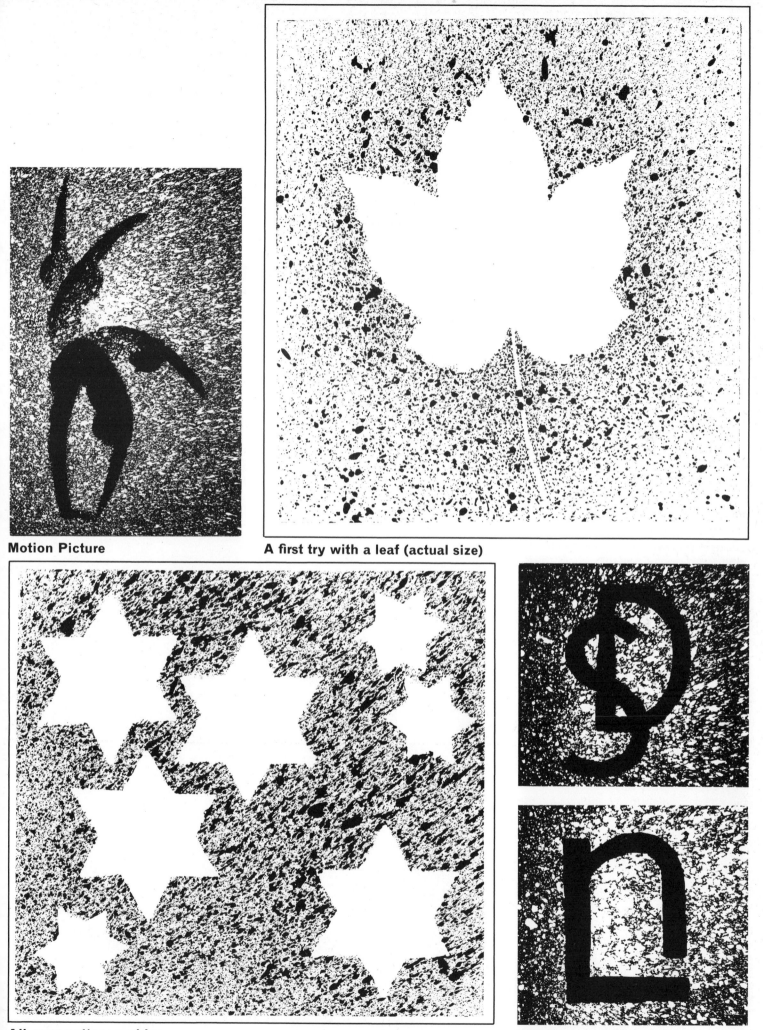

Motion Picture

A first try with a leaf (actual size)

All-over pattern making

Initials as motifs

Ink Blown

Materials: coloured inks, stencil paper, drawing pins, cartridge or sugar paper, scissors, easel, spray diffuser.

This process is an extremely simple one, but because it allows for greater control over direction and depth of colour, is a natural extension to brush spatter technique discussed on the previous pages.

Cut a shape from the stencil paper and firmly pin this on to an easel. Using a mouth diffuser (see illustrations) apply a fine colour spray around the design. Best results will be achieved if it is sprayed from a distance of between 12 in.–15 in. Carefully remove the design and re-pin it so that it slightly overlaps the first spray pattern. Select an ink of another colour and spray once more. Large free patterns can be built up in this way—especially if a variety of coloured inks are available. To prevent the inks from becoming "muddy", provide a diffuser for each colour. Alternatively, rinse the diffuser in water before each colour change.

An extension of this "edge" spray technique is to use stencils to produce the basic design and background colour for a group picture. Detail is then drawn into the shapes with oil pastel or wax crayon. "The Diver" (illustrated here), part of a panel 12 ft. × 3 ft., was worked in this way.

If the motif for the edge spray design has been cut from the centre of a piece of paper (i.e. cut through a fold), interesting effects can also be obtained by pinning this on to the easel and spraying inside it. The third photograph shows the tree design being used in this way. Intricate pictures and patterns are possible by using edge and hole stencil shapes together in one design.

Incidentally, older children will quickly appreciate that by masking parts of their stencil (with pins plus paper), it is possible to colour the picture with a great deal of accuracy. Thus the delightful colour blends which characterize spatter work can be preserved within a much more formal framework.

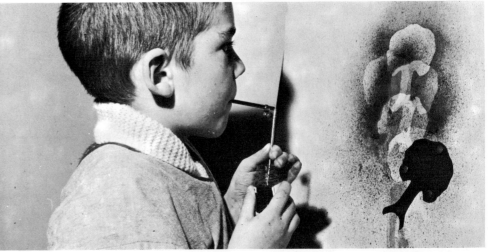

Pattern made by spraying round stencil shape with coloured ink

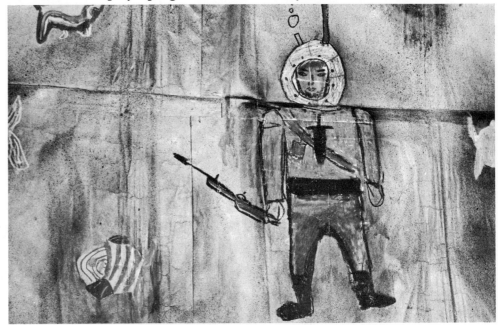

Edge stencil picture using spray and oil pastel

Pattern made by spraying inside stencil with coloured inks

. . . . . And Resisted

Fig. 1. Drawing the design

Fig. 2. Inking the design (note completed picture in background from column of the same carving)

Resist designs

Wax crayons are now playing an ever greater part in the art environment of young children for, used with discrimination, they provide a whole range of varied activities on all types of surfaces from simple line drawings to resists, rubbings and impasto paintings. Experimenting recently with resist techniques a group of eight-year-olds discovered that fascinating results could be achieved by almost "solid" drawing, using carved and moulded designs for inspiration.

The photographs here clearly illustrate this process. The group were taken to a local church where there were some fragments of an eighth century Saxon cross. A design was copied from its base using white crayon on grey sugar paper. The crayon was applied heavily, the indentations of the stone work being left undrawn (Fig. 1).

When the design had been completed a wash of ebony stain (water colour or ink will do equally well) was brushed over the whole sheet. This wash was resisted by the crayoned areas (Fig. 2).

The finished picture (Fig. 3) has unusual strength of line and something of the character of a brass rubbing.

Fig. 3. "Leaping dogs"—a design inspired by a carving on a Saxon cross.
8 year old

Note: Ebony Stain is marketed by Dryad Ltd., Northgates, Leicester, and is sold by the pint.

Pictures in Crayon

"The exquisite touch which renders ordinary commonplace things interesting." So wrote Scott of Jane Austen, but the remark applies with equal force to the young child's interest in the everyday things which surround him—both natural and man-made. This interest needs little stimulation and in fact can be used as the starting point for exciting creative work.

Almost everything has texture—leaves, wood, bark, stone, brick, coin, metal, fabric. To take a rubbing—to capture and record the "exquisite touch"—all that is required is a wax crayon (Freart, Finart) and a sheet of thin white paper. Detail paper is the most suitable, although kitchen paper will give quite satisfactory results. The paper is laid over the textured surface and a crayon or oil pastel rubbed lightly but evenly over it. Initially the rubbings will tend to be in a single colour, but it is possible to make attractive pattern sheets (suitable for book-covers or for backing classroom displays) by taking a number of rubbings on one sheet, using colours which will blend well together, e.g. green, yellow, blue.

Once children have mastered the art of taking clear rubbings, and have thus gained an appreciation of surface texture, resist techniques may be introduced. Here the

rubbing is made in white crayon on white paper. The wax must be heavily applied. To reveal the rubbing a wash of ebony stain (or thin water colour) is brushed over the paper. The white crayoned areas will resist the stain which will darken the surrounding paper (so revealing in great detail the texture of the original surface).

A further development is to encourage children to take rubbings from surfaces or designs they have themselves made. A pattern worked on a sheet of craft foil (Reeves Neo-Fol) will give excellent results, as will texture boards made from such things as string and cotton, cardboard, sandpaper and fabric scraps. Again, after allowing for exploratory doodles, quite elaborate pictures may be made. Shapes are cut from heavy paper and glued on to a piece of board. A rubbing is then taken in the way described above. The illustrations here are taken from Laye Andrew's book *Creative Rubbings* (Batsford) and show the delicate effects it is possible for quite young children to achieve. One great advantage of rubbings over other picture-making techniques is that the design may be repeated at will—making it easy to produce covers for magazines and play programmes.

Materials

Finart/Freart Crayons
Cosmic Crayon Co., Ampthill Road, Bedford.

Filia Pastels (oil)
Winsor & Newton, Harrow, Middlesex.

Ebony Stain
Dryad Ltd., Northgates, Leicester.

Neo-Fol Plates
Reeves & Sons, Lincoln Road, Enfield, Middlesex.

Bibliography

Henry Pluckrose
Introducing Crayon Techniques, Batsford

. . . . And in Powder Paint

Powder colour is probably the most widely used art material. Its attraction lay originally in the fact that it was comparatively cheap to produce and easy for the teacher to dispense. Today, however, these considerations are less important—particularly with the advent of paints to meet all possible needs from solid colour blocks to poster and acrylic colours in transparent tubes and plastic dispensers.

The great range of paints which we can buy, however, should not lead us to suppose that powder colours no longer have a useful part to play. The trouble is, of course, that for too many children the term "powder colour" is synonymous with dry paint in dirty bun trays. It has lost its excitement through term after term of uninspired daubing in endless sheets of grey sugar paper with size and hog hair brushes.

Now before I attempt to indicate some possible methods of mixing powder colour, may I suggest that even if water (and not any of the other wetting agents listed below) is used, some thought should be given to the paper on which the children are to work. Need we always use sugar paper and need it always be the same colour, size and shape? Will painting on newsprint, wall paper, lining paper or blotting paper help any of the group who never achieve success on more conventional papers? What will happen if we paint on paper which has been soaked in water immediately before the painting is begun? If this is attempted is it easier to handle if the paint is mixed to the consistency of thick cream or thin soup or used dry? I could go on to ask how the colour is to be applied—by sponge, roller, fingers, knife, fabric scrap or offcut of wood, plastic sheet or Polystyrene block? Probably, though, the hog hair fitch will remain unrivalled!

Having encouraged children to experiment with different ways of applying colour on a variety of papers, some time could then be devoted to methods of paint preparation using a range of wetting agents. For example, if Lepages gum is used instead of water the resulting mixture will dry with a hard semi-gloss—ideal for painting on papier mâché, wood or cardboard. Liquid detergent, varnish, cold water paste are other wetting agents which are worth experimenting with.

Even if used only for ordinary picture making in paint, each of these mixtures will behave in a subtly different way. For example, detergent and powder colour will give a mixture suitable for knife painting while

Gum, powder colour and sand   **Eight year old**

varnish and powder colour dries slowly, its tacky surface being ideal for texturing with glitter, sand, small stones or scraps of egg shell.

Paste and powder colour is ideal for "combing" (patterning when wet with the fingertips or with a scrap of card or a twist of heavy cord). If this is done quickly prints may be taken from it by laying a sheet of newsprint over the design while it is still wet, rubbing lightly with the hands before pulling off.

If this simple process interests the group monoprinting using powder colour with Vaseline (or even dubbin) might be at-

tempted. Roll out some Vaseline on to a sheet of Perspex or plate glass. Sprinkle some powder colour on top and roll it into the Vaseline. Lay a piece of duplicating or typing paper on to the mixture and draw a design on to it in pencil. When the design has been completed carefully remove the paper, pulling it back from one corner. The design will appear in colour, a gentle blur of line against a fascinating texture caused by the marriage of Vaseline, roller and paint.

Powder colour is a unique media offering us tremendous scope for worthwhile experiment and discovery.

Pictures in Poster Colour

Over the years the emphasis in art has changed from conventional picture-making with paint to child-centred learning through self-discovery about the way materials behave. We have not dispensed with paint—we have merely encouraged children to be more adventurous in its application.

On page 59 I discussed several ways in which the qualities and characteristics of powder colour might be altered to give greater variety to the children's art work. But although powder colour is cheap it is not easy to dispense quickly, nor are young children particularly successful in handling it dry. Indeed if the art programme is to be sufficiently varied there is a case, I believe, for the occasional use of poster colour instead. I recently heard of a school which had used poster colour over the last five years for all art work. A careful check on cost was kept so that a fair comparison could be made of the two mediums. The results showed a small saving by using poster colours in spite of rising costs.

Poster colours are sold by most artists' colourmen. They are, of course, water soluble and may be used in thin, almost transparent washes or applied thickly with roller or knife. The advent of specially prepared acrylic medium (from John Keep and Sons) adds further dimension to the work. Mix the medium and the poster colour in equal quantities (by volume). This will also give the paint a great degree of resistance to cracking. If more than 50 per cent of medium is added to the paint, exact colour mixes will be more difficult to achieve (although pretty pastel shades will result). Since acrylic medium is an excellent adhesive poster colours mixed with it will also be adhesives and therefore suitable for all types of collage and montage work.

In addition to painting, poster colour is particularly suitable for printing with vegetables, tree bark, leaves and scraps of Polystyrene. Its viscosity gives added texture to smudge prints (produced by folding paint between a sheet of cartridge or pastel paper) for monoprint designs, finger painting and for simple stencil work.

Young children will enjoy combing patterns into thick layers of wet paint with pieces of card, loops of twine or scraps of twig. Prints may be taken from this pattern by laying a sheet of paper over the combed design and after smoothing it down gently on to the still wet design, separating the two papers carefully. Experiments with paper of varying texture and thickness (e.g. pastel, wallpaper,

ceiling paper, newsprint) are well worthwhile—as is using damped paper for some of the "pulls".

Another interesting medium which may be added to thicken colour (powder, poster, solid block) is Ropasto. This is a white, water soluble paste which gives body to the colour allowing it to be applied by roller, knife or brush on any grease free surface. Colours which are mixed with Ropasto tend to dry in pastel shades. Young children to whom I introduced this medium produced some fascinating pictures—particularly when working on fabric covered oil painting boards.

Materials

Poster colours: marketed in 27 colours plus black and white in 20 fluid ounce tubes.

Acrylic medium: for poster colours.

Both from John T. Keep & Sons, 15 Theobalds Road, London, W.C.1.

This company is also making an *additive* which makes poster colour suitable for *screen printing*.

Ropasto medium: George Rowney & Co., Percy Street, London, W.C.1.

Finger painting   **5 year old**

Left. Using poster colour on junk
Below. Ropasto being mixed with dry and solid colour

. . . .And Polymer

Over the past three years I have been using Polymer colours (see list below) with children of Primary school age and have been tremendously satisfied with the results obtained. More important, the children using them have been delighted by the thickness of the colour, its range and density and the ease with which it can be applied by brush, roller and knife.

First it must be stressed that I am not recommending a wholesale flight from powder colour, poster paint or tempera blocks. On the grounds of expense alone it would be impossible to let all the children use polymers or acrylics all the time for everything. But it is important to present children with a range of art media so that they are better able to judge what they can handle most successfully.

The peculiarity of polymer colours lies in the fact that although they are very much like oil colours in the way they can be handled, they are water soluble. Yet though water soluble when wet they are virtually waterproof when dry. Most artists' colourmen market various additives to complement the colours and extend the range of activities which are possible with them. There is a medium (or binder) which is sold in containers varying in size from 5 gallons to 500 cc. tubes. The medium may be mixed with the paint (up to 50 per cent by volume) to extend its coverage. Care must be taken not to add more medium than this as the pigmentation of the paint will be thinned to such an extent that its density will be impared. There are also pastes available which when mixed with the paint make it almost thick enough to model with and which are excellent for adding deep areas of texture to paintings and models.

Another fascinating characteristic of this paint is that it is an excellent adhesive and may be used to join almost any grease-free surfaces together (e.g. leather, wood, plastics, paper, card, clay, china, metal, foil, string, fabrics). This means that it is ideal for all types of collage work with young children.

Before using these paints I would stress the following things:

1. The paint may be used straight from the tube, intermixed with other colours, or thinned with water.
2. It may be used on any surface—wood, paper, card, fabric, plaster, tissue, cellophane—and no priming is necessary.
3. It is an adhesive which will allow the paint to be textured as it dries with almost

A colour wheel built up with a palette knife. Red is in the centre and there are graduating bands of orange, yellow, green, blue, indigo and violet

Painting with thin Polymer colours on wet cartridge paper   9 year old

Below. Stencil pattern. Colours used straight from tube   7 year old

anything from lentils to gravel and sharp sand. It also means that the painted surfaces can be married with other materials for collage work—paper, wood shavings, cotton reels and wire.

4. Brushes must be soaked in water immediately after use (otherwise the heads will harden and they will become useless).

Some of the results of the children's experiments are shown here. The explanation beneath each picture will indicate how each was achieved and will, I hope, encourage readers to experiment with this fascinating new medium for themselves.

Painting with Polymers:
Details

PVA/Cryla
George Rowney & Co.,
Percy Street, London, W.C.1.

Marvin
Margros Ltd.,
Monument Way West, Woking,
Surrey.

Temperapolymer
Reeves & Sons Ltd.,
Lincoln Road, Enfield,
Middlesex.

Pictures in Pen and Pencil

The problem of creating an environment in which creative work will flourish is one which continues to cause many teachers considerable heartache. When I talk at refresher courses the question most often posed is not whether it is right to give children a rich variety of materials with which they can experiment but rather how to achieve this desirable end when so little money is available for its implementation. It is this argument, it seems to me, which lies at the root of our problems and assuming that most materials are too expensive for children of Primary school age to use without waste, last year's order of powder colour, grey sugar paper, hog hair fitches and charcoal is repeated . . . and painting becomes once again the main outlet for the child to record graphically his feelings and experiences.

Now while I would not quarrel with those who regard painting a unique method of expressing thoughts, fears and fantasies, I have always had in my classes many children who can draw well but who find it almost impossible to colour their drawings when paint is the only media available. These children become frustrated, particularly after repeated failure to master brush and wet paint. It is as a result of situations like these that the child's natural inventiveness and spontaneity atrophies (and these surely are the very qualities which should be fostered if we regard the development of a creative environment of importance in our schools).

I would suggest, therefore, that our approach to picture making need not be tied to any one material. We should not regard it as our task to teach *art* but to teach *children*. And this of course means that we must first discover the particular interests and abilities of the children which make up our group. There will be some who will delight in producing drawings in fine line, some will be most successful painting with a knife, others will have gifts which are best applied to detailed work with pen, scraper tool or fine brush, while for some fabric scraps, scissors and a reliable adhesive are the most satisfying materials for self-expression.

Let me now return to my opening remarks and examine a few of the materials which are suitable for line drawing. The least complex is the pencil. But do we provide sufficient variety in the type of pencil we offer children? The HB (usually obtained at cost from the L.E.A. supplies department) is by some regarded as an instrument suitable for recording the whole range of childhood

Picture making in chalk, using a charcoal pencil   **9 year old**

Life drawing using water colour markers   **10 year old**

experiences—from Number and English to Art and Craft. I have found that by providing one good set of pencils per group in a variety of grades (3B through to 2H) the children's appreciation of line texture and tone is developed considerably. All of the leading suppliers carry a good range from the leading manufacturers. George Rowney, Venus and Eagle market products of excellent quality which stand up admirably to the rigours of school life. If we are to provide pencils of quality then we must also give those children who wish to draw good quality paper on which to work—cartridge is not unduly expensive, particularly if bought in bulk.

Felt tipped pens offer challenge of quite another sort. Water based markers are most suitable for school use as the colour does not evaporate if the cap is left off. (Although spirit markers are excellent for working on a greater range of surfaces they are prone to dry out very quickly.) Water markers are available in a variety of points made from fibre (Pentel, Pentouch, Eagle) and felt (Platignum, Gem, Eagle). They are useful for life drawings, simple illustrations and diagrams and poster designs. A group

of children in my class experimented by using the markers in conjunction with washes of water colour and also by drawing with them on dampened cartridge paper. In both cases the results—fascinating blends where the colour from the pens "bled"— were most rewarding.

The wax crayon is another drawing material which is very under-rated. It can be used indoors and out, will adhere readily to the cheapest paper without fixing and is suitable for a whole range of techniques. These include resists (using ink, ebony stain or powder colour), chalk and crayon transfers, designs cut in crayon, and pictures on fabric. Details of all these processes are contained in an excellent publication from Cosmic Art Workshop (details on page 63).

If some of the materials mentioned here are made available to young children in addition to paint, there is much greater likelihood of each child in the class discovering which material is right for him. It is upon this self realisation that the skilled teacher creates an atmosphere in which the child feels free to express himself in picture, model, dance and words—the tangible signs of an exciting, purposeful learning situation.

. . . . And Hot Wax

Wax Painting

Stubs of wax crayons need not be wasted, but can be used as a medium for wax painting.

The materials for this type of painting are a candle, wax crayons and cardboard. The candle is lit, the wax crayon is melted over the flame and is allowed to drip or is pressed on to the cardboard.

The outline of a picture can be drawn on the cardboard beforehand or a picture can be built up without this aid.

The candle should be cut in half and stood in a saucer for safety's sake, then, if it is accidentally knocked over, it will fall in the saucer. Another saucer is useful for holding the crayons. There are usually some odd saucers at home which mother is willing to get rid of.

The crayon can be attached to a wire holder to prevent burnt fingers. The holder is made from a short length of thin wire pushed into a cork or a piece of balsa wood for a handle.

Remove any paper from the wax crayon stub. Heat the tip of the wire in the candle flame and it will go easily into one end of the crayon.

The cardboard should not be too large—about 10 in. by 12 in.—as the process is a fairly slow one and the children may get bored with covering too large an area.

The drawing on the cardboard is done in outline only—a thick outline gives the clearest guide. The subject should be kept simple: single trees or flowers are good starting subjects. A portrait is more ambitious.

Painting can be built up without a preliminary outline. Children can be encouraged to work as they wish. Some discussion with anyone about to start a painting without an outline will be found useful in helping to promote ideas.

These paintings usually turn out on the dark side and they can be enhanced by framing them in light card. Tempera colours can be brought in to help lighten up areas. The paint is sprinkled on in powder form and blended with the wax.

Tip of wax crayon about to be melted　　　**Applying the wax**

Below. Some examples of wax painting finished and unfinished

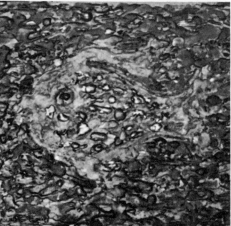

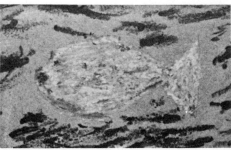

Bibliography
Creative Crayon Craft
Cosmic Art Workshop

Take a Crayon

Wax crayons are, perhaps, the most taken for granted art medium available, yet they possess outstanding characteristics, the greatest of which is the beautiful waxy surface they produce when applied with firm pressure.

Let me start with the most common use of all—drawing and sketching.

Outdoor sketching

Nowadays, with the accent in schools on relating classroom work to actual experience, much more school time is spent outside the classroom. For outdoor sketching a medium is essential that gives a wide colour range, is easily carried and needs no "fixing". I would suggest as a basic sketching kit:

1. Tin of crayons (Finart), pencil.
2. Paper that will not easily tear, e.g. sugar or cartridge.
3. Stiff cardboard or hardboard, clips.
4. Viewfinder (explained later).

What shall I draw?

Many children find difficulty in deciding how much of a particular scene they can actually get on to their paper. A simple viewfinder, made by cutting a rectangular hole, about 5 in. by 4 in. in a piece of sugar paper, will help them to select that section which will fit into the rectangle of paper.

On the whole I have found that young children, especially, will tackle sketching in a most spirited way, but can be easily discouraged from producing lively work. A sketch is merely a quick impression of something that catches the child's interest, and, therefore, criticism of faulty proportion and perspective is unnecessary at this stage, and can always be corrected in the class, if need be. However, for children who find difficulty in portraying something to *their own* satisfaction these pointers may be useful:

1. Use the viewfinder to help you to decide what to draw.
2. Pick out the *main* shape or shapes and draw these first, (this may be part of a building or a tree).
3. Look carefully at the shapes that fit around the main shape, and draw these.
4. Colour in the darkest areas.
5. If there is time, add details and textures.

64

Crayon drawing with strong lines added to paint

The Visit

The children will probably prefer to pursue their investigations in pairs or small groups each group being responsible for making sketches of a particular aspect of the place. Back in the classroom, the skill of the teacher can help to bring the children's various discoveries together, and links with other branches of the curriculum pointed out.

Crayon sketch with water colour added

Working from their sketches, the children may build models or produce more accurate and impressive pictures which could either be framed separately or mounted in the form of a large class survey book. A straight-forward painting, when dry, can be greatly enriched by drawing over it with wax crayons; perhaps to add shading and texture likewise,

A painting enriched with colour

details, highlights, silhouettes, etc., can be painted over a crayon drawing by adding a brushful of soap to the paint. (technique used for illustration, left)

Stained glass

Studies made for stained glass windows may be treated in the following way. Draw the outline of the design on to cartridge paper. Using black crayon, colour the outline and also the lead lines about $\frac{1}{4}$ in. thick, then colour in heavily the rest of the design. Place the design, face down, on to newspaper and lightly rub cooking oil into the back of the paper with a piece of rag. The oil will make the paper translucent. Finally cut a window-mount for the design and hang against a window. The result is usually most effective.

Bibliography.
Introducing Crayon Techniques
H. Pluckrose, Batsford

Drawing with a Needle

Children should be given the opportunity to use a needle and thread in the infants school. "Drawing" with a needle can be as much fun as drawing with a pen or pencil and a few simple stitches can be taught in the process.

The first example shown here was made by a six-year-old girl. Stitching has been kept to a minimum much of the material being glued down. Without actually being aware of it, the little girl has learned back stitch, cross stitch, running stitch and a binding stitch.

Before beginning the lesson, the children were told the Christmas story and looked at pictures and reproductions of famous paintings illustrating various aspects of the story. (This little girl copied the idea of having Jesus's head and arms peeping above the crib from a book illustration.)

A large piece of hessian was used for the background and a needle with a big eye used for the sewing—a darning needle will do very well. The children should be shown how to thread their needles, although casting on and off may have to be done by the teacher.

All the material was put in a central place accessible to everyone. It was sorted into piles and boxes and the children moved about freely taking what they required. Some of the material was cut into small pieces for easy handling, and the cotton and wool was cut into suitable lengths. No distinction was made between paper (which could be glued on), and material and there were many interesting sorts of paper available for use, as well as materials.

As you will see in this example, the angel's wings are made from pieces of a doiley. The little girl noticed at once that the centre of this particular doiley formed a star and that there were many more stars around the edge. She has used the centre one as the Star of Bethlehem and the others as ordinary stars.

The sewing of the earth took quite a while. Guide lines were drawn for the outline of the stable.

In the second example, cotton wool has been used for Father Christmas's beard and for the snow. When the pictures are completed, they can be sewn to a backing cloth, or glued to a piece of card.

Some Thoughts on Picture Making with Young Children

Collage

Primary schools today are tending to think less and less in terms of subjects and increasingly in terms of children learning from first hand experience. All the various forms of expression—language, movement, sound, drawing and painting, work with materials and so on become ways of recording experience and exploring it further. Each of these forms of expression provides its own kind of experience. Each has its own problems to be explored, and children need opportunities to explore each form of expression for its own sake as well as exploring it as a way of recording experience. If there are broad and rich opportunities for exploring materials, for example, children begin to build mental pictures of what materials can do and so become increasingly able to select what they need for a particular purpose.

This article will therefore be concerned with the possibilities of three different kinds of art and craft activity, collage, work with paint, and printing.

The materials available today are many and in addition to working with all kinds of bought materials, teachers and children are becoming very inventive in the use of scrap materials of all kinds. At Christmas time we tend to seek ways of transforming our normal environment, perhaps by hanging traditional decorations, perhaps by attempting to turn the classroom into an Aladdin's cave or a jungle or an underwater world or something of the kind, perhaps by taking the traditional figures of the Christmas scene and making friezes or models or stained glass windows of the stable, the shepherds and the wise men, with Mary and Joseph and the baby Jesus.

We are often helped in our attempt to make the classroom gayer than usual by the fact that there are a number of materials available which are normally hard to come by. There are usually all kinds of wrapping papers and tape in various metallic colours, and some of these may find their way into the classroom before Christmas. Quite a number of things sold as Christmas decorations may also lend themselves to other work. I am therefore planning to look particularly at some of the possibilities of collage, which lends itself to the use of these materials. Many schools make friezes and large Christmas pictures and some of the following ideas might be tried:

1. A collage might be made using varied papers and cards, such as metallic paper, corrugated card or paper, paper from the

A visit to the Zoo. A fine example of mixed materials

packing of biscuits and sweets and so on.
2. The same sort of idea might be carried out with fabrics, sticking fabric to fabric with paste and doing some stitching where suitable.
3. Collage using natural materials, such as bark, pine needles, nuts, seeds, ash and sycamore wings, cones, twigs etc. These can be glued to a background or pressed into rolled out Plasticine.
4. Heavy collage using stones, shells, broken glass and china. This needs to be carried out on hardboard, using tile cement to stick the materials. It needs to be done on a fairly large scale and the pieces must be placed close together. It is easiest to do this by letting the children plan roughly in chalk on the linen surfaced side of the hardboard and then lay a number of the stones or other material in place before they stick, so that they can get the idea of what it will look like. These can then be lifted section by section and tile cement put on and the stones pressed into it. Once they have grasped the idea, there is no reason why they should not stick as they go. This gives a fairly permanent result which can stand out of doors if the edges are protected.
5. A kind of collage can be made with both clay and plaster. Let a group of children each roll out a slab of clay and decorate it by impressing it with such things as stones, shells, bottle caps, etc. Let the clay dry out under a piece of wood (so that it does not

curl) and then take the pieces and arrange them on a piece of board. When the children are satisfied with the arrangement stick the pieces with glue. Slabs made in this way can be made in the shape of people or houses or parts of a picture.

A more permanent way of doing this is to put a wall of clay around each slab and to fill the hollow created with plaster of paris. The slabs made in this way can then be stuck to a background with tile cement.

Yet another way of casting is to fill a box with damp sand and to impress shapes in this and fill them with plaster. These shapes also can be stuck on to hardboard with tile cement. Dry powder colour can be sprinkled into the hollow before casting. Plaster can be coloured by adding powder colour to the dry plaster.

Materials

Cold water paste or polycell will be suitable for the paper and fabric collages. The natural materials need a glue. Gluak is very suitable. Tile cement, obtainable from hardware stores, is probably better for heavy collage.

Books

Mosaic Making. Helen Hutton. Batsford.
Fabric Pictures. Eugenie Alexander. Mills & Boon.
Creative Clay Craft. Ernst Rottger. Batsford.
Some chapters on these ideas in:
Art and Craft in the Primary School Today. Joan Dean. A. & C. Black.

Creative Themes   Water

My ten year olds have just completed a most exciting period in their primary school life. With so many children (over 100) we were able to have two school journeys—one to Broadstairs and the other to Swanage. The remainder of the children were grouped together and they decided to use the River Thames as a theme for project work. The work for each theme began with weekly meetings from January, and then full time involvement for two weeks before the school journeys departed, and continued for the same period after the completion of the stay in the holiday resorts. The "home team" enjoyed six excursions along, on and under the Thames. Naturally, their impressions were recorded in a variety of ways—on film, still and movie, on tape, in pictorial and written form, and through model making.

Model making is not a subject for Friday afternoon or the end of term but one which has equal claim on any time allotted to creative work. When well produced these models provide one of the most comprehensible means of communication of knowledge. Model making also enjoys the advantage of being one where group activity can be positively encouraged without anyone getting disturbed about copying or conversation. Finally the activity serves so well as a bridge between subjects even in schools where only a limited amount of integration takes place.

Let me now return to the activities of April and May, when I was able to share some of the work of all three groups. In every case the activities were dominated by water. In Swanage the party hired a boat at Wareham and travelled down the Trent to Poole Harbour and landed at Brownsea Island; later the party did a beach nature trail among the sand dunes, and on the following day spent time on the beach. At Broadstairs the children also did a beach and rockpool study and then had a most exciting "flight" on a Hovercraft, landing for half an hour on the Goodwin Sands. The Thames group visited the dock area in North Woolwich, the Cutty Sark in Greenwich and the Maritime Museum and then lower down the estuary to Gravesend, where they were able to comb the foreshore at low tide.

With each of the groups in turn I was able to spend time assisting them as they began to translate their experiences into reports, pictures and models.

Each team of two, three or four members discussed the models they had in mind,

Barges on the Sharpness and Gloucester Canal

referring to the many text books, guides and postcards that were available to them.

The approximate size of the model was decided upon, and a baseboard selected from the store of hardboard and timber kept in school. Boxes and other scrap material were assembled and tools, nails, scissors, adhesives made available.

I would like to describe a few of the models that the children produced. The Coot was a bird the class has seen on the marshes bordering the Thames, and a show case, 15 in. x 8 in. and 30 in. high was made. Earth and reeds were added to the model after the background was painted. Using a piece of chicken wire, the shape of the body was formed. A smaller piece was rolled into a short neck and then another piece fashioned into a head with beak. Newspaper was stuffed inside the wire, and then small

pieces of tissue paper were stuck on the bird starting from the head and neck. At the tail end the boys discovered that they had to stick the end of the paper into the wire to get the right effect. A text book had to be referred to for the colour of eye and the white marking over the beak. The same book gave the right markings for the egg. Chicken eggs were painted and placed in the nest.

The model of the Frost Fair on the Thames which the party saw on their excursion to the London Museum fascinated a number of children. They chose a piece of hardboard 1 yard by 18 in. as a baseboard for their interpretation. Rolled newspaper provided the banks for the Thames, and while two boys produced a simple silhouette of the buildings on either bank, three girls began to make stalls from balsa wood and scrap pieces of

Dinas Dam, S. Wales

Arkwright's old mill

cotton. A slight crisis arose when they decided to include St Paul's in the scene. Did it have a dome in place that year? And were there houses on London Bridge too, or had it fallen down? They resolved these problems with reference books.

The largest model needed a 5 ft. x 4 ft. base board and lots of boxes, for this was to be the story of a river. The boxes were piled at one end of the board and their contours were softened with rolled up newspaper. Then sheet after sheet of paper was pasted and draped over the model until five or six layers were in place. Overnight this dried and then a thick white paint, given body with paste, was applied over the model. When this had dried, details were added. The snow line was established, heather added to the highest slopes, trees planted where only they could grow. As we moved down the mountain so agriculture took over with fields growing crops. But the dominant feature was the river which began on the mountain side and tumbled down to the sea. First in long straight runs and then as it reached the plains meandering its way to the ocean. Bridges, towns, roads, boats were added as the children recalled features they had heard about and seen.

Other groups in this section made a dock and ship being unloaded; a tug and laden barges; a London dock with lock and unloading facilities for dozens of craft; an estuary scene with shipping and the correct distribution of buoys.

The Swanage party agreed that Lulworth Cove was a spectacular formation and two boys used white card to form the great circular basin. They found the aerial view in the guide book refreshed their memories and helped them to cut the shapes to join with Sellotape to make an excellent likeness of the feature. Papier mâché was added to the basin to simulate the sea. This was painted when dry. Balsa wood was used for the houses of the village. For beauty on the water, it is difficult to surpass the swan. To see these birds in great numbers is certainly an exciting experience and our party enjoyed their visit to Abbotsbury Swannery at nesting time.

Two girls chose to do a life size model of a swan. To do this they made a double cut-out of the shape of a swan. The tail and bottom of the neck were joined with Sellotape and paper used to fill the shape out. The card left over from the original cut-out was used to provide wings which were fixed over the top of paper filling. Twigs and reeds were collected to make the nest.

The Broadstairs party were able to get leaflets and postcards from the Hovercraft firm at Ramsgate and also a plan of the machine from a reference book. They decided to work as accurately as they could to scale. Around a cardboard hull they wrapped carefully folded newspaper to represent the cushion or skirt. Balsa wood shapes were used for the cabin and on this was drawn the faces of the passengers inside. Card was used for the propeller and

rudder and tail plane sections. Papier mâché formed the rough sea and cotton wool the spray which rose up the sides of the vehicle. Chicken wire suitably moulded and stapled to a heavy baseboard 2 ft. by 2 ft. made the shape of a rockpool. This was covered by large sheets of pasted paper. Muslin and plaster squares would also have been satisfactory. It was then painted to make the rock formation more realistic. Shells and other dried finds from the beach were added to the model and they had just enough of the smell of the sea about them to transport one back again to the Kent coast.

All these models, along with paintings, brass rubbings, photographs, spoken and written reports were presented in the middle of May to give a series of personal impressions of places and things seen.

The children you teach will have spent their holidays by the sea, or possibly in the country near a river. Perhaps your school stands near a canal or a pond. Can the children visit it—make sketches, and when back in school get their minds and hands to work to show others how they felt and what they learnt when they looked at **water**?

The river and the sea

The world beneath the sea is a subject which never fails to interest children of Primary School age. Moreover since it is wide ranging in content, a great variety of picture making methods may be introduced.

The simplest method of making fish pictures is to use coloured sticky paper and loop it to give the impression of scales, the outline shape of the fish having been first drawn on sugar or cartridge paper. It is best to discuss the peculiar qualities of fish with the group before they begin to work. What do fish look like? Are all fish the same shape? What do fish have in common? Provide photographs for the children to study—photographs showing different types of fish (e.g. swordfish, shark, carp, plaice, Siamese fighting fish, angel fish, eel).

Having introduced the subject through paper montage techniques, ask the children if they can think of other ways in which it could be treated. All sorts of materials will be suggested—postage stamps, eggshell scraps, milk bottle tops, fabric oddments, ceramic chips, glass mosaic tessera. Obviously the only relevant considerations here will be: (1) The mounting material, (2) the adhesive. I have found that PVA adhesive (now obtainable from the main art suppliers) is suitable for glueing almost anything—from broken earthenware to tissue paper.

The type of mounting board (which could be as light as pastel paper or as heavy as chipboard) will of course be determined by the materials used in the picture (the heavier the "junk", the heavier the mounting board).

If children are working with paper on paper or thin board the fish shapes may be cut out and arranged to make a group picture. The shapes may be mounted flat or glued on to matchboxes and then mounted to give dimension to the picture. Raffia, paper, wood or wool scraps arranged between the fish, with a "floor" of glasspaper or coarse hessian can be used to complete the design. Fish cut outs are also invaluable for giving the group some experience of display. Here a pea or bean net draped across a corner of the classroom or in a window recess will give the children tremendous scope for self discovery.

How best can the shapes be grouped? What is needed for the background? Could a table covered with shells and sand be incorporated into the display? What other things could be made—a diver, a mermaid,

Fish in netting　　　　　　　　　　　**10 year old**

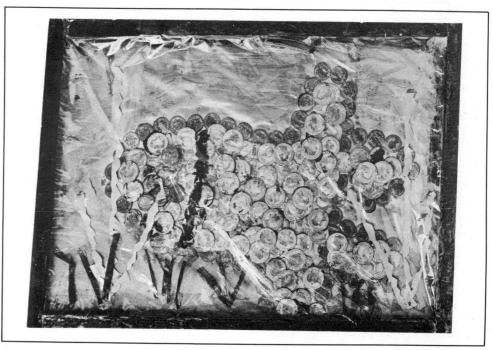

Card money　　　　　　　　　　　**8 year old**

a treasure chest, the figurehead from a sunken galleon? Could some of the fish be suspended from the ceiling so that they swing freely above the netting?

Development of picture making along the lines indicated above will often result in pictures of unusual quality. Compare the "Sea Dragon" painted by a twelve year old in heavy layers, of aquapasto and water colour with "aquarium fish" built from cardboard money by an eight year old.

If the sea is taken as a general theme it is obvious that the group should not be restricted to underwater pictures. "The galleon" was drawn by a seven year old in felt tipped pen, while his less gifted contemporary was equally proud of his boat made from dried pulses and temperapolymer colour. (See page 70.)

Galleons fighting (felt pen)　　　　　　**7 year old**

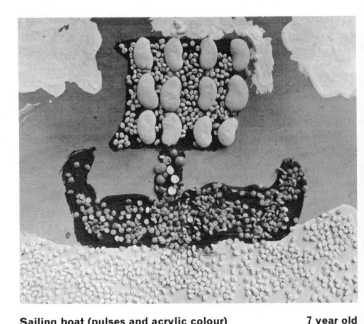

Sailing boat (pulses and acrylic colour)　　　　　**7 year old**

Sea dragon　　　　　**12 year old**
(aquapasto and water colour)

Our primary pupils these days are great in science and mathematics and their enthusiasm arises in part from the fact that these subjects, as now regarded, admit of a certain amount of messing about with water and other basic materials; natural and productive activities which for so long have been among the childish activities put away at the mature age of seven plus.

If we postulate—very reasonably—a teacher who has aroused a great flow of interest by a series of experiments with water, we may imagine his considering how to make use of it. If he reflects on Margaret Greaves' observation that "In the classroom one should begin from the immediate environment and first-hand knowledge, *but it is a mistake to be always limited to it*" (One World and Another, Teachers' Book—Methuen) and if he knows his Sybil Marshall (Experiment in Education—Cambridge) he might well decide on a "topic" on Holland.

At some stage in the complex of writing and reading and painting and modelling (with the Dutch and Flemish schools of painting thrown in as a bonus) he might wish to throw emphasis on the elemental nature of water, in which case he would do well to reflect on the use he could make of poetry and music. I do not claim that to do this is a fundamental of classroom practice, but my observation and experience indicate that it affords a means of imparting a very desirable richness of texture, so to speak, to teaching content.

Treating of music first, our teacher would be very foolish to expect his children to sit solemnly listening (or more likely uproariously not listening) to long pieces such as Smetana's "Ma Vlast" just because it is "about water" although it is music which he would certainly wish to make use of in some way. I am inclined to the belief that he would do well to acknowledge the debt we all owe to the B.B.C. and introduce his music through movement, at least in the early stages. He might prefer to tape selected passages, of course, which prompts me to express the hope that colleges of education will ensure that students are trained in the use of tape-recorders and mechanical aids in general.

There is no difficulty, when we turn to actual items, in finding some very good storms: the overtures to the "Flying Dutchman" and "William Tell"; the Fourth Movement of Beethoven's "Pastoral" Symphony; the chorus "He gave them hailstones" from Handel's "Israel in Egypt"; the Interlude in Britten's "Peter Grimes"; and those which occur in Britten's "Noye's Fludde", Berlioz "Trojans" and Rossini's "Barber". If our teacher chooses any of these we may assume that he is concentrating on the struggles against tempest and flood which punctuate Dutch history, in which case he need not confine himself to excerpts in which composers specifically set out to illustrate such happenings. Where is conflict and terror better expressed than in the "Dies Irae", "Tuba Mirum" and "Rex Tremendae" of Verdi's "Requiem Mass", or in "The Ride to the Abyss" from "The Damnation of Faust" by Berlioz.

For the sea in its "dragon-haunted" aspect, which would include the adventures of all the great naval explorers from Jason onwards and including those whose efforts resulted in the making of the Admiralty Charts (and not forgetting Sir Francis Chichester), I recommend "Neptune" from Holst's "Planets" Suite, Debussy's "La Mer", Mendelssohn's overtures "Hebrides" and "Calm Sea and a Prosperous Voyage", the "Dawn" and "Moonlight" interludes from Britten's "Peter Grimes", the Triton music from Respighi's "Fountains of Rome", Variation XIII from Elgar's "Enigma Variations", Balfour Gardiner's "News from Whydah" (if available) and Stanford's "Songs of the Fleet" and "Songs of the Sea" (with the same proviso).

Sea shanties seem too obvious to mention but it should be pointed out that some of them are very suitable to our need and they enable the children to take an active part in the proceedings; which reminds me to warn the inexperienced that children react to the human voice in "serious" music in unexpected ways, if it is not their own. And if you listen to, say, the "Rhinemaidens" or a Verdi tenor and try to shed adult sophistication as you do it, you will understand why children often laugh at a first hearing.

If our teacher became ambitious and as his children became more experienced, he might turn to the more domestic aspects of water, in which case Smetana's tuneful geography lesson, "Ma Vlast", would be invaluable. Liszt's "Au bord d'une Source" and "Fountains at the Villa d'Este" describe water in its pastoral and decorative aspects and Schubert's "Die Schöne Mullerin" is full of the chatter of streams and the noise of mills which "Clack so busy by the brook". His song "Die Forelle" and the variations on it in his quintet should please the anglers and might be coupled with Wolcot's poem which ends

**"And when an angler for his dish,
Through gluttony's vile sin,
Attempts, a wretch, to pull thee out,
God give thee strength, O gentle trout,
To pull the raskall in."**

The "Song of the Volga Boatmen" and "Ol' Man River" deal directly with work on or by rivers and the latter seems to lead to Tom and Huck, who, with a river to play with, hardly needed all a teacher's careful planning. They remind us, though, that much

of this music has obvious literary connections. Neptune reminds us of the history and legends of Greece, Mendelssohn of the Celtic myths, Noah of Bible stories and tales of the saints—Liszt has a piano piece "Légende" describing St. Francis of Paola making his miraculous crossing of the Straits of Messina.

We need not confine ourselves to literature which has a connection with music, of course. A teacher with present knowledge or the time for extensive reading may turn to source books such as Hakluyt but the poets and novelists have already taken the facts and raised them to a higher power of concentration and inspiration than can be achieved by someone (this is true) who has merely experienced and suffered. The Browning tag—

**". . . we love
First when we see them painted, things we have passed
Perhaps a hundred times, nor cared to see;
And so they are better painted . . ."**

generalises on the matter and Lowes' great book, "The Road to Xanadu" examines in detail the particular case of "The Ancient Mariner", in which he shows how Coleridge achieved an accuracy in describing what he never saw, which we are told amazes seafaring men. It does not matter to young children that he derived his information from reading Hakluyt and his like and talking to Nelson's admired Captain Ball; but they will respond to passages such as

**"And now there came both mist and snow
And it grew wondrous cold
And ice, mast-high, came floating by
As green as emerald.
And through the drifts the snowy clifts
Did send a dismal sheen."**
And
**"The ice was here, the ice was there
The ice was all around
It cracked and growled, and roared and howled,
Like noises in a swound."** And
**"Beyond the shadow of the ship
I watched the water snakes:
They moved in tracks of shining white,
And when they reared, the elfin light
Fell off in hoary flakes.
Within the shadow of the ship
I watched their rich attire:
Blue, glossy green and velvet black,
They coiled and swam: and every track
Was a flash of golden fire."**

In fact, eleven year olds at least will respond to the whole poem, well read (I recommend Burton's Argo record) and if they have the text before them (a good rule with "difficult" or long poems), it is hardly necessary to comment on the attraction of the colours in the excerpts.

Other passages of value are the opening scene of "The Tempest", Ingelow's "High Tide", "The Forsaken Merman", the end of "Off the Ground" and "Sunk Lyonesse" by de la Mare (with Debussy's "Cathedrale Engloutie" as illustration), ballads too numerous to specify (but including those odd ones about seal women), Flecker's "The Old Ships", Gibson's "Flannan Isle", Squire's sonnet "There was an Indian" and "The Ship", Dobell's "How's my Boy?", Davies' "The Child and the Mariner", which tells—shades of the Torrey Canyon—of how

**"The sea's sharp needles, firm and strong
Ripped open the bellies of strong iron ships,"**

and John Gray's "The Flying Fish", the "scaled bird" which leaps "with a silken swish" and dies panting "in crystal and mother-of-pearl".

Kipling's "Smugglers' Song" is a standard piece and I would think his poems worth further investigation, especially as he writes of steam ships more than most. Someone may discover a poem called "Big Steamers"! (This a joke for the benefit of the middle-aged and beyond.)

Masefield, too, offers richer freight than "Cargoes" (though it is not the bad poem that Robert Graves makes out) in poems like "Spanish Waters" and in many passages in his narrative poems, for he, of course, had direct experience of what he wrote about the life of those who man "the tall ship, under topsails, swaying" on the sea.

For prose reading, there are "The Wind in the Willows", "The Borrowers Afloat", the adventures of Sindbad, Crusoe and excerpts such as the typhoon in "The Caine Mutiny" and the rising of the flood in "The Elephant and the Kangaroo".

Enthusiasts for mime could try "The Sorcerer's Apprentice" with Dukas' music and the crossing of the Red Sea with choruses from "Israel in Egypt".

Looking at Pictures

JOSEPH MALLORD WILLIAM TURNER
1775–1851

Life

Turner was the only child of a barber who kept a shop at 26, Maiden Lane, Covent Garden, and it was in the window of this shop that the work of the young Turner was first displayed for sale at prices of two or three shillings apiece. His earliest known drawing, dating from his ninth year, is of Margate Church. His schooling was very elementary. His father taught him to read, and although he journeyed to the continent frequently in later life, he never mastered any foreign language, indeed he scarcely mastered his own. His childhood was not particularly happy, the Turner home being disturbed by the ungovernable temper of the mother, who ended her days in an asylum. This may account for much that was eccentric and unsociable in Turner's character. He was, however, devoted to his father, who ran his son's studio from 1800 onwards, stretching canvases, preparing the palette, varnishing the finished work, and from 1812 attending to the gallery attached to the house in Queen Anne Street, where Turner's pictures could be both viewed and purchased.

Turner said, "If Tom Girtin had lived, I should have starved". He had met the watercolourist, Girtin, born in the same year as himself, at the house of the art patron, Dr. Munro, who later purchased from the artists at the cost of their suppers and half-a-crown apiece, copies of Cozen's watercolours, drawn by Girtin and painted by Turner. Turner became Girtin's companion on sketching expeditions, when they made topographical studies of buildings and landscape in different parts of Britain. Girtin's premature death in 1802 brought an end to the friendship, but Turner gained something from Girtin's originality of style, and the power he brought to watercolour painting.

Turner's earliest employment was colouring prints for engravers: after this he was admitted to the Academy Schools exhibiting his first work in the Academy, a watercolour of Lambeth Palace, at the age of fifteen, and from 1790 onwards he was a regular exhibitor until within a few years of his death. He was made an A.R.A. at the age of 24, a full Academician at 27, and Professor of Perspective at 32. It is said that his Academy speeches were "confused, tedious, obscure and difficult to follow"; but his opinions were always treated with respect.

In his long life, Turner did not have many close friends; he was by temperament secretive, and did not encourage intimacy. His person was small, insignificant, and being sensitive about this seeming inferiority, he sought solitude in his work. It is also said he suffered a disappointment in love in his earlier days. Returning from an absence of several years when he had been busy increasing his reputation, he found the lady of his choice wedded to another. This episode did little to improve his relations with women, and he remained unmarried, employing a housekeeper, Hannah Danby, to look after his establishment in Queen Anne Street on the death of his father in 1830. His two important friends and patrons were Lord Egremont of Petworth House and Walter Fawkes of Farnley Hall. He stayed with both, having a studio for his use at Petworth, where he painted frequently until the death of Lord Egremont in 1837, and where a group of his paintings may be seen today.

By inclination, Turner lived a very simple life and cared nothing for society or the social life of the art world. On sketching tours, bread, cheese and beer made an adequate dinner. Then, after a few hours' sleep with his head on an inn table, he would be out to sketch the sunrise. He worked in snow storms, storms at sea, wind and rain. He left his carriage when crossing the Alps in the snows of January to sketch mountain ridges and deep gorges. He could walk twenty or thirty miles a day with ease. He was devoted to his art, and no personal discomforts deterred him; the nineteen thousand watercolours in the British Museum and the series of engravings "Liber Studiorum" bear testimony to the fervour of his industry. Many stories are told to his discredit accusing him of avarice, but he could also be exceptionally generous, though his acts of generosity with his usual reticence he did not disclose.

He made several prolonged visits to the continent, the first during the lull in the Napoleonic Wars, 1802–1803, when he recorded his first impressions of Alpine scenery. War prevented continental travel until 1815, and it was not until 1819 that he at last reached Italy. He had been painting imaginary Italian scenery for years, so he was fascinated by the original, and the country and art made a lasting impression on him and his work. Here, with phenomenal zeal, he completed fifteen hundred detailed drawings and watercolours in Rome alone. His second visit was in 1828, and in 1843 he made a farewell tour, wandering from place to place, an ageing and solitary figure.

By 1827 he had reached the pinnacle of success. He could demand excellent terms for his work, and even refused to sell any picture he particularly liked, sometimes buying back his own work, which was stored in the gallery in Queen Anne Street, in growing dirt and disorder, until after Turner's death, when Ruskin, opening up the gallery, said, "Nothing since Pompeii so impressed me . . . the finest productions of art, buried for forty years".

From 1830 to 1840 was a period of most intense activity for him and some of his most famous oil paintings date from this time, pictures such as "The Fighting Temeraire", "The Parting of Hero and Leander", "Ulysses deriding Polyphemus". Nonetheless, the change towards abstraction is increasingly apparent in these years, until in the work of his last period he seems to float films of colour across his canvases, submerging all detail in a hazy light.

He became more and more of a recluse and ended his life known as "Admiral Booth" in the obscurity of a small house along the water front at Chelsea kept by his old Margate landlady, Mrs. Booth. He died there, aged 76, leaving a large fortune to found a home for the support of "poor and decayed male artists", and bequeathing his pictures to the nation, on condition they were exhibited in rooms of their own, to be called "Turner's Gallery". A large selection of these paintings may be seen in the Tate Gallery. The terms of the will were confused, and the fortune was wasted in legal expenses. The residue went to his next-of-kin, to whom he had not wished to leave a farthing. A simple stone marks his grave in the artists' corner in the crypt of St. Paul's Cathedral.

Snow-storm at sea

The full title of this work is "Snow-Storm: steam boat off a harbour's mouth making signals in shallow water, and going by the lead. The author was in that storm the night the *Ariel* left Harwich". Many of Turner's most celebrated works are marine subjects and nearly all his pictures include at least a glimpse of water. Sometimes he chose tranquillity; the smooth silky-finished surfaces of lakes, Venetian canals and the empty sea shore at dusk; or, in his own unique style, he described the unleashed forces of nature, the waves whipped into a whirlpool of elemental fury.

Snow Storm at Sea. Reproduced by courtesy of the Trustees of the National Gallery, London

For this picture, Turner, aged 67, was lashed to the boat's mast; this is almost the only visible structure in the work, and around it in a great whirling vortex spins the sky, sea and smoke, indivisible, and creating a cavity of light just right of centre in which the helpless boat can be vaguely discerned. "I did not expect to escape," said Turner of his four hour ordeal, "but I felt bound to record it if I did". As he conveys this fearful experience, he expresses his feelings of man's hopeless weakness when caught in the uncontrollable and destructive violence of the elements.

Turner's development as a painter

Turner's early work is full of exact detail, but as he grew older he discarded topographical accuracy, working towards a broad and free handling of colour. The clear outlines of forms are dissolved into his luminous atmosphere of "tinted steam", and the power of colour transcends form. Nevertheless, his development would have been impossible but for the immense detailed knowledge he possessed of the forms he painted. He had made such studies of wave forms, that he was able to recreate them at will; and he could draw the most complicated man o' war, complete with guns and rigging, entirely from memory.

Turner also painted many classical subjects. A great epic from antiquity such as "Hannibal crossing the Alps" would seize hold of his imagination and by addition of a snow storm and with dramatic rending of dark clouds, he could turn his theme into an apocalyptic catastrophe of Wagnerian proportions. Other subjects, fires, plagues, avalanches, deluges, stormy shores, volcanic eruptions, all show his deep interest in the dynamic forces of nature and the transitory quality of human life amid overwhelming odds.

To emphasize the inner meaning of his work he often added poetic quotations to his titles, mainly from his own incomprehensible poem "The Fallacies of Hope", which has, despite its poor grammar and poetry, a lofty, if baffling, grandeur of thought and sentiment.

The Nativity (1)

The "Mystic Nativity" by Botticelli

Botticelli, the son of a Florentine tanner, born in 1444 (or 45), is really called Alessandro di Mariano dei Filipepi, but nicknamed Botticelli, or "little barrel", possibly taking the name from an elder brother with whom he lived and who was similarly named. He is referred to in a document of 1457 as aged thirteen, of weak health, and still at school. This would indicate a fairly extensive education in those days for one of his status. His first work was probably with another of his brothers, a goldsmith and gold leaf beater. But his talent for painting being early apparent, he was apprenticed to Fra Filippo Lippi, probably remaining with him as an assistant until 1467, when Lippi finally left Florence.

In the fifteenth century Florentine Art was mainly concerned with sculptural form, the play of light on rounded surfaces, and the painted illusion of three dimensional space by the use of linear perspective. These ideas had been originated by Giotto in the early fourteenth century and were developed by Masaccio, Piero della Francesca and Verrocchio. Botticelli was also influenced by these ideas, but developed an individual style which is characterised by the vigour and beauty of its line, Botticelli's principal means of expression, and his art has therefore something in common with the art of Siena. He did, nevertheless, frequent Verrocchio's workshop, a busy and sociable place, noted for bronze casting and stone carving as well as painting. Here he became friendly with the young Leonardo da Vinci, who was later to unite the two trends of Italian Art, the linear beauty of Siena with the sculptural form of Florence, into the supreme art of the High Renaissance.

Botticelli never married, but generally lived at home with his brothers, though he set up his own workshop, and his first independent work dates from 1470. One of his pupils was Filippino Lippi, the son of his old master. Although he was never rich, he was never poor enough to feel distress, and benefited by the patronage of both the Pope and the ruling family in Florence, the Medici.

He painted his two most famous works, the "Primavera" (1477-78) and the "Birth of Venus" (1485-86) for the decoration of a Medici Villa. At this time the study of antique remains was only in its infancy, and both these pictures show a new pagan delight in bodily beauty and movement.

In 1481 Botticelli was summoned by the Pope to Rome to decorate, with other noted painters, the walls of the Sistine Chapel. Here he completed three large frescoes, often overlooked by present day visitors marvelling at the magnitude of Michelangelo's work in the same chapel.

In the late 1480s signs of agitation of spirit became increasingly perceptible in Botticelli's work. His linear rhythms became straighter expressing a tension and emotional turbulence which increased on the death of Lorenzo II Magnifico in 1492 and during the rule of his worthless son which followed. In Rome, a Borgia, Alexander VI, by immense sums spent on bribery, was elected to the Holy See. He regarded the papacy as an instrument for his worldly schemes, had no thought for the religious duties of his position, and by his greed, his debauchery and the murders committed in his name, brought the Church to its lowest level of degradation. In Florence, Savonarola, a brilliantly intellectual Dominican friar, with superb powers of oratory, thundered great apocalyptic sermons from the Cathedral, full of the wrath and vengeance of God about to strike down the wickedness of both Church and Pope. One of Botticelli's brothers came under the Fra's influence, and became a devoted follower, as did Botticelli himself after the martyrdom of Savonarola in 1498. The religious ecstacy manifested in Botticelli's work of his last years clearly shows evidence of the great spiritual turmoil through which he lived. After 1500 very few documents relate to the artist, but we do know he served on the committee 1503-4 to decide on the placing of the marble statue of David by Michelangelo. At his death in 1510, Botticelli was buried in Florence. He was probably regarded by then as a somewhat old-fashioned artist, and for this reason his work was lost in obscurity until rescued from oblivion in the nineteenth century.

The "Mystic Nativity"

The Holy Family, the ox and the ass are seen in the centre of the composition under the roof of a simple shelter built against a cavelike aperture in the rock. Enclosing the background, a typical Botticelli device, is a grove of trees, probably myrtle, the tree used in antiquity to symbolise love. On the stable roof are three angels, Grace, Truth and Justice, referred to by Savonarola in his Christmas sermons of 1493 and 1494, when he urged those who wished to see Florence as the new Nazareth to go spiritually to the manger and rediscover these virtues attending the infant Christ.

A heavenly field of gold in the sky is filled with the angelic choir, who, with hands joined and a fluttering of draperies and ribbons weave a chain of eternal dance, reminiscent of the painter's three graces in his "Primavera", where the undulating linear rhythms rise and fall in a similar circular movement.

The three robed men in the ecstatic embrace of angels in the foreground are often thought to portray Savonarola himself and his two fellow martyrs, but this view is not universally held by critics. Along the topmost edge of the picture, not shown, is painted in Greek an epigraph, beginning, "I Alessandro, painted this painting at the end of 1500 during the troubles in Italy", and goes on to refer to the eleventh chapter of the Revelation of St. John and the liberation of the devil, expressing a hope the devil would soon be chained and "trod upon just as in this painting". And, indeed, under the rocks in the foreground can be discovered several devils, transfixed by shafts, the one on the extreme right being particularly unmannerly.

The arrangement in three registers on the flat surface gives a curiously archaic look to the work. The figures in the foreground, although nearer the spectator, are smaller than the more distant Virgin, thus conflicting with our ideas of perspective. This brings the figure of the Virgin to the surface of the picture plane, so that while the work has very little of the three dimensional depth much admired at the time, it has, in compensation, a superb two dimensional design on the flat surface.

Botticelli has arranged his central figures in a triangular group. These fit into the space created by the cave entrance which also serves to separate this group from the rest of the picture. The seated, folded figure of Joseph, the ox and ass, build up one side of the triangle. The kneeling figure of the Virgin, enclosed by the taut linear edges of her mantle, with submissive dedication fills the second side. The Child rests in the centre of the group, held in an even smaller triangular unit within the lines formed by the Virgin's robe and the neck of the ass. And the ass, symbolic of all that is most dull and stupid in human life, pauses in his munching, arrested by the appealing gesture of the Child, and with a vague suspicion that something out of the way has occurred.

In his early work Botticelli's style has a peculiar strain of haunting beauty and melancholic grace; "The sadness of the exile" characterises Botticelli's work, wrote

Page 74. The 'Mystic Nativity' by Botticelli
Above. Detail of centre part

Pater. The superb draughtsmanship, the light, decorative colouring, the inventive charm and poetic lyricism make him a unique and individual artist. As he developed and was caught in the religious controversies of his day, his work took on a vehemence of expression, a passionate excitement. In his later years, instead of gentle waving rhythms his lines shoot and leap over the picture with an angular abrupt-ness, and a disturbing energy tosses his figures about in an agony of drama and torment. In the " Mystic Nativity", although it is among his last works, a less frantic note is struck.

The Child reaches out his hand in a gesture of both supplication and blessing, a symbol of spiritual giving and receiving which is, after all, the special message of Christmas-tide.

Packing tubes and light bulbs make impressive figures   9 year olds   . . . as do bottles dressed with felt

Christmas is a time when the pressures upon the teacher are often at their greatest (carol concerts, parties, nativity plays, school entertainments and the like) taking toll upon stamina and ingenuity. This invariably means that something goes overboard and more often than not it is the art and craft activities of the group which suffer. This is not to say that craft is ignored (in fact it is usually embraced with enthusiasm in the most unlikely quarters). The hall has to be decorated, properties made for the school play, table centres prepared as well as the inevitable run of Christmas cards and calendars for the new year.

The danger, when such a wealth of activities are of necessity crammed into a few hectic weeks, lies in the fact that the teacher in an attempt to "get everything done" follows a plan which was successful in previous years. This means that instead of the Christmas story providing opportunity for experiment with things new, it provides nothing more than the excuse for the rebirth of old techniques (and sometimes even the resurrection of last year's pictures, mobiles, displays and models).

Think for a moment of the possible ways of making the figures for a Christmas crib. I had always thought (until last year) that with young children, clay was the most successful medium for making figures. I had always used clay, the results were pleasing, the material was clean in use and easy to handle. Was there any need to be exotic or experimental? What happened last year to make me change my mind? I went into a nursery class (the children were all aged between 3 and 4) and saw a large crib scene. The figures were made from paper bags. Each bag was partially filled with rubber foam scraps, then twisted (an elastic band held this in place). The filled portion represented the head, the rest of the bag, opened fully at the base the remainder of the body. A touch of paint here and there, completed the figures, which spoke as eloquently of the birth of Christ as anything I have seen in cathedral or parish church. It is, of course, possible to achieve variety by varying the base used for the figures from year to year. (The base selected will give a certain uniform character to the figures.)

Thus wire (chicken or galvanised) might be chosen, Here the figures will tend to be simple in form, although how the armature is covered will to some extent determine the degree of detail obtained. Among the many different materials which could be used plaster and scrim and papier mâché come high on my list. Egg trays, soaked in water and broken down into a thick cream, forms the base of another excellent covering medium. Into this stir an equal quantity of premixed Polyfilla. This Polyfilla+egg tray mix may be pushed onto the wire with the hands and textured with knife and brush. When hard (it sets overnight), rough patches may be smoothed with glass paper. Bottles (wine, large medicine, cordial) are another useful base. When they have been given a head (from Plasticine, clay paper twist) they may be covered (i.e. given body shaping) in strips of paper soaked in paste, butter muslin or thin cotton fabric soaked in plaster of Paris or vilene soaked in Polyfilla. Alternatively the bottle could merely be given a head and then dressed in a costume made from felt, linen or cotton.

Neo-Fol is another excellent material for Christmas figures. This is a heavy foil marketed by Reeves Ltd. It may be cut with scissors or knife, folded, textured (by drawing onto it with a clay tool or dry bits) painted, glued with an impact adhesive and stapled. Indeed, it may be used instead of card or paper for all types of dimensional modelling. It has the added advantage that when bent into gentle curves it holds its shape.

So much for the figures—what of the base? The most satisfactory results are often

77

achieved when the setting is discussed with the group before they begin to work. Is the scene to be traditional with the figures displayed in a stable? If so, a large cardboard box forms the most easily constructed base particularly if it is faced with strips of balsa wood before painting. A cave made from layers of newspaper is another possibility (readers with a mechanical turn of mind can achieve interesting results here by lighting it within using a dry cell battery). Sand, small stones, a lock or two, straw, raffia will be needed for the base. If the figures are a little unstable (as they might well be if made by very small children) a thick bed of sand will do much to keep them upright.

This brief article is not meant to indicate a process in detail but to encourage experiment. The Christmas story, which after all is about a homeless family often suffers from a sentimental approach (compare for example, the typical "Jesus meek and gentle" nativity scene with the ideas expressed in T. S. Eliot's "Coming of the Magi"—"This birth was hard and bitter agony for us, like death, our death"). If the children can be encouraged to think to experiment, to express what they *feel* about the story (instead of echoing a sugary adult approach) then Christmastime can provide a unique opportunity for art and craft work which is both purposeful and alive.

Working with wire and plaster   11 year old

Angel in Neo-Fol   10 year old

A Christmas Crib

9 year olds

The Story of Christmas Cards

New Year and Christmas have always been in the nature of family festivals. In Ancient Egypt and Rome all members of a family group visited each other at this time of the year to exchange greetings and small gifts. Throughout the greater part of the Middle Ages travel was very limited and few people ever moved away from their villages or town and it was still very easy to make personal visits. However, from the 16th century onwards as travel became easier families began to spread and there grew up a need for some substitute for the personal visit.

Around the middle of the 15th century there developed, apparently in Germany, the custom of sending an engraved greeting at New Year. Most surviving examples include some reference, directly or indirectly, to both Christ and the New Year and angels, birds, flowers, ships and, of course, the Christ Child, are included in the designs. The habit of sending such greetings seems to have been abandoned during the 16th and 17th centuries for very few examples have survived. This change may have been due to the current religious atmosphere or perhaps just a change in habit.

Early in the 18th century some people sent out calendars or large prints at the end of the year and there also appeared the quodlibet. These were sheets showing some of the wares offered by printers. Many of these

'The Magi'. Sold in aid of the funds of the British Red Cross Society

Sold in aid of the Save the Children Fund

were sent out in the form of a New Year greeting often with an appropriate illustration figuring prominently at the centre. These seem to have been common over most of Europe and were in the nature of advertisements soliciting business.

Somewhat similar were the begging broadsheets distributed by local parish servants such as the bellman, watchman or night beadle. These were produced certainly as early as the 17th century and continued well into the 19th century. Most of them were large, often about 12"x18" and at the top and sides were a number of small woodcuts illustrating the Annunciation, the Nativity, the shepherds, the Massacre of the Innocents or similar religious scenes, whilst others were edged with a floral theme. One such example, dated 1800, is entitled A Copy of Verses Humbly Presented To All My Worthy Masters and Mistresses In The Parish of West Ham in the County of Essex, by William Meade Bellman and Crier. It has some 21 verses dedicated to a variety of patrons including St. Michael, St. John, Christmas Day, The Queen, The King, but the crux of the matter is to be found in the verse headed "To My Masters" which reads:

My gen'rous masters, when you're safe in bed,
With spouse in arms, and pillow under head,
When love and peace your manly breasts invest,
Your cares beguil'd, and sinking into rest,

Think of your Bellman, cold, and void of ease,
Without one comfort, save his hope to please,
And let not this old adage 'scape your minds,
"Labour best sweetens the reward it finds."

Broadsheets were sold by printers and used by school children and by the Parish charity boys who hoped to collect small rewards for their skill in colouring and penmanship on these ready printed sheets.

In Europe a number of smaller cards primarily intended for New Years greetings were common. The cards were small being more or less visiting cards with an appropriate greeting added. The invention of lithography in 1798 made possible the more faithful reproduction of artists' work and there was naturally a great increase in the use of this new technique. Engraving was commonly used in the production of greetings and some issued early in the 19th century were designed so that they could be used for a whole variety of occasions. They simply bore the words Anniversary, To, From, with a space for the insertion of a date, so that it might be used for birthdays, Christmas, New Year and so on.

It was in the 1840s that the first Christmas Card as we understand it today was produced. The stimulus for the idea apparently came from Sir Henry Cole who was a man of strong principles and, in some ways, considerably in advance of his own time. He was interested in education and was very keen

'The Journey'. Sold by Christian Aid

'Mexican Toy Fair', the design contributed to UNICEF, the United Nations Children's Fund, by the Swiss artist, Trudi Weber, for the 1968 card sales

on producing good quality, cheap, illustrated children's books and he was also anxious to restore to their pride of place some of the old traditional stories and rhymes that had been neglected by educationists of the early 19th century. He is also credited with the first children's commercial paint box as well as sets of construction playing bricks. It was this desire for better quality artistic values that led Sir Henry Cole to suggest to a friend, John Calcott Horsley, that he should design an attractive form of greetings card. This was done in 1843 and the lithographed, hand coloured card, printed in Holborn, shows a family group surrounded by vines and obviously sharing in good cheer with the conventional Merry Christmas and a Happy New Year printed below the picture. The card itself measures approximately 5″x3″ and is on a single stiff piece of cardboard. There is a space for the name of the addressee and the back of the card is quite blank. About a thousand copies were retailed at the expensive price of 1/- each. Several others have been credited with the first card but Horsley's example has the strongest claim.

Once the first step had been made others began to exploit the idea. Printed coloured cards did not immediately catch on and in the 1850s they were still relatively uncommon, but the habit gradually spread and by the 1860s a number of publishers and printers were producing a great variety of
80

cards and by the 1880s they were well established in popular taste and fashion. As the demand grew so the variety increased and they were supplied in every shape, size and style, large, small, embossed, folded and usually sold with an appropriately sized and decorated envelope. The Robin appears about 1862 whilst holly and mistletoe, as befits their great antiquity, appear on the very first of the Christmas cards. Padded and pull-out types both appeared during the 1860s and 70s and photography was soon being used. The numbers swelled yearly and the original 1000 in 1843 has now grown to millions, but in the process the Christmas Card has lost something of its true purpose and become far less personal and far more a social habit.

Bibliography
The History of the Christmas Card by George Buday 1954.

The custom of buying Christmas cards, issued by charitable societies in aid of their funds, is now universal and their output provides a wide selection of attractive and colourful cards. We can show only a few but readers who wish for further information (or who may wish to order cards) should write

to the societies enclosing a stamped addressed envelope.

Action for the Crippled Child

Christmas

The Nativity. Folded card figures

These figures are made with cartridge paper.
Fold an oblong or square of any size in half
and cut out a triangle—see diagram.

The face is also cut from a folded piece of
paper, as is the crown.

Arms are strips of paper with hands glued
to the end. If a cloak is required, this too
should be cut from folded paper. Hair and
beards made from wool or cotton wool and
wings made from foil or a doiley can be
added.

Prose, Poetry and Music

The graft of the birthday of Christ on to the
pagan Yule Festival has not blossomed quite
as the Fathers of the Church hoped. Mac-
Neice speaks of the herald angels begging
for copper coins and of Christians "letting
the belly have its say, ignoring the spirit".
He might have added that the only spiritual
manifestations of which most people are
aware at Christmas are the school nativity
play and carol service. All who agree will
also agree that its production demands
every care for this reason alone.

Some teachers cast round for novelties in
the telling of the story, such as making
Herod the principal character or inventing
a new one such as a soldier who could have
killed the Baby but refrained or a shepherd
who got left behind. These are not gimmicks
but the product of a feeling of despair at
yet another angel-blond in a blue snood and
carrying a doll, yet another gaggle of bare-
legged, hessian-clad shepherds and so on;
and with older children (say 13+) may well
be used. But with younger children it should
be remembered that a plain narrative has
all the delights of novelty.

By plain narrative, I mean the sequence
which consists in full of the Annunciation,
the journey to Bethlehem, the refuge in the
stable, the shepherds and the angels, the

Magi and Herod, the Birth and the adora-
tions, the warning from the angel, the
slaughter of the innocents and the flight
into Egypt (which most people firmly believe
appears as such in the Gospels). The ways
of dealing with this are manifold but a good
start is to take a good long look at as many
paintings from Giotto to Spencer, as possible (and in the company of the children who
are to be the performers).

The use of the actual words of the Bible
presents difficulties. What Bacon calls the
pencil of the Holy Ghost is often very cryptic
from the point of view of the producer, but
it is not easy to find words which, compared
with it, are not vapid, so that it is essential
not to use them in dialogue.

On the other hand, it would be interesting to
use some of the recent modern translations,
where the contrast between, for instance,
the pronouncement of the angel and the
words which might be put into the mouths of
the shepherds, would be less marked.

When it comes to looking for poems and
music to embellish the narrative, the pro-

ducer has to decide what use should be
made of carols. Mostly, they are confined to
the Service of Carols and Lessons, but they
could be used effectively in much the same
way as Bach uses his chorales, or as prelude
and postlude.

Similarly, poems can be used to set a scene
or to round one off. The poems to be considered are mainly oblique in approach,
presumably because poets have measured
their strength against that of the authors of
the Revised Version and given them best.

Perhaps the best is Hardy's "The Oxen"
(though not particularly devout) and could
be used as a reading to precede the scene
in the stable, just as the search for lodgings
could be preluded by part of the anonymous
poem set to music by Thomas Ford, which
begins "Yet, if His Majesty" and ends
"Christ cannot find a chamber in the inn.
We entertain him always like a stranger
And as at first still lodge him in a manger."
Elizabeth Jennings has a fine poem, "The
Annunciation", probably too difficult for
our age group, so that Sansom's "Mary of

Nazareth" would be preferable. Eliot's "Journey of the Magi"—almost hackneyed now—is not so difficult as some would think. Other poems which should be considered are "Innocent's Day" by Nicholson, "A Song for Simeon" by Eliot, "Bethlehem" by Phyllis Hartnoll, "The Circle of a Girl's Arms" by Caryll Houselander, "Epstein's Madonna and Child" by Geoffrey Dearmer, the Mac-Neice already referred to ("A Week to Christmas"), "Jesus and his Mother" by Thom Gunn, "Christmas Landscape" by Laurie Lee, "Christmas Day" by Andrew Young, "Carol" by W. R. Rodgers, "The Burning Babe" by Southwell and Milton's "Ode".

In looking for music, other than carols, we will not, as previously, be necessarily looking for music which we hope will sharpen the apprehensions of the children concerned, but it will be all the better if it does.

It should be remembered first that Berlioz and Handel between them cover almost the whole story. From the Pastoral Symphony from Messiah, up to the chorus "Glory to God" makes up a sort of tone poem; "Behold the Lamb of God", fading out at the four-

teenth bar, would make a good introduction to the Adoration scene; and the prelude to "The trumpet shall sound" could announce the entry of the Kings.

Berlioz' "L'Enfance du Christ" includes an ominous "Night Patrol" of soldiers, which could be used in the Massacre section, or to announce the entrance of Herod; a cabalistic dance for either of the same purposes; a chorus of angels warning Joseph and Mary to flee; a chorus of shepherds worshipping; a superb orchestral section called "Le Repos de la Sainte Famille"; and a delightful trio for harp and two flutes, supposed to be played by the Ishmaelites who succoured the Holy Family in Egypt, but perfect for the shepherds before the angels arrive. (It will be observed that Berlioz was not afraid to add to the plain narrative.) Other suggestions:

The Annunciation. The beginning of Weber's "Oberon" Overture: the second movement of Haydn's Symphony No 104: the opening of the Larghetto of Beethoven's Violin Concerto; the horn solo which opens and closes Britten's "Serenade".

The Arrival at Bethlehem. Musette from Handel's Concerto Grosso Op 6 No 6: the

second part of Janacek's "Fairy Tale".

The Stable. Schumann's "Child Sleeping" (from Kinderscenen): the seventh variation from Brahms' "Haydn" Variations: Pavane from the "Capriol" Suite by Warlock: Ireland's "Holy Boy":

For the Shepherds. Minuet and Trio from Haydn's Symphony No 88: Pastoral from Beecham's Handel Suite, "The Faithful Shepherd":

The Angels. The by now celebrated Creed by Gretchaninov.

The Kings. Alla Marcia from Sibelius' Karelia: the Sonata Pian'e Forte for brass by Gabrielli: opening adagios from Haydn's later symphonies:

Herod. First part of "Der Freischutz" Overture: the trombones from the beginning of Berlioz' "Francs Juges" Overture.

The Massacre. I would suggest electronic music here (accompanying a shadow mime?); the Bach Toccata in D minor, either on the organ or orchestrated:

The Flight. The allegro of the Unfinished Symphony or the second movement of the C major (of Schubert).

A Medieval Christmas

Our domestic Christmas stretches from somewhere about mid-December to December 27th or 28th. New Year is regarded as a separate event and Twelfth Night is remembered only as the occasion on which decorations should be removed. This is a very attenuated Christmas compared with that of the medieval festival. To the people of the Middle Ages, Christmas started with Advent and ended at Epiphany or Candlemas and during the whole of this period there were a number of celebrations and customs to be observed. Christianity was, for the common people, still a mixture of the old pagan beliefs and the new faith and in many cases Christianity took over and adapted the old beliefs. One such example was the decoration, both inside and outside the house, with bunches of holly, ivy and mistletoe. Since mistletoe is regarded as representing the female element and holly the male it was thought imperative that both should be present. Mistletoe had not completely outgrown its old pagan connections and during the Middle Ages it was never allowed inside a church with the exception of York Minster. There a branch was ceremoniously laid upon the altar on Christmas Eve and allowed to remain and whilst it stayed a general pardon was extended to the city.

One of the most unusual of Christmas customs was the election of a Boy Bishop—a practice observed at most of the cathedrals, choir schools and in a few of the smaller parish churches. A member of the choir was nominated as the Bishop and in some places he actually took the service excepting only those parts which required the presence of an ordained priest. The Boy Bishop wore the full regalia of a bishop and served out his term of office until December 28th, Holy Innocents Day, when he was given a ceremonial feast and then led a whole cavalcade through the city bestowing a blessing as he passed. In some places he also preached a sermon on this day. The custom was continued until July 22nd 1541 when Henry VIII commanded that henceforth "all such superstitions be extinguished". Although there was a brief revival during the reign of Mary this marked the disappearance of a most curious and obscure custom.

With the start of the Twelve Days of Christmas on December 24th one of the first jobs was to clean the house thoroughly and especially the implements of brass and pewter. Certain tasks such as spinning were forbidden. With Christmas Eve came the

A group of mummers

midnight Mass at which hymns and Christmas carols would be sung. One of the earliest of the Christmas hymns was written by Ambrose, Archbishop of Milan, who died in 397 and a free translation of this is given in No. 55 in Hymns Ancient and Modern, whilst No. 56 also dates back to the 4th or 5th century. Both these hymns would, of course, have been in Latin and it is not until the 15th century that there is any indication of Christmas verse written in English.

On Christmas Day the feasting began, but many of our present-day foods were, of course, unknown in the Middle Ages. One of the most important of Christmas specialities was the boar's head which was brought in with due ceremony and the custom is still continued at Queen's College, Oxford, complete with its own Christmas hymn. Poultry was eaten although the turkey does not seem to have reached this country until the late 16th or early 17th century and goose was probably the most usual. Then there were the cakes and pies, some of them quite enormous requiring bushels of flour and pounds of butter. One popular dish which has now disappeared was frumenty—this was made of wheat, boiled in milk and seasoned with sugar, cinnamon and other spices. Certain parts of the country had their own specialities; thus East Riding of Yorkshire had a Yule Cake and in Shropshire "wigs" or caraway buns dipped in ale were peculiar to Christmas Eve. Mince pies seem to have a very long history and there are references to them as far back as the 16th century, whilst Christmas pudding is usually considered to date from the late 17th century. In the great houses of the nobility naturally the choice was greater and there was

venison, peacocks, and sides of beef offered for Christmas food. Drink was largely of ale mixed perhaps with milk, whilst the Wassail bowl contained hot spiced ale and toasted apples. Many old English carols mention wassail and the groups of singers, the waits, who paraded the streets expected to be plied with this drink.

For entertainment there were the mummers or guisers, who toured the district presenting their strange, Christian-pagan play or their Morris dances. Then there was the bringing in of the Yule Log with its ceremonial kindling, with a remnant carefully preserved from the previous year.

However, all seasons had their end and for most, Epiphany marked the end of the festivities. The day following Epiphany was known as St. Distaff's or Rock Day and this was the time when women recommenced their spinning and the Monday following was Plough Monday when the men began their farm work again.

There is evidence that at the Royal Court festivities might continue right up to Candlemas, February 2nd, although one feels they must have had a rather jaded air by then. Many of these old customs lingered on until the mid-19th century but the great majority have now passed into memory and Christmas is probably the poorer for this.

Bibliography
Christmas and its Customs. C. Hole. R. Bell
4,000 Years of Christmas by E. W. Count. 1953.
Christmas in Ritual and Tradition by C. Miles. 1912

Craft notes for Christmas

One of the most useful presents any teacher can get for Christmas, is an ideas book. This begins as a book of blank pages and gradually is filled up as ideas accumulate. I come across ideas for art and craft in various places—in the pages of this book for instance, and other professional journals, in colour supplements, in adverts on the side of a bus and so on. One of the best times for gathering ideas is during Christmas. At this time most shops make some effort in their window display and in the case of Regent Street and Oxford Street some theme is adopted throughout their length. Christmas cards, wrapping paper and various types of decoration can be looked at with an eye to its potential use in the classroom. The great value of the notebook is that it can provide for the lean years as well as those of plenty! Nor need, or should, the ideas be slavishly followed. The same materials may not be available, nor the original entirely suitable to your own situation.

While in no way diminishing the pleasures of Christmas pudding, parties and the like, the importance of the Nativity is paramount in the Christmas scene, and children do enjoy preparing a stable with Mary and the Infant Jesus. The nature of Eastern dress encourages one to select for the models a suitable shape for the body. Bottles—glass or polythene can be used, and gay, striped material can be draped around the shape and stitched into place. A little Plasticine can be used for facial modelling and more material draped over the head as the burnous. Animals can be made as simple cutouts of card to stand in the background. The stable itself can be made from a large cardboard box turned on its side.

Dioramas can be made to flank this model of the Nativity, showing the shepherds and their flock, and the three wise men on their camels. On a number of occasions we have presented these and other models to the local church as part of their Christmas display, a gesture as much appreciated by our own children as the vicar.

Paper sculpture can be employed to produce some simple and effective figures for scenes of the Nativity, as table decorations for the parties in school or at home. Those who have already had experience in cutting and folding paper may be able to produce some very elaborate forms, but for the beginner, the cone of paper might be tried. A large cone forms the body, and on to the apex of this a smaller cone is inverted and interlocked. A simple fold of paper is stuck on to the

This classroom frieze, made by the whole class taking part, is described opposite

back as a pair of wings and a similar shape to the front to show the arms in praying position. Let the children experiment with the shapes of arms and wings, until they are satisfied with them. These can stand freely, be pinned to the wall, or suspended as a mobile.

An even larger shape can be attempted, using white card instead of cartridge paper. Instead of the upper cone, a balloon can be inflated and fixed in position. Butter muslin can be stuck over the balloon to provide the right "complexion".

The star is the favourite Christmas feature and card shapes can be used for these. A pair of shapes can be interlocked by making slots in each one. A third shape can be added after some experimenting with scissors. Snowflakes are also an attractive geometrical shape and can be included either in paper or in the new very cheap Polystyrene tiles which are available. Cutting can be done with a very sharp knife, but a simple battery operated cutter can be bought for about 7s. 6d. from most handicraft suppliers. Make sure you get some spare wires with the kit. A warmed hacksaw blade will also cut the Polystyrene. The material is used increasingly as a packing material and many shops are pleased to give it away. The shapes are often irregular but they are usually larger than the tiles one can buy, and the children will enjoy shaping them into snow covered scenes.

Cotton wool is another cheap material which will be extensively employed for models at this time of year. Snow men are examples of typical use of the wool. As well as models,

these snowmen can double as gift boxes, with the ball of wool used for the head being removable.

Father Christmas is very much the festive figure for the season, and a large figure can be created on a chicken wire form. This is a useful idea for a hall decoration. Red crepe paper can be used for the costume, if other material is not available.

A large sack can be made from brown paper and from it, can come tumbling parcels. If the school collects gifts for children in needy circumstances, this model in the corner of of the hall, can act as the central depot, each day seeing a change of arrangement of the parcels around the central figure.

One of the simple ideas I jotted down in a notebook some years ago was a Father Christmas made from a box. This formed the head and body combined—a diagonal line across one corner showing the division between those two parts. A matchbox was stuck on as a nose. Through the front edge, pieces of card were stuck as arms and at the bottom, two more pieces of card protruded as legs. On some of the models they were straight out, while in others the leg pieces were bent at the knees. The boxes were painted over with plaster to give a good painting surface, and then the red, black and white paint was applied to make the costume and facial features.

These were placed in various places in the school—on cupboards, shelves, windowsills, etc., and made a gay splash of colour wherever they were used, either singly or piled one on top of another in totem pole fashion.

Christmas Decorations

A Nativity Frieze

The theme of a traditional nativity frieze can be used to great advantage to create something exciting and imaginative. With just a few scrap materials and a little enthusiasm one can make a picture which comes alive to the children, the whole class can take part in the making of the frieze and therefore one group does not take all the credit.

Preparation of the background is very important. White paper must be used for the lower half of the frieze and blue paper for the top. Figure 1 shows the finished and prepared paper. Make sure both pieces are well glued together and then the sky can be made more interesting by adding a few silver stars and one main star with two angels. To make these stand out more, cut out the shapes of the main star and the angels and pin them with straight pins to the paper. Spray around the shapes with silver spray. Leave the paint to dry and remove the shape. This leaves the shape of the star in blue with a silver halo. This can be seen in figure 2.

Cut out the shapes for the figures in the nativity. Arrange them in the order desired. Shapes can be chosen from camels, palm trees, shepherds, kings, Mary and Joseph and the baby Jesus. Pin the shapes to the paper in the same way as before and using plastic hair spray bottles half filled with paint of a chosen colour, spray around the shapes. Use different colours for each figure so that the paint will mingle on the paper and give a good background colour. (Figure 3.)

When the paint is dry, take the figures off the paper and the figures can be filled in with various materials. An example of this can be seen in figure 4. In the picture the king has been filled in using the following materials, gummed paper, black paper, cotton wool, velvet topped red paper, gold

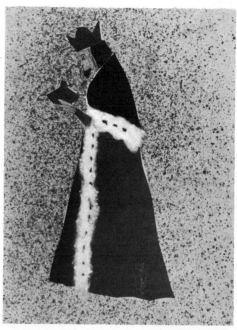

paper oddments and the rest is filled in with wax crayons.

The rest of the frieze can be filled in with all kinds of oddments. A selection of materials can be used and the following list can be kept in order to keep them in stock.

Tissue paper, foam rubber, silver paper, silks, cotton materials, paints, cane oddments, gummed paper, felt, raffia and Fablon or contact oddments.

Left. Fig. 3   Above. Fig. 4

Below. Fig. 1   Right. Fig. 2

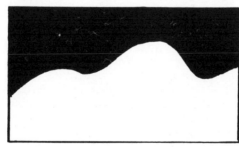

Christmas Tree Ornament

Materials required: stiff card or used greeting cards; Christmas cards with nativity scenes; coloured foil or wrapping paper; a few inches of narrow ribbon.

Instructions

(1) Cover a card circle of 7 in. diameter with gold, silver or coloured foil (alternatively plain coloured paper or suitably designed gift wrapping may be used).

(2) Trace the star shape and central hole on to the reverse side of the circle and cut out (a).

(3) Select a small Nativity scene from a

Christmas card, cut out into round, square or oblong shape according to the picture chosen, taking care to cut the picture a little larger than the hole. At the same time make sure that it is cut a little wider at the sides so that it can be folded inwards as shown (b).

(4) Positioning the picture carefully over the hole on the reverse side tape down the outermost edges so that the picture stands about $\frac{1}{4}$ in. away from the card.

(5) Complete the ornament by punching a hole in the top of the star and thread a ribbon loop (c).

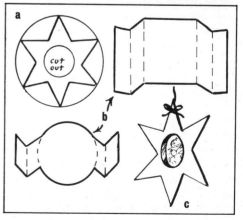

The Nativity (2)

Masterpieces from time past

The illustration of the Christian story was, for over a thousand years, the main labour of the European artist. In south-eastern Europe the work was generally large and public; it was done in mosaic during the Byzantine era, and in later years in fresco, providing an open book from which the illiterate masses could learn the Christian doctrines. In north-western Europe the artist was employed on work of a more intimate and private character, namely the illumination of holy manuscripts which became the highly-prized status symbols of the thirteenth and fourteenth century art-patron, and the painting of small, portable altarpieces, richly decorated and intrinsically valuable.

Of course, art is not only an expression of the prevailing mood of the age, nor is it just a remnant of reality from time past, captured and set in amber to surprise us. Nevertheless, art does relate us to the thought and values of the past in a unique way, a way which can be both a strange and beautiful experience.

Painting number 1, in the style of Orcagna, is the left wing of a triptych; for this reason the main lines of composition flow downwards from the right. Orcagna worked with at least three brothers and had a number of pupils, so the exact attribution of this work is uncertain. He was a Florentine, a follower of Giotto, but at a time in the fourteenth century when Sienese painting was in the ascendency, thus enriching Orcagna's style with its charm of line and colour. The clear surface design indicates no strong interest in volume or space, except in so far as these contribute to the production of a satisfactory formal abstraction. Time also is used by the artist to suit his purpose. At the top of the panel the angel appears to the shepherds, and below, the same easily recognizable shepherds are in the stable. The stable itself is a light portable structure, its supports too elegant to last out a winter's night. But there is no winter's night here; the Virgin, in her gold-embroidered mantle, is no breathing reality, but a visitor from some rarer life.

The picture, by its formal aesthetic qualities, conveys an idea of the pure, spiritual beauty brought by the coming of the Christ Child.

Piero della Francesca's "Nativity", painting number 2, has also a clear, abstract beauty, but this has been achieved by the application of intellectual theories. Its scientific

In the style of Orcagna   **"The Adoration of the Shepherds"**

truth is based on a knowledge of anatomy and perspective. The angels stand solidly in three dimensional space; the Virgin, though idealized, has ample sculptural form to her figure; the Child conveys an idea of roundness altogether missing from the previous picture; and there is a use of diminution to create distance in both the landscape and in the fifteenth century Umbrian townscape. Piero was a mathematician famous in his day for his treatises on geometric solids and perspective. It is not surprising then, that his pictures always have an underlying geometric construction of squares and rectangles; note, for instance, the vertical line running through the wall of the shed and the left hand angel, or the horizontal passing through the angels' mouths and the horizon. His figures are locked into the geometry of his composition, giving his work an inflexible timeless quality, which is further emphasized by the serious, inward expressions of the faces. Christ in this picture has just assumed the human form, and to the Renaissance mind, man and his intellectual powers were the measure of all things.

Gerard David, picture number 3, was almost the last of the Flemish altarmasters, and follows a line of famous artists who, in the early fifteenth century perfected the use of oil as a medium, thus enriching their colour with a remarkable jewel-like beauty. They are noted for the exquisite refinement of their work, in which they added detail to detail to rebuild a mirrored representation of the visual world, a development of the miniature-painting used earlier in illuminated manuscript. David's "Adoration of the Magi" is set in a ruined building giving a view through to a quiet Flemish townscape, where the ox and ass are seen grazing, and people go about the street on their daily tasks. Minute windows, doorways, turrets and pigeons are all painted with that close observation characteristic of Flemish altarmasters. The details of gold, jewellery and fabrics are done with such care one would suppose the final effect to be worldly and materialistic in the extreme. Yet there is a simple piety about this picture, an innocent belief in the story as told in the Bible, but here taking place amid the contemporary court life of Bruges.

Giorgione's "Adoration of the Magi", picture number 4, is a small narrow panel, possibly a predella to an altarpiece. Giorgione was a sixteenth century Venetian painter, and originator of the Classical

Venetian style, though as he himself died of the plague in early manhood, his ideas were later developed by Titian. Little is known of his life, excepting his love for music and for women, which has become legendary. His painting has a dreaming, romantic quality. Many of his subjects are mysterious. Lapped about by soft twilight landscapes, his figures are suffused with a mood of melancholic reverie; an indolence and sensuous charm pervade his scenes. It is said he first laid out patches of light and dark colour, using no drawn outline, space and light being his main ideas. His lack of definite subjects puzzled his contemporaries, but in this picture we are not left in doubt, though even here there is a lack of purpose about his magi; one cannot suppose they have travelled with much effort for any distance, and each figure seems enfolded in his own enchanted dreams. For Giorgione's Nativity, though attired in fashionable contemporary dress and given substance in visual terms, has the elusive quality of a dream. The coming to earth of Divine Love is but a distant hope, an ideal, probably imaginary and altogether unobtainable, except in the visions of the artist.

Of all the pictures considered, picture number 5, "The Adoration of the Shepherds" by Rembrandt probably follows the Bible story most faithfully, although it is, of course, translated into terms of a seventeenth century Dutch interior. It is a humble scene, a barn or cattle stall, with harness and ladders picked out here and there in the glowing radiance. The shepherds and Holy Family are also a humble race, no gold embroidery or courtly costumes for them. These are the ordinary peasants with whom Rembrandt, as a miller's son, had been familiar since his childhood. But the important subject in this picture is light. The source of illumination is not clear, but there is a brilliance overflowing from the manger where the Child lies which illumines all around it. The light seems to pour from the Christ Child Himself, penetrating the surrounding darkness and lighting it with the simple reality of His presence.

Models for the Primary Class

Nativity Play

"And, lo, the angel of the Lord came upon them, and the glory of the Lord shone round about them:. . ." St. Luke, chap 2, verse 9.

Preliminary discussion will be necessary to ensure that all the characters are being made. With a certain amount of tact and discretion, it should be possible to arrange that the best speakers make the most important characters.

Spare children can swell the heavenly choir, or they can be extra animals and people, bringing gifts to Jesus.

The head of each puppet is half a toilet roll centre. Make two tubes of paper—one to fit over the thumb and one over the little finger (older children can do this themselves). Diagram 1.

Let the children choose a suitable piece of material or felt for the character they are making—place one hand on the material and draw around it (as in diagram 2), then cut out. The glove is then glued on to the finger tubes and the neck is glued into the head.

Glue paper hands to the top of each finger tube. Diagram 3.

The faces are decorated according to the character—wool, straw, raffia or cotton wool being used for hair.

Some of the puppets could have legs. The glove should be cut a little shorter and legs and feet of thin card or paper glued to the inside of the glove.

When all the puppets have been made, the children can begin to make up their parts.

A simple and effective theatre can be made with two tables, one being placed on top of the other. Cover with a cloth or blanket (which can be brightened up with silver stars or flowers pinned over it).

The children stand, or kneel behind the tables and reach up. Keep the movement to a minimum and let each speech and appearance be as short as possible—little arms get tired very quickly!

If a background is required, this can be stretched across a blackboard or stand of some sort. A crib can be made from a box painted appropriately and a child is bound to have a tiny doll at home to use as the baby Jesus.

A very simple stable can be made from card. The ends are fixed firmly to the table so that the card forms a curve, the top is then covered with raffia or straw as in the illustration.

Magic

Materials: One large balloon, Polycell paste, newspaper, Plasticine, powder colour, Marvin Medium, thick string or binder twine, scrap Polystyrene, manilla card, hemp (used for lagging pipes).

Method: Cover a large balloon with six or seven layers of paste and paper. Keep the balloon warm on a radiator to prevent it going down.

When the layers of paste and paper are absolutely dry, deflate the balloon and remove it from the hard shell.

Make a simple paper template of the eyes, place it onto the shell, draw round it and using a very sharp knife cut out the shapes of the eyes. Cut out a hole big enough for a child's head to fit through, so that the head can be worn.

Make a hooked nose and a chin from Plasticine, glue these on to the face and cover with two layers of paste and paper. Using rolls of Plasticine, make the mouth. Glue on to the face and cover with two layers of paste and paper.

Mix enough powder colour and Marvin Medium to paint the entire head. Dark green is very effective. Using either a stiff brush or a small trowel, spread the mixture over the head and leave to dry. A heavily textured effect can be attained using this technique. Paint the mouth bright red, using a mixture of powder colour and Marvin Medium.

Cut large teeth from Polystyrene and glue into position. A simple method of cutting Polystyrene is by using thick wire stuck into a large cork and heated over a candle. Use thick string or binder twine to make eyebrows.

Tease out the hemp, which can be obtained from most hardware stores, and glue it into place to make the hair. This can be dyed black or blue if so desired. Natural hemp makes a good contrast with the dark face. Make the hat from a large cone of manilla card, gluing on a brim of the same material. This can be fixed firmly to the head using an impact adhesive.

A simple dress can be made from a suitable heavy material—preferably dark in colour. Hessian makes an excellent shawl and pinafore. (Old sacking can usually be obtained from a local farm or grocer's shop.) A pair of old black gloves, with huge Polystyrene nails glued into position make effective hands. These look most impressive when used in a drama lesson, making the witch look even more fierce.

If the head only is made, flashing red lights

90

Positioning the eyes and mouth

Trying it on for size

Spreading the mixture

can be put in the eyes. A Christmas tree flasher and two 15 watt bulbs connected to the mains by a suitable plug can be connected up—a link with science—and will serve very well. Red Cellophane can be glued to the inside of the eyes to give even greater effect. An interesting decorative mask is made even more exciting by these flashing lights.

If required, a broomstick is easy to make. The school caretaker can usually provide an old stake from a brush. Twigs or pea sticks bound tightly to one end of this with binder twine or thick string are very effective. Children will have great fun making this witch, and she can be used to spark off drama, poetry writing and oral English, and to stimulate the imagination of the young child.

Getting ready

In action. This witch's mask is three feet tall, including the hat

A Witch and her Cat

No Hallowe'en is complete without witches and broomsticks and cats. The witch's body, the cat's body and the cat's legs are made from tubes of corrugated paper (A). The witch's hat is a circle of card with a paper cup on top. The broomstick is a long, thin roll of corrugated paper which is "sliced" at the bottom before being rolled. Her hair is tangled wool. The cat's face is a circle of paper to which ears have been added. The eyes are green foil and the whiskers thin strips of paper.

These lessons have been carried out with both Infants and Juniors and have always proved enjoyable and usually successful. Sometimes, though not always, models made by the teacher have been left on view a day or two before the lesson to give the unimaginative or inexperienced some ideas. This has been entirely dependent on the particular children involved.

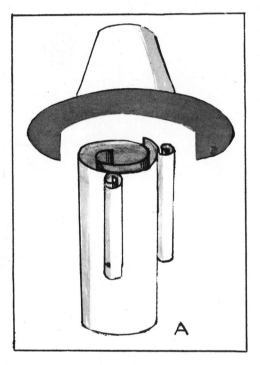

All purpose Witch

Cream is now sold in small plastic bottles and in similar glass jars which are not returnable. These, together with a ping-pong ball make unusual storage jars, perhaps for a girl's dressing table.

First wash out the jar thoroughly and decide on a character doll; the rest is up to the ingenuity of the maker and the contents of the junk box. The doll illustrated here, a witch for Hallowe'en, most disgruntled, needed only scraps of material, thick wool for hair and pieces of felt and stout paper, costing nothing at all.

See that the ping-pong ball is not greasy, sponging over if necessary with meths before painting. Then poster paint or watercolour can be added to the face section covering the rest with suitable wool stuck on with **Uhu** or **Bostick**. Any hat or bonnet can be pinned into position with ordinary pins through the celluloid. The head is not fixed to the body but left separate to act as a lid.

Dressing the doll is simple. Cut some stiff material wide enough to frill round the jar and long enough to reach the ground with additional turnings; and stitch into a tube. Make a hem and gather up the top to tie round the jar top. In the case of a plastic bottle this garment can be fixed in position by piercing the top with needle and thread. Small felt or cardboard feet and hands can be stuck or stitched in place as required. Other things like aprons, cloaks, scarves or ruffs can be added later.

These little figures lend themselves to the designing of stage sets, historical costume and puppet plays—though it must be pointed out that they are more suitable for female characters with long skirts. For male characters cover the jar with a dark tight-fitting tube and suspend separate trousers or breeches in front.

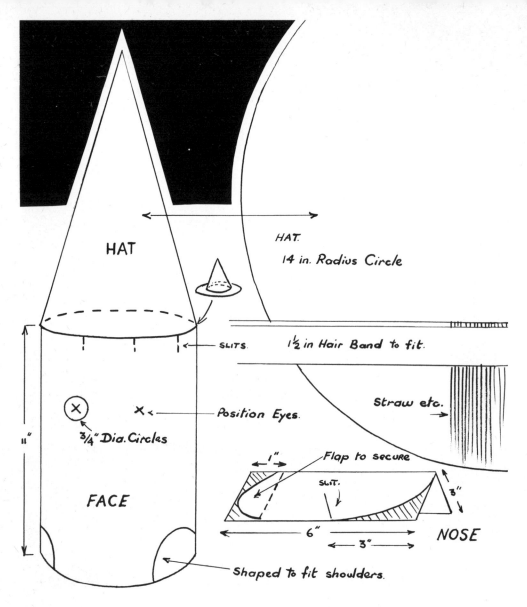

HAT

HAT.
14 in. Radius Circle

SLITS.

1½ in Hair Band to fit.

Straw etc.

Position Eyes.

¾" Dia. Circles

X

11"

FACE

1"

Flap to secure

SLIT.

6"

3"

3"

NOSE

Shaped to fit shoulders.

Witch's Mask

Given a few basic ideas everyone should be able to produce a mask of great individuality which will hide the identity of the wearer and immediately create a lively party atmosphere.

Collect as many large sheets of reasonably thick white or coloured card as possible. Sources of supply may include your local printer, stationer, or bookshop. Raffia, rope, thick string, and straw will also be required together with a stapling machine, brass paper fasteners and strong glue.

A card cylinder can be made out of card measuring approximately 28 in. by 11 in. This can be overlapped to suit the size of head it is to cover, and then pieces can be cut out of the lower edges to allow it to sit on the shoulders. Fingers can then be used to locate the eyes whilst it is being worn, and these can be cut out as ¾ in. diameter circles. The nose is made as illustrated and stuck firmly into place.

A 14 in. radius circle is cut out of firm card and made up into a tall cone which is then fitted to the face by paper fasteners thrust through both face and cone. A good fit is ensured if the top edge of the cylinder is slit occasionally to allow it to be more pliable whilst fitting together is taking place.

Two long strips of card 1½ in. wide are used to sandwich straw, raffia, wool, string, etc., as hair and then this is fitted into place at the top of the cylinder. A hat brim can then be devised to complete the construction.

Decoration is very much a matter for the individual. Any original touch such as dead leaves glued to the hat will add a great deal of character.

The Cat

A piece of black card is measured and cut as shown in Fig. 1. The thin strips are gathered together in pairs on top of each other working each side of the odd centre strip. The latter is then used to cap the rest, and all are pinned by a brass fastener. This shape makes the top half of a mask. A pair of black ears are made as shown in Fig. 2 and eyes are positioned and cut as ¾ in. dia. circles. The nose is cut out and secured by staples and is allowed to bulge slightly below the lower edge of the mask. Brush-bristle whiskers are then added. The eye holes are then surrounded by an area painted yellow as shown.

½ - 1 - 1 - 1 - 1 - 1 - ¾ - 1¼

1

EYES.

8"

BASIC SHAPE

10"

¾" DIA.

2

EYES.

1"

2"

3½"

½"

1"

EARS.

2¾"

2"

NOSE

Fire

1. Yorke house.
2. Durham house.
3. New exchainge.
4. Savoy.
5. Somerset house.
6. Arundel house.
7. Essex house.
8. Temple.
9. Baynards cast.
10. St Andre in Holb.
11. St Pauls Church.
12. Boo Church.
13. Guild hall.
14. St Lorentz Poultney.
15. the Roijal exchainge.
16. St Michael.
17. St Petrus.
18. St Duston in the East.
19. Alhallows harking.
20. Cystom house.

A German print of the Great Fire of London

C. E. Montague, a journalist, critic and short story writer highly thought of in his day, but now almost forgotten, wrote* "Among the mind's powers is one that comes of itself to many children and artists. It need not be lost, to the end of his days, by anyone who has ever had it. This is the power of taking delight in a thing, or rather in anything, everything . . . just because it is what it is . . . No matter what the things may be, no matter what they are good or bad for, there they are, each with a thrilling unique look and feel of its own, like a face; the iron astringently cool, the painted wood familiarly warmer, the clod crumbling enchantingly down in the hands, with its little dry smell of the sun and hot nettles; each common thing a personality marked by delicious differences. "This joy of an Adam new to the garden and just looking round is brought by the normal child to the things he does as well as those that he sees . . .

"The right education, if we could find it, would work up this creative faculty of delight into all its branching possibilities . . ."

Like most of us, Montague found it easier to point out what is wrong than to suggest remedies; and besides, he was not a teacher.

*Disenchantment, 1922.

"To make this large, gay book of fairy-tales, the earth, dull and stale to a child importunately fingering at its covers might seem a task to daunt the strongest. But many of the teachers of our youth are indomitable men. They can make earth's most ardent small lover learn from a book what a bore his dear earth can be, with her . . . insufferable tale of flax and jute," he adds.

From his fiction we gather that his solution is for all children to have wise and rich parents, living in quiet, handsome houses surrounded by trees on the banks of rivers, who would not send them to conventional preparatory and public schools. No one would argue with the theoretical soundness of this diagnosis; and, indeed, is not a good deal of our best teaching aimed at remedying the very deficiencies in life as most of us have to live it which prevent us from exercising this "creative faculty of delight"? Is not this the purpose behind school journeys, educational visits and the sort of work in the classrooms which is urged upon us by people like Sybil Marshall, David Holbrook, Denys Thompson, Henry Pluckrose and Rosemary Beresford?

If our putative teacher followed up his work on water by similar studies of earth, air and fire, it need not be because of a misplaced

logic, but because it had come to him how radically we are divorced from contact with the elements in vital forms. Water comes, flat and tame, from a tap and is only drunk if nothing else is to be had and there is very little of Rupert Brooke in the chlorinated liquid in a swimming bath; fire is humbled and squeezed through wires and pipes (no wonder children rhapsodise over bonfires); we are insulated from the air by central heating and from the earth by slabs of concrete.

It is impossible to give children all the contacts they should have with the elements in natural surroundings, where they can see how man has tamed them and produced the landscape of field and farm and church and woods and added to it roads and railways (which the accustomed eye accepts, but rebels at pylons!). As I have said, school journeys and visits (at least in the hands of teachers who look upon them as vivid extensions of study and not as cheap holidays) make a contribution towards remedying these deficiencies and one which shows its value when the children have returned to the classroom with the knowledge that phrases such as "Roll on, thou deep and dark blue Ocean" and "the coloured counties" and "I go on for ever" and "the ribbed sea sand" really have meaning. But the main foundation must, of necessity, be meaningful teaching which calls to its aid the rich help of the world's artists.

Imagine, then, our teacher considering the aspects of fire, as illustrated by the Fire of London and the Fall of Troy, the holy flame on the altar, the domestic hearth, the work of the smith and the potter and the cook, and the pillar of fire by day and the bush which burned but was not consumed. His sources will be the Bible, Homer, Pepys and the myths and legends which tell of Prometheus, Vulcan, the Titans, the Gnomes (but not of Zurich), Wayland Smith, Loki and Siegfried, Hallowe'en and Beltane fires and the flames of Hell. He might consult Dickens for cosy domestic scenes and Macaulay for "the red glare on Skiddaw" which told the burghers of Carlisle that the Armada had been sighted on its way to a destruction—in which fire-ships played some part. But I have not found that the lyric poets afford much help in this instance. (And here I might point out that it is to be hoped that no reader will accept this dictum.) Wider knowledge and more patience than mine may well be able to contradict it and, speaking generally, it should be made clear here that my intention is not to provide a syllabus to be followed doggedly, point by point, but to set at least a few colleagues at searching the anthologies and the catalogues

for their own selections, which they will be able to present with conviction. I recommend them not to despise the second-rate (by usual standards of criticism) for composers such as Suk, Weber, Prokoviev and Kodaly, to name the first four which come to mind, may well provide the material we are looking for, rather than Bach or Beethoven. Nor do titles matter. One of the most tumultuous pieces of music I know is the second movement of Haydn's Symphony No. 40 (said, but not by Haydn, to represent the crowds demanding Crucifixion for Christ and freedom for Barabbas).

In respect of fire this last remark is particularly apt, for the most incandescent music I know is to be found in the opening section of Berlioz' "Romeo and Juliet", in passages from Tchaikowski's symphonies and tone-poems, the codas of the quick movements of Dvorak's Concerto for cello and the first movement of Mozart's Symphony No. 25.

Some of the chilliest music ever written is Stravinski's 'Fire Bird' and it is run close in this way by Wagner's Fire Music, for both deal with magic fire; and, conversely, I have heard the first part of the Fire Bird used most tellingly at the entrance of Judas in a passion play.

Elsewhere I have referred to the difficulty experienced by many teachers in persuading young children to listen to music with any profit, mainly because they had forgotten

how tiresomely elaborate and repetitive much of it seems to childish and untrained ears. I suggested ways of overcoming this difficulty but this seems the place to point out that the habit of listening should gradually be acquired, both because it is good for the children in itself and is extremely convenient in the classroom. For instance, if children are going to paint "Bonfire Night" (which is bound to happen, come to think of it) the teacher will wish their flames to leap on the paper and will first endeavour, as Marion Richardson advocated, to build up a keen desire to put brush to paper. If he decides to call in Berlioz, it is clearly much more convenient just to be able to put a record on the player than to have to introduce devious means to persuade the children to listen.

The lack of specific musical items and short poems about fire is odd but not complete. Brahms' song "The Blacksmith", Verdi's "Anvil Chorus" from "Il Trovatore" and Siegfried welding his sword are all evocative and de la Mare has a poem on "Making a Fire"—

Scatter a few cold cinders into the empty grate;
On these lay paper puffed into airy balloon,
Then wood—parched dry by the suns of Summer drowsy and sweet;
A flash, a flare, a flame; and a fire will be burning soon—
Fernlike, fleet, and impetuous.

Craft notes on Fire

There has been a most serious falling off in the standard of Guys in recent years. We can tackle this problem on two fronts. By witholding our contribution to the collectors until the level of work improves and/or seek to effect an improvement in school! In a Festival of Fire one November, we held a parade of Guys, which were wheeled or carried around the hall for all to see. The prize was quite a small firework but this was only one incentive, for competition provided the main spur.

For the guy, to be carried in an old pram, the question of support hardly arises. A sack filled with old material or newspaper will soon fill out into a torso. For the classroom a costume can be made using tissue paper. The hat will need card for stiffness. A papier mâché mask can be made over a face modelled from Plasticene, and be a refreshing change from the bought variety one sees at

this time of year when the only variety seems to be in the choice of colour.

Costumes, props and backcloth all need to be prepared for a drama performance of the Gunpowder Plot. History books and other documents will need to be referred to for detail of costume, weapons, appearance of cellars, etc., and their production assigned to members of the group.

The shape, form and colour of many fireworks appeal as much as the effects on the night of November 5th, and a rummage in the junk box should produce a variety of box shapes which can be covered, built upon, and then decorated. Rockets, jumping jacks, Catherine wheels will only require a little more ingenuity. The arrangement of these around a class Guy makes an exciting November model for the Hall. By the way it is an offence to manufacture fireworks or other explosive material. I was sharply reminded of this last year when I heard from the Chief Inspector of Explosives, Home Office, after I had written quite innocently to the British

Fireworks Manufacturers Association for advice on how to make a volcano work! We had used chicken wire to take up a conic form and stapled it to a wooden base. Onto this pasted paper had been applied. Plaster of Paris had been poured down each side to represent laval flow, and paint applied. So it had to be an extinct volcano in our Exhibition of Fire.

The problem of space often deters the model makers in school and the answer can often be found in the low relief model built up in a 4-in. wide frame. This technique was used for a Fire of London model. Inspiration came from a number of book illustrations, and a visit to Room 14 of London Museum where in the diorama, the fire still seems to be burning as it did in 1666. It is fantastic to think of a conflagration which destroyed so utterly nearly 100 churches and over 13,000 private dwellings. In card streets, houses were drawn and coloured in the design of the period. The scale of the houses varied and when arranged inside the frame, perspective was given by placing those at the front which were largest. Matchboxes and toothpaste cartons were used to give further depth to the scene and act as "separators". St. Paul's and other churches were introduced to the model and then the "fire" was started. Paint was added in red, blues, blacks and yellows to represent flames and smoke. Then cotton wool and wire wool were teased out, and gummed to the houses and background, to show the effect of the fire with a wind fanning the flames.

A fire of London at a later time, 1940, inspired a similar scene; this time the effect was heightened by the use of black card for the St. Pauls and other buildings cut-outs. White paint was used to show searchlight beams picking up tiny aircraft suspended from the top of the model. The silhouette form was further developed by cutting away a section of the back of the frame at the bottom, and allowing a small amount of light to filter in from the window, the sill of which is ideal for this kind of model.

The phoenix is often taken symbolically to represent the rebuilding of a bombed or otherwise destroyed city, like London, Plymouth or Coventry. This mythical bird makes an interesting subject for a Festival of Fire. Using the simple technique of cutting its shape out of card on the stained glass window principle of leaving bars, following the contours of the wings and feathers, two of our boys produced an effective design. To the back of this they stuck all the warm tissue paper colours, and fixed their "bird" to the classroom window. Cane, No. 8 size, can be used to produce another form of the bird, through which is woven raffia and tissue to represent the flames. The Golden Salamander has an almost mythical story told about its ability to walk unharmed through fire. Reference to an encyclopaedia gives details of its size and colour (and doubt about the story), and this will provide a child with the necessary information to model in clay and cover with papier mâché for later application of paint.

Without a doubt this is an exciting topic and should produce striking results in all creative branches, and therefore it is impor-

tant to remind them that "Fire is a Bad Master and Good Servant". A series of simple models can be evolved to show the various ways of making fire and how fire outbreaks can be quickly dealt with. The making of fire-engines through the ages will provide a number of ideas for models. A fire in a private house or factory is also a subject for a group model, with fire tenders, hoses, ladders and other rescue techniques shown. The firetenders on the river, and the forest fire are also models which will provide a stimulating opportunity for the class, in fact one might be forgiven for saying the whole subject should set them alight!

Useful publications:
The Conquest of Fire—Burke Press.
Gunpowder Plot; The Plague and Fire of London—both in the Jackdaw series—Cape.

Diorama of the Fire of London (London Museum)

Air

From the earliest times man has viewed with envy the apparently effortless ease with which birds moved through the air. So great was the impression and so miraculous did it appear that man credited his gods with this wonderful power and hoped that one day he might simulate their feats. Legends and myths telling of man's attempts to fly abound in most cultures and the best known is probably that of Icarus and Daedalus.

Most of these stories tell how man tried to copy the birds and fly by flapping wings and this line of thought was to predominate for many centuries. A limited understanding of mechanics prevented the realisation that the power developed was hopelessly inadequate to lift the weight producing that power. All attempts to emulate the birds inevitably ended in disaster and even Leonardo da Vinci was unable to design a practical flying machine.

It was not until the late 18th century that man made his first faltering leap into the air and the way was pointed by two French paper manufacturers. Tradition offers several explanations for their first interest—a shirt billowing out when drying or the lifting of a paper cone thrown on the fire. Etienne and Joseph Montgolfier were convinced that these effects were caused by a gas lighter than air and they were equally sure that this gas was produced by combustion. To achieve best results they burned such evil-smelling items as damp straw, old shoes and rotten meat. In fact the same results could have been obtained by any form of combustion for it was the expansion of warm air and consequent loss of weight per cubic foot that produced the lift.

In November 1782 the Montgolfiers constructed an envelope of silk with an open end beneath which they burnt some paper. No doubt to their delight the bag swelled and rose to the ceiling and when the experiment was repeated out of doors their balloons reached a height of 70 feet. Their greatest triumph was in June 1783 when one of their large models reached a height of 6,000 feet, flew for ten minutes and covered a distance of a mile and a half.

News of these quite incredible results reached Paris and stirred the Academy of Science to attempt a similar experiment. They were under the impression that the Montgolfiers were producing inflammable air which had first been discovered in 1776 by Henry Cavendish and which Lavoisier was to name Hydrogen in 1790. The Academy proposed that a balloon of rubber coated

silk 12 feet in diameter was to be filled with hydrogen produced by nearly 500 pounds of sulphuric acid and a thousand pounds of iron filings. This complex and dangerous operation was successful and the balloon tethered by a rope, floated up one hundred feet on the 26th August 1783. Popular interest was enormous and extreme measures of security were needed to safeguard the balloon and when it was finally released for free flight it was watched by most of Paris. It stayed aloft for some 45 minutes and landed 15 miles away when it was destroyed by a fearful band of peasants.

Not to be outdone the Montgolfiers planned to carry out an ascent before King Louis at Versailles and on September 9th 1783 their balloon, tastefully decorated in blue and gold and bearing the royal insignia, was ready. An exciting new factor was present for this balloon was to carry passengers—the king had forbidden human passengers so that a basket containing a duck, a cock and a sheep was to brave the terrors of the air. The flight was successful and the animal passengers survived the height of 1,700 feet and the 8-minute journey.

Once it was proved that life could survive such hazardous trips it was not long before men were pressing to be allowed to fly. Originally the French king gave permission for two condemned criminals to be used as guinea pigs, but two adventurous men persuaded him to give them the opportunity to be the first to fly. Their vehicle was 46 feet in diameter, again in blue and gold but bearing on this occasion the signs of the zodiac and beneath the open neck hung a wicker gallery on which they were to ride. On the 15th October 1783 Pilâtre de Rozier made a captive ascent of 80 feet and on the 20th November he and the Marquis d'Arlandes made the first free flight by any human. They stayed up for 25 minutes reaching a height of 2,000 feet and narrowly avoided death when the fabric began to burn.

The feat was repeated by a hydrogen filled balloon on 1st December 1783 when J. A. Charles floated along for an hour and covered 27 miles. It was this balloon which first used the now traditional system of a spherical envelope and the basket suspended beneath it although Charles had his gondola fashioned in the form of a chariot.

Progress was now rapid and the first woman aeronaut made her flight in June 1784 reaching the height of 8,000 feet and remaining aloft for three-quarters of an hour.

Lilienthal gliding in 1896
By permission of the Science Museum, London

In Britain interest in these French follies was slight and it was in fact an Italian who made the first ballooning experiment in this country. It was also an Italian, Vincent Lunardi, who made the first aerial voyage in September 1784 when he took off from Moorfields, London, in a hydrogen filled balloon accompanied by a dog, a cat and a pigeon. His red and white vehicle carried him as far as Ware, Hertfordshire, and his landing spot is still marked by an appropriately inscribed monument. In October the first Englishman to fly, James Sadler, took off at Oxford and in January 1785 the Channel was crossed by a balloon.

To the early balloonists the biggest problem was one of control for the free balloon was at the mercy of the winds. Paddles and sweeps were suggested as means of giving the vehicle some headway which would allow steering but it was not until September 1852 that a steam engine was attached to a long pointed gas envelope and dirigible, or steered flight, became a reality. Here was the beginning of the airships such as the R.101, Hindenberg and the Zeppelins which flourished until the dangers of such large volumes of inflammable hydrogen made them too unsafe to use.

Soon men's ideas were turning to aeroplanes and in December 1903 the Wright brothers made their first 12-second flight at Kittyhawk. Progress, spurred on by two world wars, has been colossal until supersonic airliners are now regarded as commonplace, so that at last man has achieved his conquest of the air fulfilling his ancestors' dreams.

Books for your reference

The Aeronauts. L. T. C. Rolt. Longmans.
The Story of Aircraft. R. J. Hoare. A. & C. Black.
Directory and Nomenclature of the first Aeroplanes 1809–1909. C. H. Gibbs-Smith. H.M.S.O.
The Fighters (World War I). T. Funderburk. Arthur Barker Ltd.
Early Aeroplanes. H. Linecar. Ernest Benn Ltd.
Aeroplanes of World War I. H. Linecar. Ernest Benn Ltd.

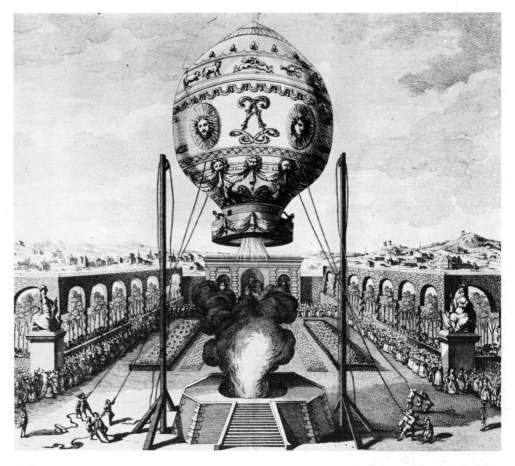

A Captive Montgolfier Balloon 1783   *Science Museum, London*

Poetry and Music

Turning to Air, we can easily slip back into a repetition of storm music, through "the brunt wind that dented the balls of my eyes" (Ted Hughes) but there are Shelley's West Wind and Kingsley's Wild North-easter to quote and illustrate with Debussy's "Nuages", perhaps; but in actual fact it is probable that flying in its various forms would quickly become a substitute. Icarus and Gagarin might well mark the beginning and end of a project which would tend to be more scientific than anything else, but a thoughtful teacher might seek for ways of making his children realise something of the "lonely impulse of delight" of Yeats's airman, though an easier (if less bold) way would be to introduce witches, "astride, the night for to ride" with Mussorgsky's "Night on the Bare Mountain" and the Sabbath from Berlioz's "Fantastic Symphony". Macbeth's witches are not airborne, nor is T. H. White's Madame Mim, but both remind us of the hut of the Baba Yaga in Mussorgsky's "Pictures from an Exhibition".

Birds are so well catered for that the mind boggles at the *embarras de richesse*. Sibelius's "Swan of Tuonela", Beethoven's

Pastoral birds, the cuckoos of Delius and Daquin, Saint-Saëns swan, nightingales in Granados and Respighi, St Francis preaching in Liszt's "Légende", the cockerel in Saint-Saëns's "Danse Macabre" and the magic cock in Rimsky-Korsakov's "Le Coq d'or", are all descriptive and it would be a good exercise to find non-descriptive passages illustrative of bird flight (in the style of "Things to do" in text-books) as described by Cameron Wilson in "Magpies in Picardy": I would suggest as a start, the opening Adagio of Mozart's Symphony No. 39 for the "slow and sombre rook".

Parts of Vaughan Williams's "Lark Ascending" are ready made, as it is intended to be descriptive of Henley's poem "Margaritae Sorori"; Shelley's "Skylark" soars splendidly and Meredith says "Lovely are the curves of the white owl sweeping Wavy in the dusk lit by one large star".

English poets, in general, are quite mad about birds, even if they sometimes use them as pegs to hang philosophising on (like Keats) or as decoration (like the Elizabethans) or incidentally, like the Adlestrop blackbirds, or the Ancient Mariner's "all

little birds that are" or Wordsworth's cuckoo. But Tennyson's "Eagle" (hackneyed though it is) and Clare's "Trotty Wagtail" are brilliant; of the moderns I can only list:

Two Peewits (E. Thomas); The Kingfisher and Jenny Wren (W. H. Davies); The Hawk Roosting and The Hawk in the Rain (Ted Hughes); The Linnet, Titmouse, Jenny Wren, and others (de la Mare); Ducks (F. W. Harvey); The Kingfisher and The Buzzards (M. Armstrong); The Wild Duck (Masefield); Gulls (C. Sansom); Heron (L. Clark); Gull (A. Llewellyn); The Robin (H. Summers) and D. H. Lawrence's "Humming Bird", "This little bit chipped off in brilliance".

Birds have their place in myth and legend. Though the Greek stories of metamorphoses are pretty dull, there are doves, storks, sparrows, ravens, eagles and swallows in the Bible, St Francis preached to the birds and St Kevin held a blackbird in his hand until it hatched its egg.

Lorenz has much fascinating lore about birds, especially geese; and in "The Sword in the Stone", T. H. White transforms Wart into a merlin so that he can further his education by spending a night in the mews: and in the revised version which appears as the first part of "The Once and Future King", he lives with a flock of wild geese, though his favourite bird was the rook, because it seemed to him to enjoy flying the way a boy enjoys swimming. And it strikes me as I write that it would be worthwhile for our teacher to consult White's remarkable book "The Goshawk".

If he has been reading these articles approvingly, he will have been doing as I have of late, listening to lots of music on a new wave length, he will, like me, have been judging it on its evocative possibilities. It is, I find, an obsessive occupation but I have emerged with some rich rewards. The French composer, Koechlin, who was inspired by Kipling's "Jungle Books", the American Charles Ives; the music for xylophones which is characteristic of coun-

tries such as Siam and is shared by a number of African nations; experiments in electronic music and various individual items such as the Prelude to "La Traviata", which seemed to me to be remarkably suggestive of the measured flight of a large bird and comparable to T. H. White's "there came a sweet, slow, straight beat of white wings close to the water . . . and he went home . . . almost afraid to say he had seen a gyrfalcon."

Craft notes on Air

A visit to the Shuttleworth Collection of aircraft at Old Warden, Bedfordshire, the aeronautical section at the Science Museum London, London airport or any other aerodrome open to the public is a most stimulating experience, and especially if in connection with a topic on *Air*. Quite the most expressive way in which the impressions of such excursions can be made is through modelling and other craft work.

Recently a class at school following such a centre of interest turned their room into an airport. An informal grouping of tables and other furniture was arranged around the perimeter of the room, so that a layout of runways, with markings, could be rolled out across the floor when required. Desks, tables, cupboards provided the framework for stand-up models made from cardboard boxes which represented hangars, airport buildings, offices, customs sheds, interconnecting transport services of road and rail and so on. Behind a model control tower, a pair of tables were made up into a desk for the traffic controllers to work at, with model radio and radar sets. Model aircraft, fashioned from balsa wood, cardboard and purchased kits, were incorporated within the classroom scene—under maintenance in the hangars, waiting on the aprons or taxiing out for take-off on instructions from the controller. Other aircraft arriving or departing were suspended with cottons from the ceiling in such quantities that one could see the sense in having air corridors and stacking at 2,000 feet intervals.

Windsocks, airport vehicles—tractors, crash tenders, ambulances, etc., provided modelling opportunities for many pairs of hands. Girls turned their hands to needlework and produced a smart air hostess jacket and skirt after discussions about colour, design,

badges, buttons, etc. They took to wearing these clothes off duty too! It wasn't difficult to see why that particular job attracted the girls.

The building of a mock-up aircraft is another exciting prospect for a young class. It's a more practical proposition to manufacture half an aircraft, with the fuselage being formed along the length of the room with one wing extending outwards into the classroom, resting upon a row of desks or tables with the engines (and propellers—if non-jet) projecting forward.

The sides of the aircraft, rudder and tail fin, etc., can be made from cardboard, and supported by battens or some such stand as a painting easel. Ordinary chairs placed inside the aircraft can be used by passengers and crew, but the rest of the equipment, control column, instrument panel, radar screens, controls, etc., should be manufactured. Pictures abound in text books, but airline companies are also forthcoming with illustrative material for such studies. A painted backcloth on each wall to be observed through · aircraft windows is an additional feature, to increase the illusion.

Flight and other movement in air is a fascinating subject and children feel a real achievement if they can produce a model which will perform in the medium for which it was intended. The parachute is a simple example to begin with. The handkerchief knotted at four corners and attached to a stone as a weight is the prototype from the playground. Panels of scrap material, light in weight, should be cut out and joined to make a semicircular form. The parachute can be "built up" over a large ball to obtain a good shape. The greater the number of panels the more circular the shape of the 'chute. From the edge of the material, at the point where

panels are sewn or Copydexed together, a nylon thread should be tied. For the stone, a figure modelled in papier mâché or other media, is substituted with all the lines tied securely above its centre of gravity. Outdoor testing of the parachutes follows with adjustments being made after trials. The paper dart is another regular schoolboy "free time" activity which can be taken over, with good cartridge paper provided, careful folding being insisted upon, and mark II, III and IV models encouraged. The alteration of the weight of the nose, the folding up or down of the ailerons and other minute alterations will all affect performance. Distance flights and aerobatic manoeuvres should form the bases for competitive efforts from the class.

Other aerofoil forms should be attempted using thin card. Large wing areas produce the better results for gliding. Nose weighting with paper sliders is usually enough.

The Australian boomerang is an intriguing article, relying on the skill of the thrower as much as the design. Experiments can be tried with cardboard shapes and even though return flight might elude one, the curving flight can be seen when the card boomerang is flicked away from the open hand. However a much more successful "helicopter" can be manufactured from two pieces of balsa wood. These have to be identical in weight and shape.

After a rough cut has been made with a knife, some fine shaping should be made with fine sandpaper to get a smooth finish and a rounded edge along the entire length of the wood. The pieces are then fixed together at right angles with an elastic band. Holding it by one arm, the "helicopter" is flicked forward into the air and within a very short while a return flight to the hand will result "to the amazement of all". Decorative features such as strips of coloured adhesive tape can be added to each arm equally—to avoid upsetting the aerodynamic balance. Transfers can also be used or balsa wood paints employed.

The kite is another ancient toy which is too easily bought these days. The very simplest requires little more than two lengths of split cane, some string and paper. Split cane is chosen because it is strong and light. A piece 12 inches long should be tied securely to a piece 18 inches long to form a cross. Using a knife or a file a slot should be cut into the ends of each of the two pieces of wood. This is to hold a length of string which goes round the entire shape. A large sheet of strong light paper (e.g. tracing paper) is cut into the diamond shape of the kite—with an extra inch allowed to paste over the

string. A tail needs to be added for balance and a length of string fixed to the upper half of a tie line which is fixed to each end of the longer stick. Experiment with other shapes—squares, octagons, etc., so that the class does not produce 40 identical kites. The box kite is a further development and for this a fabric is recommended for the double band of material is fixed at the top and bottom of the four canes. These are held apart by two crossed canes which are tightly braced across the middle of the framework. Colour and design are further individual variations which can be applied to the paper and fabric used.

Chinese flying fish

Yet other flying forms come from the Chinese. These are the fish and other shapes which are made in tissue paper and are a type of open envelope. For example the

shape of a fish is cut out twice in tissue—at least 24 inches long. The mouth being about 6 inches in diameter. A thread is attached to each side of the mouth and then tied to a single string. This is then towed at high speed around the playground; as it fills with air, it floats behind the puller.

If the study of air and flight is an extensive one, the shape of seed forms and birds will be included. Large reproductions of the winged forms of the ash, sycamore, plane, maple, most conifers, dandelion, rosebay willow herb, etc., can be made and suspended in an interesting mobile. Bird cut-outs, either in flying position or perching can be drawn on card, and coloured after reference to appropriate books. Birds of various habitats, e.g. the seashore, moorland, river valley, etc., can be mounted in diorama scenes with other attendant features, plant forms, etc.

The French version of Concorde, 001, takes off on its first flight from Toulouse (Fox Photos)

The Wheel

The wheel presents such a wealth of suitable material for picture making that the danger lies in trying to embrace all within the confines of one short article.

What lines of development are possible? In many an infant school nowadays there are displays based on specific themes. Sometimes they are based on colour. A "blue" corner will comprise, for example, of a whole collection of blue objects as varied as fabric lengths, wallpaper, children's paintings, a reproduction or two, balls of wool and cotton, book dust jackets, pots, toys, kitchenware—anything, in fact, in which blue predominates. While I would not suggest that "wheels" is as easy a theme to develop as the one I have described before, an attempt would be well worthwhile if only to help the children to appreciate the peculiar quality of the wheel—its shape and its purpose. Pram wheels, cog wheels, wheels which contain ball bearings, wheels from toys, wheels from washing line pulleys and perhaps even a car wheel could start the collection. It is not enough, however, merely to put all these things on a table, arrange them attractively and wait (like Micawber) for "something to turn up". The teacher will need to be involved and interested when the children handle and discuss the objects.

This may lead to an interest in the circle and in curves. Where else can they see similar shapes in the everyday objects which

"Machine" made from metal junk held in position with acrylic paint

surround them? What is the peculiar quality of a curved surface? Boys in the group might direct their interest to tyres and the patterns which tyres of different types make on the road. This in turn could result in pattern making and even the making of plaster casts. All of this will encourage children to look for and to appreciate more than they might otherwise have done, the many colours, shapes and patterns in the world

in which they live.

With young children the idea of shape (circle, square, triangle) is most easily explored through paper. For example tissue circles cut in various sizes may be pasted on to a sheet of sugar paper (see photograph). Glossy paper may be used instead of tissue (or in conjunction with it). By overlaying one circle upon another quite sophisticated patterns can be built up.

Our civilisation runs on wheels but the wheel is not a primary requisite of civilisation. The Peruvians devised a perfectly viable way of life without a wheel in sight and loads were moved and pots made and corn ground before an axle turned. But the wheel has made possible the rapid growth of the technological age, as a labour saving device and a means of directing power.

An extensive plan of work might be built on the wheel. Its shape alone introduces a mathematical connotation and one which might well be used to link mathematics with other aspects of school work, as a recent Reith Lecturer urged us to do. The historical and geographical aspects are obvious (embarrassingly so) but any teacher might welcome help when he thinks of turning to the poets and musicians for assistance in promoting free writing, in building his pupils up to that state of "headlong, concentrated improvisation" (Ted Hughes—"Poetry in the Making". Faber & Faber) when

they will startle even the expectant teacher with their use of words.

It so happens that I can offer a package deal to any teacher dealing with the heavy wooden wheel of the primitive farmer. In Sackville-West's "The Land" there is a fine passage beginning "He who must yoke . . ." which finds a perfect parallel in the section of Moussorgsky's "Pictures from an Exhibition" called "Bydlo" (The Ox-cart), whether in the original piano version or orchestrated by Ravel. This suggests the story of Samson, "Eyeless in Gaza, at the mill with slaves" and vv 6–7 of E. B. Browning's "Cry of the Children" where again the wheel symbolises slavery.

In Biblical days the chariot of war seems to have been associated with tyranny and it was not until the days of David that the Israelites emulated the Egyptians, Philistines and other baddies, by using them, though in due course they produced Jehu, the prototype of furious drivers, and a traffic problem in

the days of Nahum, who speaks of "the noise of the rattling of wheels and of the prancing horses and of the jumping chariots".

The last section of Respighi's "Pines of Rome" depicts the march of the legions but could as easily be taken to depict an army of chariots such as Tamburlaine riding "in triumph through Persepolis". Other choices are Siegfried's "Journey" and the "Night Patrol" from Berlioz' "Childhood of Christ".

The farm-cart, it is significant, has produced poetry as well as the war-chariot. We have Herrick's "Hock Cart", Masefield's "The Wagon-Maker" and the verses from his "Joseph Hodges", beginning "Now the brown horses". Moussorgsky's ox-cart could give further service and Balfour-Gardiner's "Shepherd Fennel's Dance" be used to illustrate a harvest-home feast.

Kipling's "busy mill", from Puck's Song and the many spinning wheels of legend can be

Pattern sheets based on curves and circles may also be made by taking prints from finger paintings. Roll water colour ink on to a sheet of perspex or plate glass. A pattern of twists and roundels is drawn with the fingertips into the wet ink. A print is taken by laying a sheet of paper (sugar, pastel, duplicating) over the pattern smoothing it on to the inked plate. Variety can be achieved in the pattern by using slightly damped paper for the print or by taking a print from the paper pull off. When dry the pattern sheet itself might be used as the starting point for a painting in which "wheels" play a predominant part.

Older children (8 upwards) will enjoy developing the theme through machines. Acrylic paints, which are now widely available through school suppliers, mean that almost any grease-free material can be used for collage—from metal scraps to strips of wire and paper plates. The use of these (on sheets of polystyrene tile) is clearly shown in the photograph.

Activities of the type described here emphasise shape and line. This may result in designs in paint, crayon or pastel based entirely upon the circle. However it is worth remembering that wheels on trains and tractors, cars and bicycles, machines and barrows can provide the inspiration for detailed pencil sketches, still life compositions in paint and on scraperboard and designs printed from lino blocks.

---

illustrated by Saint-Saëns' "Le Rouet d'Omphale" (but not all of it—it is long and tedious. And, by the way, do not count on his "Samson and Delilah" to help in the context mentioned above). I would prefer Schubert's Impromptu No. 3 (D899).

On wheeled transport the poets are helpful. I list: "Sunday at Hampstead" (Thomson); "From a Railway Carriage" (Stevenson); "Puffing Billy" (Hassall); "Night Mail" (Auden); "Morning Express" (Sassoon); "Cynddylan on a Tractor" (Thomas); "Song of the Wagon Driver" (Johnson); "The Flower-fed Buffaloes" (Lindsay) and the Mail Coach verses from Masefield's "The Landworkers".

Among the musicians, Honegger wrote "Pacific" and Britten has two fine passages in the finale of "Let's Make an Opera" and the second scene of "The Turn of the Screw". The French cavalry charge in Walton's "Henry V" music could be conscripted

Oil pastel designs based on circles and curves. Nine and ten year olds

Using tissue paper for collage based on circles and squares

and there is an enormous amount of 19th century symphonic music which could be thought of without strain as illustrative of travel on wheels. To see what I mean listen to the Etudes of Chopin, the beginning of Schubert's "Satz" Quartet and the Préambule to Schumann's "Carnaval".

Wagner has a Spinning Chorus, Schubert is full of millwheels and Mr. MacColl has a fine "Fitter's Song" and a "Fireman's Calypso".

For teacher's reading, I would suggest H. J. Massingham's "Where Man Belongs".

The development of wheels

Wheels are of such fundamental importance that it requires no imagination to appreciate the degree to which modern living depends on this basic device. Mechanically it may be defined as an infinite series of levers each with its fulcrum at the rim and the load and effort centred at the hub but practically it is the mainstay of most moving machines. For such an important device its early history is, perhaps not unnaturally, very obscure.

It seems reasonable to conjecture that the first form of "mechanical" transport was some form of sledge—perhaps one like the travois of the North American Indian. The next step was probably the inclusion of a simple system of rollers. At some time in the distant past an unknown genius or inspired opportunist developed the idea of thin slices of rollers fixed to the load. This development was not without its disadvantages for the grain of the wood runs concentrically and this does not make for strength—any sharp sideways knock would have shattered such wheels.

One means of overcoming this great drawback was to construct the wheel with the grain running across but to cut the wheel from one piece of timber presented too many problems to the primitive wheel-

The Craft of the Wheelwright being carried on at Bratton, Wiltshire

wright and the normal method was to fashion the wheel from three planks, cut to shape and fixed together. This step was almost certainly taken first in the area of Mesopotamia and graves dating from about 3500 B.C. have yielded such wheels made from three planks held together with copper clasps. Set in the centre of the middle plank was a thick hub through which passed the axle. The wheels were held in position by a wooden linchpin passing through a hole at the end of the axle. Durability and strength were often increased by fitting a metal rim, studded and held in place by metal clasps. Solid wheels were quite serviceable and satisfactory when speed was no necessity since their weight was considerable. To lighten the load some of the excess wood near the hub was cut out—often in the form of a crescent—to produce a crude spoked wheel. By 2000 B.C. such wheels were in use, for clay models found in tombs of this period are fitted with them. By 1500 B.C. the Egyptians were fitting light six-spoked wheels to their war chariots and similar types are recorded in China about the same time. It was some time before such wheels reached Europe and one of the first recorded was in the tomb of a Swedish chief who lived around 1000 B.C.

Despite its apparent simplicity the fitting of spokes presented a number of constructional problems to the wheelwright and soon Celtic craftsmen gained a reputation for the quality of their product. Certainly the Romans appreciated their worth and made great use of them. Wear was greatest at the hub and the Celts devised, within their technology, a very efficient bearing by cutting channels into the hub and then inserting free rotating wooden rods. The Roman system consisted of bronze rings on axle and hub—a far cruder system. But the sixteenth century wheel design had evolved the broad rimmed wagon wheel which was now dished for greater strength. Dishing is the form of construction in which hub and rim are not in the same plane so that the wheel assumes something like a saucer shape. The wide rims caused a great deal of damage on the roads and were often banned from towns. Generally the spokes numbered from six to ten but in China some had as many as forty.

Besides its obvious use in transport the wheel has been adapted for many domestic uses and once again the majority of these innovations originated in the East. Spinning wheels were used in India as far back as

1000 B.C. but they were unknown in Europe until the Middle Ages. In the same way the simple wheel-barrow long used in the East did not appear in Europe until the late thirteenth century. Persian windmills were spinning happily in the tenth century but are not recorded in Northern Europe until the twelfth century—probably introduced by returning Crusaders.

Today the craft of the wheelwright is rapidly becoming a lost one but in the past it was a demanding skill. Timber had to be chosen and cut at the right time of the year—beech in November, ash in the winter, oak in the spring but elm could be cut at any time. For the hub oak or elm was preferred but for the spokes only the tough oak was right: for the sections of the rim known as the felly any of the four woods might be used. Each spoke was fixed to the stock or nave at the centre by means of a mortice and tenon joint whilst the other end was shaped to a round tongue which engaged with the felly. Metal tyres were made slightly smaller than the wheel and heated until the expansion allowed it to slip into position. When it was cooled the contraction forced home all the joints and the result was a product that was sturdy and good for many years of trouble-free service.

Craft notes on Wheels

I had decided to take the Wheel as a theme for a series of assemblies, and also to retell that very moral and entertaining tale *The Wheel On The School* by Meindert de Jong, and so felt it very necessary to have a cart wheel. I spent a travelling holiday and visited many rural districts but found it impossible for a variety of reasons to obtain an old cart wheel. In despair—it was nearing the beginning of term—I found myself in Beresford Square market, Woolwich, and surrounded by wheels. It was then quite easy to find the blacksmith who repaired these and obtain from him a wheel! Get one if you can and let the class see the workmanship that has gone into it. The felloes of ash—seven of them altogether making up the rim; the spokes—two to each felly, always made of oak, and then the hub or nave of the only wood which could stand the constant strain of the turning wheel—elm. Around the rim a perfectly fitting iron tyre. What a bit of craftsmanship! From balsa wood get them to try to make up a wheel to the same pattern. The history of the wheel is almost the history of civilisation, and to illustrate this in a series of models of the development of transport, careful research will be needed into the way the wheel has evolved from rollers to solid wooden wheels, to spokes, pneumatic tyres and so on. The cruder forms can be fashioned from wood, but the more developed forms will be better drawn and cut from cardboard to add to the model of a carriage or other vehicle.

The flanged wheel of the railway engine can be made by sticking a disc of cardboard to the section cut off a dowel rod of smaller diameter.

The building of a watermill with wheel can be an exciting prospect if the material chosen, e.g. hardboard, is later varnished, and the model used in running water at the sink.

An overshot model would perhaps be more convenient, as the flow of water passes over the wheel, turning the paddles. The same type of wheel construction can be used for the production of a paddle-steamer.

One of the interesting features of such a topic will be the "I-Spy"-Wheels-in-use, and their subsequent modelling. The potter's wheel and the spinning wheel are two which come to mind, which would incorporate the modelling of a figure in costume at work, with examples of completed work in miniature, e.g. pots and spun wool.

The ship's wheel is yet another example, but in this case you might decide that you would like a life size model. An old bicycle wheel can be pressed into service here, with card being used on both sides to simulate the spokes and rim. Wooden dowel rods can be added, screwing them to the rim after a number of the spokes at critical positions have been removed. A wooden frame can be made up and the wheel supported in this by a six-inch nail through the axle hole. Modellers might well feel they would like to go on to model other bridge furniture after the completion of the wheel.

The fairground is always an exciting and colourful place, and wheels certainly keep turning there. A group exercise could be built up around such a situation. The Big Wheel or Ferris Wheel would be a very challenging model to attempt. Once again the discarded bicycle wheel can form the core of this particular model, and smaller wheels, e.g. from perambulators, the bases for roundabouts. If all models are carefully

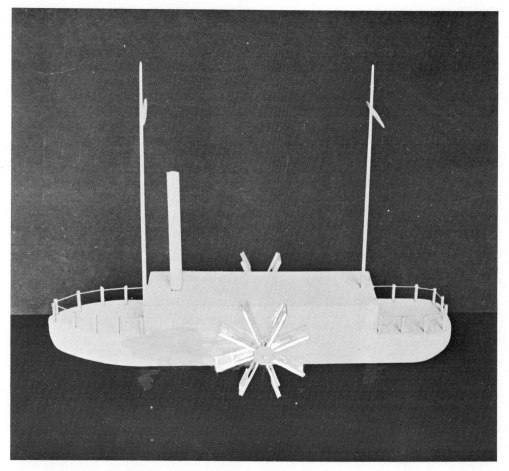

This balsa model is based on Robert Fulton's steamboat "The Clermont" 1807

mounted in wooden frames, they will turn, and so allow the whole model to come to life.

An amazing collection of scrap wheels can be made by a class during a project like this and various imaginative sculpture forms can be attempted—animal and human forms as well as Emmett types of machines can be made from such scrap material. Even if science is not part of the school curriculum, children will inevitably discover some most interesting facts while building such figures, low relief sculptures, engines and so on.

The transfer of motion from one wheel to another raises some interesting questions. A wheel can be fixed close to another to provide a fraction drive, while a second experiment can be set up which will require the use of a fan belt. Wide elastic bands are useful for this work. Crossover linkages can be incorporated and other wheels introduced. The cogwheel can next be tried. Crown corks can be positioned on a board with nails so that they can mesh into one another, but the work can develop to a further stage by making wheels of wood and nails or small

dowel rods around the edge to mesh with similar cogs or those of a different diameter to watch variations in speed which result.

Ways of starting wheels, with various types of handle, and the very fast method using a string coiled around the axle, and then methods of stopping them with different forms of braking device, all present opportunities to the modeller. The efficiency of many of the wheeled machines can be measured, e.g. by testing home-made cars on an inclined surface to see which will run the farthest, providing incentives to the modellers to improve their machines.

Still in the scientific field, simple pulley wheels can be made by fixing two hardboard discs around a core of a section of dowel rod and various experiments found in science books to show their uses and advantages.

By work such as this, by exploring the various ways in which the wheel can be used, and having had to manufacture the form in which they needed it, the class will come to have a very much better understanding of its importance in our lives.

The Harvest

A bale accumulator being towed behind a baler

I have worked in a city school for the whole of my career and have, like many another teacher, found it difficult to make the children really appreciate the ever-changing cycle of nature (which surely is part of the country dweller's rich heritage). I have had the usual run of classroom pets—rabbits, hamsters and the like; I have grown things in pots, bowls and glasses, taken groups to stay in small country towns. Yet the sum total of all of this is hardly enough to show the imperceptible change from seed time to harvest, the changing colours of the countryside, of the stark silhouettes of trees in midwinter and of their flowing forms in high summer.

But in spite of all this, harvest is celebrated in town schools with as much enthusiasm as their country counterparts, what is lacking in country produce being made up for with tins of soup and cans of fruit. Although we might argue that the whole thing is rather synthetic, unrelated as it is to the natural ebb and flow of the seasons, there is much gained if the produce collected by the children is given to people less fortunate than themselves.

For the harvest assembly the hall will need to be decorated. I have tried several approaches, all of which have enjoyed reasonable success. Perhaps the most satisfactory method for the older age range in the Primary Department (and Lower Secondary) is to begin by discussing with the group who are to be responsible for the preparation of the hall, what sort of things we are saying "thank you" for. Firstly there is food which is grown on the land—fruit, corn, meat. How can this be represented visually?

A painting of a farm springs to mind but this is rather commonplace. Try leading the group towards some form of simple dimensional representation—a large scarecrow, perhaps. This is simple to make from two broom handles, with a turnip for the head and dressed in a few old clothes. If picture making is attempted a collage of limitless size could be made by cutting food pictures from glossy magazines and mounting them on frieze paper. Take care to group the shapes so that the overall effect is one of brilliance of colour (rather than make a design which presents the idea of food in a whimsical way).

Then the harvest of the sea might be suggested. Here there is tremendous scope for lively picture making—trawlers in rough seas, harbour scenes and seascapes, collage work based on fish shapes cut from

metalic papers and sea creature mobiles (crabs, lobsters, shells) made from manilla card and suspended form hoops hung from the ceiling. The whole display could be draped with pea or bean netting to give extra dimension to the children's work. Lobster and crab pots, if available locally, would also add much visual impact to the display.

A more difficult conception for young children is the harvest we reap from the earth—coal, oil, precious stones, clay, metals. However, if this aspect is drawn to the attention of the children they will quickly appreciate its relevance. In some areas it will be possible to build a display around the tools of the miner's craft (his light, his helmet, his pick) and the harvest he helps win (coal). Paintings of a pithead or careful plans of an underground working would be appropriate pictures for this section.

If the school is in an area far from pits and coal-faces, the most important local industry could be featured. Obviously, it is facetious to suggest that Hatton Garden Primary "do" diamonds—but it would surely not be inappropriate for a school in Bedfordshire to feature brick-making, or a school in Stoke-on-Trent to include some pictures and craft work on ceramics and the many uses of clay.

It is of prime importance—if the hall is prepared along the lines suggested above—that the harvest assembly embraces all the aspects which are featured. To have a mining picture dominating one corner of the room and only to include poems about fields of golden corn and prayers about our brave fishermen is obviously nonsensical. Thus it is wise to begin by discussing the pattern of service and the display together so that each will complement and give meaning to the other.

For younger children—in infant departments and transition classes—the approach outlined here might well prove a little too

difficult to implement successfully (though much could be done by giving each group a specific theme to work around). But even if the conventional "Farmer's Year" type of service is to be used, picture-making can range from imaginative countryside paintings to cut out friezes illustrating ploughing, reaping, threshing and bread-making.

Let me in conclusion stress the underlying reason for presenting this article in the way I have. Often we are given golden opportunities to unify and vivify the whole curricula through corporate experience in which a school assembly is used to mark some special occasion. All too often we ignore the challenge and so prevent the children's experiences and joyful self-expression being as deep as they might otherwise have been. If we can use the harvest *this* year as a time when the children are stimulated orally (through music and verse) and visually (through displays of pictures, models, gifts of food and fruit and flowers painstakingly arranged) then the lives of all the members of the school—both pupils and staff—will have been made that much richer.

The Origin

Except in Africa and the East the harvest is no longer the occasion for celebration that it was, but at one time to all men it was a supreme festival. Upon the harvest might depend the community's whole future; life and death, peace and war all were dependent upon the harvest. It was the culmination of months of work and care. It is not, therefore, surprising that man has always celebrated collection of the fruits of the earth with elaborate ceremonies and rituals. In Christian countries the harvest festival is still celebrated with gifts of food to the Church and this is no more than the parallel of sacrifice in pagan countries. Indeed it could be argued that the harvest was the foundation on which civilisation was built since people on the move seldom produce great thinkers or inventors. Before man has settled into fixed communities in the near East there will be little hope of a lasting culture developing.

The first crops were probably wild grasses, found over much of the Middle East, gathered haphazardly and cut with flint sickles. Some 7–8,000 years ago the plant was domesticated and as the men hunted or fought it became the women's job to tend the seed and plants. This feminine association may well explain why agriculture was so often regarded by the Ancients as being under the care of a goddess rather than a god. She went by many names among them: Isis, Demeter and Ceres —the origin of our modern cereals. By 5000 B.C. there was settled farming in Egypt and Mesopotamia and soon celery, rice, barley, carrots, beans and wheat were being cultivated. Egyptian wall paintings show the reapers at work using small hand sickles in identical poses to those still used up to a century ago.

Roman farming seems to have developed but little and strangely enough it is not even certain that they had the scythe, although their Gallic neighbours were at that time using a mechanical harvester. A cart with the rear end fitted with an iron toothed comb, adjustable to the height of the corn, was pushed through the growing wheat by an ox harnessed at the rear. As the comb engaged the stalks they were pushed against the teeth which pulled off the ears and allowed them to fall into the cart.

Life changed but very little over the centuries and the routine on the medieval manor and that of the 18th century farm were essentially the same. Harvesting of the corn was normally undertaken in late summer and barley, the second crop, in the early autumn.

On the Feudal Manor at harvest time the villeins were liable to carry out extra work for the lord—boon work. Not only the villein but all members of his family, with the exception of his wife, were expected to turn out at such times. The only obligation of the lord was to provide food for the boon workers, an obligation continued until very recently in the form of Harvest Home. All the crops gathered on the lord's demesne were his sole property and as such were consumed or sold by him.

The introduction of mechanical harvesters changed the entire pattern of rural life and the centuries-old traditions began to wither. By the 1920s nearly all the old customs had gone or survived only in a very attenuated form. Prior to this when harvest time

arrived all available hands were pressed into service; the day began at first light and continued until darkness and even beyond if it was a moonlit night. A harvest horn was sounded as a signal to start work and the leader, usually known as the Lord of the Harvest, set the pace as men and women worked with scythe and sickle. Food and drink were supplied by the farmer and in many cases there were seven meal breaks during the day—dew-bit, sun-bit, 'levenses, nammet or noon-bit, nuncheon, dinner (beaser in Suffolk and progger in Kent), and fourses. Ale or, more commonly, cider, was on hand all the time in some form of harvest bottle or costrel. These might have been old leather jacks, small barrels or glass bottles enclosed in a wicker frame rather like the modern chianti bottle. Work continued as long as there was corn standing until there was but one last bunch left. This last stand was regarded with particular veneration and the customs associated with

its cutting were numerous. On some farms the man who actually cut it traditionally stood and crowed like a cock—an interesting connection with the common straw figure of a cock once found so often at harvest time. In other parts of the country it was known as the Mare and when cut was sent as a derisory gesture to a neighbouring farmer who had not yet completed the harvest. In other parts this last stand was used to make the Harvest Queen or the Kern Dolly, a straw figure bedecked with ribbons and carried home in triumph on the last cartload of wheat to the Harvest Home. This was the culmination of the harvest, a great communal feast held in the largest barn or farmhouse kitchen, when all the labourers and their wives, sweethearts and families were feasted and feted, traditional games were played; toasts were drunk and there was a true feeling of deep satisfaction that something worthwhile had been achieved and that all had just cause to celebrate.

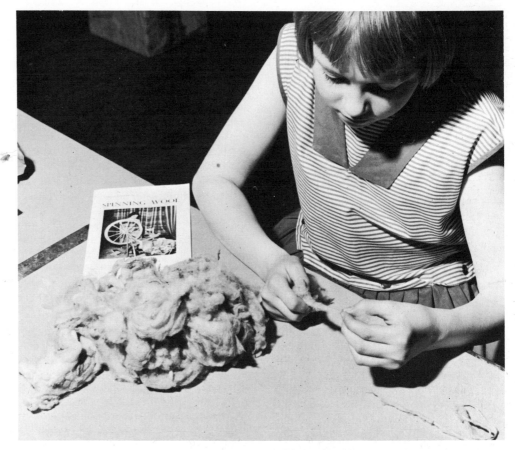

"All good gifts around us . . ." Need the harvest always follow last year's pattern? Could we not include raw wool or synthetic fibres in our harvest-time displays around the school? Above, child "teasing" wool

Craft notes on the Harvest

It is a delightful experience to sit and watch a country craftsman practising his trade or to see reconstructions of his workshop. The Chair Bodger's Shop in High Wycombe, the Basket Maker and Woodturner at St. Fagan's Museum, Wales, and the Wheelwright's Shop in the Science Museum in London come to mind in this context. One immediately thinks how wonderful it would be to learn some of these crafts and teach them to children. But not only would one need the tools and materials, one would also need the time, years of time—an apprenticeship. But this does not apply to quite all the crafts. Last summer I came across one which was reasonably easy to learn and then pass on to children. This is the art of Corn Dolly making.

There are two very useful books on the art; Miss M. Lambeth's *The Golden Dolly* (Cornucopia Press) and Lettice Sandford and Philla Davis' *Decorative Straw Work* (Batsford). Both are well illustrated and extremely clear in their instructions. A smaller pamphlet by the last two authors is available from the Herefordshire Federation of Women's Institutes, Hereford.

A number of museums have examples of dollies on show and there are an increasing number of churches which feature them during their Harvest Festival celebrations.

Many children will have been able to watch the farmers at work in their fields gathering in the crops, especially in the more southerly counties and they will in most cases see the efficient way in which the combine harvesters get to work. These machines make good subjects for modelling from card and scrap materials. Opportunities should be taken to look at reference books showing older methods of cropping—the reaper binder and the sickle, with the thresher at work in the farmyard when the crop has dried out. These old threshers were fascinating machines and will present a delightful challenge to two or three boys with a box of wheels and rubber bands. If a picture can be obtained for guidance a large model could be built up with the thresher at work (a small electric motor may be an anachronism—but it would provide just that vital factor to make an exciting scene). The stack of wheat, the barns, the horse-drawn wagons, the farmhouse and the cutout figures of the men and women are other details to add. This type of model makes a

colourful centre piece for a school or church harvest festival.

Lines of workers in the fields using primitive means of harvesting can form another diorama scene. Foam rubber—yellow, but with touches of colour added—can be purchased quite cheaply and used to suggest the crop. And talking of crops, vary these as much as possible. Potatoes, growing in a model field with the special harvesting machine which turns up the vegetable and stones which look like them, and the lines of bent pickers selecting them for the carts to take them off to the clamps, is a good scene to model.

Try a hopfield too. A piece of fibreboard needs to be carefully drawn up with a series of lattice lines, an inch and a half apart. Drill holes at all the interstices, large enough to take 4-inch lengths of dowel rod (a collection of round lollipop sticks will suffice). The "poles" now have to be threaded up and pieces of green tissue paper twisted around the threads to simulate the growing hop bines.

The collection of the hops is made by itinerant workers putting the crop into baskets. Although the men on stilts work earlier in the year during the stringing up, one or two of these high above the harvesters will create an extra point of interest.

Also high above ground level will be the apple and other fruit pickers, working on ladders against the trees. Once again the trees have to be laid out with geometrical precision in their rows and lines. (Who said that they never saw a ruler in a craft lesson these days?) Pieces of wire, bent in two, are twisted together. After an inch or so, pieces of tissue or material are placed inside the wires and the twisting continued. The tree shape can be trimmed with scissors afterwards. Small balls of tissue can be glued into position as the fruit. Alternatively small twigs can be gathered from trees and these covered with tissue paper or foam rubber pieces.

The opportunity can be taken to give a different line of interest to the Festival of Harvest by looking at the work of the farmers and fruit-growers of other countries. Thus an orange grove in Israel, or a vineyard in southern France, or a cocoa plantation in Ghana are all extensions of geographical study and group exercises in craft. To arrange these around the hall during celebrations would cultivate a less insular attitude among the children, and suggest the interdependence of one country upon

another for food supplies. The building of a fleet of cargo vessels bringing the food from overseas is yet another facet of this single topic.

Occasionally the work of the fisherman can be highlighted in a special Harvest Festival of the Sea. A fleet of drifters or trawlers can be made by a class, to be exhibited returning to their harbour well laden. A table can be filled with sculptured fish shapes made from manilla card or cartridge paper. Some of these can be used in a mobile, either suspended from the ceiling, or underneath a large table, on top of which is sailing the fishing boats.

Finally the harvest of the hedgerow and woodland should not be neglected. There are usually some very good warm dry days in October to take a party out foraging for fruit and berries, foliage and fungi. Many attractive arrangements can be made up by young children and the beginner in this field can be recommended to choose a theme, or be limited in the variety of material that can be used, e.g. three items only or only red berries, etc.

In ways such as these, the harvest will indeed be a rich one.

Notes

It may be assumed that this subject would be dealt with round about the time of the year when harvest festivals take place but the festival could reasonably be either the starting point or the culmination of the scheme of work.

In both cases we may assume that very few people these days are satisfied with a perfunctory "hymn and a prayer" festival and that the poets and the musicians will be pressed into service. In my day, it used to be "Big Steamers", "Behold, a giant am I" and "We plough the fields and scatter". (I was quite old before it struck me that we do not just "scatter", but "scatter the good seed".)

Nowadays, with record-players and tape-recorders available we can be rather more ambitious. An excellent overture would be Purcell's great chorus, No. 35 in "The Fairy Queen", entitled "Hail Great Parent", perhaps preluded by a trumpet tune. This could be balanced by a choral finale, Nos. 22–24 from Haydn's "Seasons". Incidentally, gorgeous, triumphant music may be needed, if a procession is part of the scheme, and I suggest either "Jupiter" from Holst's "Planets" or the second part of the "Mastersingers" overture, commencing with the section based on the Apprentices' Dance. The first entry of the tremolando theme in Elgar's "Introduction and Allegro" might well suggest a wheat field rippling in the wind and the magical passage where four pizzicato notes simulate the chime of distant church bells could be used to introduce one of the readings suggested. If modern methods are referred to I can think of nothing better than the opening of Brahms' First Symphony to suggest a combine harvester pounding over the fields where men once worked with scythes.

MacColl's "Shoals of Herring" refers to another sort of harvest.

Marvell's well-known garden could be used to introduce the idea of the lushness of harvest and Swift's saying about two ears of corn to stress the economic note, but omitting the snide crack at politicians. Other readings could be drawn from the following: "The Land Workers" and "Joseph Hodges" by Masefield; "The Hock Cart" by Herrick; "Summer" from Bloomfield's "The Farmer's Boy"; "Harvest" from Vita Sackville-West's "The Land"; the opening of Arnold's "Scholar Gipsy"; the translation of Pasternak's "Haystacks"; the relevant lines in Hopkins' "Hurrahing in Harvest"; Laurie Lee "Apples" and the beginning and end of the Masque in "The Tempest".

Keats' "Autumn", of course, is unrivalled in its conjuration of an atmosphere of ripeness, but it might be thought rather languorous for a harvest festival, sounding as though all this fruitage had just happened, without toil and sweat or risk.

Hood touches on crops in his "Autumn" but deals mainly with Autumn as the presage of winter.

I have seen a dramatisation of the story of Joseph used most effectively as the centrepiece of a harvest festival and the second chapter of the Book of Ruth and the Parable of the Sower provide suitable readings.

A hint for a different approach is given in the "Ballad of John Barleycorn" and if it is found rather cryptic for children, there is another version of it in Longfellow's "Hiawatha", where Hiawatha wrestles for three successive nights with a young man clad in green and yellow. On the third night, Hiawatha kills and buries him and from his grave grows maize.

A combine harvester discharges wheat grain into a trailer

Houses

Give a small child a sheet of paper, some colours and a brush and leave him quite free to paint what he likes and more often than not he will make a picture around a house, a person and a tree. Throughout childhood this preoccupation seems to remain and it is as well to acknowledge this interest from time to time in their picture making activities. I suppose part of the attraction for painting houses, street scenes and towns may be attributed to the fact that these are comparatively easy things to paint. The lines are uncomplicated and straightforward and it hardly matters what colours are used provided there are some windows, a door with a number and a chimney belching smoke.

And yet could not houses—the houses round the school, the houses in the town or village in which the children live—be used as a starting point for some very basic art teaching? In my opinion it is part of our task to help the children we teach to look carefully at the world around them, and having looked, to *see*. I remember taking a group of nine-year-olds on to the roof playground of the four-decker Victorian building in which I worked. We had been talking about houses through the ages, their changing style and function. I noticed that in illustrating the houses in which they lived almost every child drew a country cottage, with door neatly centred between four curtained windows, while from the roof smoke curled

upwards from a small chimney stack. This from children living within minutes from the Elephant and Castle in London! We looked at our drawings and then went on to the roof playground, pencil and paper in hand, just to look at roof tops, chimney pots and the pattern of the skyline. The children drew the different roof styles—some houses had flat roofs, others were gabled, some were slated, others tiled; some chimney pots rose up singly from the end of a building, others were grouped in great batteries, some were straight, some twisted, some cowled, some tall and thin, others short and squat. The children looked and saw, and when they went back to their classroom, bubbling with interest (over what for me was quite a mundane experience) they wrote down and illustrated their observations. Next day several came with sketches of their own house, quite different from the country cottage they had thought would satisfy me.

I often wonder whether we use the children's immediate environment enough to throw light and purpose on our teaching and to keep the whole business of learning alive. I have always advocated (wherever it is possible) going to look and touch (and thereby experience) rather than rely on acquiring knowledge second-hand through books. One occasion for example, I took a group to Norwich Castle. We went to the dungeons and, standing in pools of water, the curator said,

"Now I'm going to switch off the lights and close the door—imagine..." Intense interest, excitement and rich verbal comment followed (and as far as I know, no nightmares!). Perhaps a castle is not a house, but we could produce a similar learning situation by taking children to wander round houses steeped in history—Burghley House, near Stamford, for example, for its fascinating kitchen; Sissinghurst Castle in Kent for its Tudor tower; Blikling Hall, Norfolk, for the splendour of its Jacobean frontage; Ickworth, Suffolk, for its Paladian corridors and great rotunda, or to the ruins of Fountains Abbey in Yorkshire for the sheer beauty of its Gothic arches. On the visit give the children time to make detailed sketches, take large sheets of sugar paper and wax crayons and encourage them to try to recapture the spirit of what they see.

In the school's immediate neighbourhood much could also be done. A simple street map of the area (useful links with maths here) could be made on a large scale, the children drawing the houses individually and pasting them in position. (See opposite.) This in turn might lead to paper collages of town scenes. By varying the type of paper used for the cut-outs considerable contrasts can be achieved. Compare, for example, the picture of the "Town at Night", with the delicate tone and pattern of "Buildings" (in which tissues were used throughout).

"Where the monks lived"   **Crayon drawing by girl of ten**

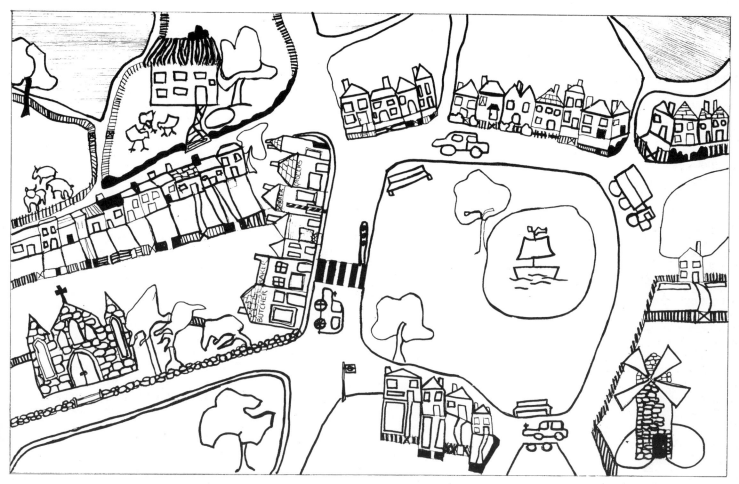

Street map. Drawing by Bridget Jackson from "Let's work Large". Mills and Boon

Tissue collage by a ten year old.

Left. Paper Collage. "Town at Night". Nine year olds' group work

109

Whatever approach to and development from this subject is made, a recurrent theme must be the idea of a house as a man-made contrivance giving protection from weather and wild beasts and human enemies, crude units of shelter at first, ameliorated by engineers and craftsmen into places of comfort. It is one which should be presented to children, for it deals with a problem so successfully answered as to prevent them from understanding that it exists, basic though it is to human life.

It is a theme round which can grow a complex of historical, geographical, scientific and artistic ideas of the greatest vitality. We have never, I think, neglected some few aspects of this complex, when we have dealt with igloos, Japanese paper houses, the black tents of the Bedouin and similar exotics, but I visualise extending it to embrace the Mile End Road and the Brandon Estate and their equivalents in the provinces.

(Older children could be encouraged to examine the effects of a temperate climate on the habits of plumbers and builders. At least, they might find out why pipes freeze in England, but not in Moscow and Saskatchewan.)

The subject is not one which has, so far as I know, brought the best out of poets and musicians who tend to stoop unduly to nostalgia. Hood's "I remember", though, is a better poem than we used to think and it will be new to our pupils—and, indeed, to most of our younger colleagues. Herrick wrote "A thanksgiving for his house" and Padraic Colum's "Old Woman of the Roads" dreams of the house she never had. "For Sale", by W. H. Davies, praises the strength hidden in the ruins of an old cottage and the now well-known 17th century poem beginning, "Yet if His Majesty", includes a bustling account of preparing a house to offer hospitality.

The house as a unit in a community can hardly be disregarded. Masefield, the indispensable, has a bright little picture of a country town a century or so ago ("Wonderings—The Town") and it can never be wrong to introduce children to "The Key of the Kingdom". Edwin Muir's "Good Town" begins with a factual description, clear and lovely, and goes on to describe the effects of,

". . . two wars that trampled on us twice,
Advancing and withdrawing, like a herd
Of clumsy-footed beasts on a stupid errand
Unknown to them or us."

This is a subject some teachers may care to follow up, especially if local circumstances make it apposite to do so.

The musicians approach the subject somewhat deviously. The houses of the Baba Yaga (Moussorgsky's "Pictures from an Exhibition") and of the witch in "Hansel and Gretel" (Humperdinck) are fascinating but neither domestic nor architectural and Beethoven's overture "The Consecration of the House" was written for the opening of a theatre.

We have here a good example of an occasion when it is essential to choose music for its sound, regardless of its title, for mime and drama and the promotion of a mood. There are no Eskimos at the South Pole, but Vaughan Williams' "Sinfonia Antarctica" suggests the struggle of man against the polar cold; Debussy's "L'Apres-Midi d'un Faune" evokes the idea of shimmering heat regardless of latitude; if we are thinking of houses as forts, any battle music will do; and there is a good supply of ominous music for wolves sniffing round the cave-mouth. The houses built, one on sand and one on a rock, teach the same overt lesson as the story of the three little pigs, come to think of it; and "The House that Jack Built" involves a good deal of social history, from home-brewing to the domestication of animals.

Craft notes on Houses

Quite recently we have had a survey team in school, inquiring into ways in which craft work will take its place in the Middle School. When will the ruler, hardly the dominant tool in primary craft, be introduced to the 9-13 year old child, and will its excessive use stifle the creative aspect which is one of the most valuable, were questions they asked.

In fact of course, the ruler is a valuable aid and needs to feature in craft work almost at all ages, when it is needed. Certainly in the theme (page 108) on "Houses" the need to measure is very real—and the child will see the reason why.

Try to obtain plans from a local architect or purchase books of house plans from the local bookseller. Small groups of children can then adopt a particular style of house they favour and then model it. Card is the most satisfactory medium to use, although those who are more proficient can use hardboard which is very cheap to purchase—especially as off-cuts. Let the groups agree upon a suitable scale, e.g. one inch to the foot, and then discuss a few conversions of this and set them to work. The basic shape needs to be tackled first, and then the "extras" added. These can be large additions like garages and conservatories, or small items like a porch or dormer windows, and older pupils will want to include these.

The setting out of the models in conjunction with one another, with the addition of street furniture, garden features and the inclusion of public buildings are all important aspects of the topic. The small classroom may have to be content with a long street along the windowsill, but one other form of display is possible and exciting. The layout can be made on the wall, with the pattern of the estate, village or city suburb drawn into position. Small flaps incorporated at the bottom of each model will enable the model to be fixed securely in place and so present a bird's eye view. Perhaps in this way the concept of mapping may become clear to the child for the first time.

The visit to a large country house or castle as part of a topic will suggest more mathematics. Even if a scale plan is available in the guide book, it is a good exercise to have the children measure the length and breadth of the building, and of course, its height by inclinometer or some other height-finding apparatus which has been manufactured in the classroom. One of our groups caused some diversion to those waiting for tickets for the Proms, when they went round the outside of the Albert Hall with a clickwheel. Large and small houses of historic interest stand in most neighbourhoods and visits to them in connection with some topic or other will naturally lead to modelling. Varieties of material can be chosen to represent the building material. Thus strips of balsa wood will be appropriate to the Tudor building, and dried grass or raffia to thatch a roof. Paint will prove to be as useful as ever in "laying" bricks and stones. Old negative film stock or cellophane can be used for windows, and ball point pens used to give leaded effects, and so on.

In addition to observation to supply details for modelling, another interesting possibility is open. To use Dickens as an example: read a description of Peggotty's house in *David Copperfield,* or of Miss Haversham's house in *Great Expectations* and then have the children bring the scene to life. If these models are large enough, then the interiors can also be modelled, with either a side hinged to open to reveal the contents, or having a removable roof, so that the furnishings can be examined. The chairs, tables, beds, curtains and tablecloths, offer many opportunities for children to model, the more easily after using well illustrated books and after visiting appropriate museums, e.g. the Geffrye in Shoreditch, London, where rooms of different periods are set out.

If the centre of interest is an extended one, then a number of lines emerge. The historical approach enables more group and individual assignments to be arranged. Models of dwellings from the cave right through the ages to the tall flats of mid-twentieth century will be required. These should be homes as well has houses, and so will need small figures, approximately to scale, so that a three-dimensional time line can be built up around the room. Direct reference can be made to those buildings in the neighbourhood which represent the period of the models.

The geographical approach is another broad canvas on which to work. For this a series of dioramas can be built up. A piece of card is curved and fixed to a segment of a circle. This will form the background and provide an opportunity to paint in other dwellings, plant forms, and even prevailing weather conditions. The model of the New Zealand whare can thus stand, made of wood, with carved doorposts and its thatched roof, in front of the painting of the village with the stockade protecting all. A New York scene can feature two or three tall columns with minute windows marked in, standing in front of a lower Manhattan skyline with Boeing jets flying overhead. Incidentally, beware of the pitfall of the anachronism of the igloo. Their last stronghold appears to be the classroom. The last speaker we had from the Commonwealth Institute, speaking about Canada, told us that the last time he had shown his film was in an Eskimo school, on a projector as new as our own.

The homes of animals can also feature within this theme, when the nests of birds, the underground sanctuaries of the badger, the moated fortresses of the beaver can be attempted using natural materials brought in from the park, woodland or garden.

If one does not find the prospect too whimsical, the *Wind in the Willows* has some fine

A nine year old working on a junk model entitled "My block of flats"

descriptions of the homes of Badger, Mole and Toad!

Finally a word about building kits. There are several such commercial products on the markets and many of them are excellent. Because the units are precision made, it is possible to create some realistic shapes and learn some building techniques at the same time. Children need to be encouraged with such kits to explore the material and grow out of the book of plans as soon as possible, incorporate them with other materials and so learn to regard them merely as another element to use in their creative modelmaking.

""Tis Folly to be Wise"

By definition a house is a dwelling place and in many ways the story of houses reflects the story of living. The Stone Age man lived in caves because they were available. He had neither the skill nor, even more important, the time to build. By far the greater part of his life was taken up with the struggle to stay alive. The demands of living left him little time for pleasure.

As life became more settled the struggle to live became less severe and man had time to think of comfort. From the 11th century onwards the pacification of Britain con-

tinued apace and by the time of the Tudors the necessity to consider defence as one of the main purposes of building no longer applied. Noble homes no longer required enormously thick walls and tiny narrow windows intended primarily as loopholes. The moated manor house replaced the castle and the 17th century saw an increasing number of country houses that were living places rather than military strongpoints. Instead of solid walls the architect offered expanses of glass so that the view became part of the home. Soon untamed nature was no longer acceptable to the owner and landscape gardening in hands such as those of Capability Brown became a matter of the artificial being made to appear natural. It was inevitable that soon the planner would seek to embellish the view even further and it is during the 18th century that the peculiarly British pastime of folly building flourished. There sprang up newly constructed classical temples, castles, towers, monuments and ruins. Britain is dotted with surviving examples ranging from a complex mathematical lodge built at the end of the 16th century to a tall brick tower built as late as 1935 and in between stand miniature colosseums, battlemented tunnel entrances and even a model Stonehenge.

Sir Thomas Tresham was possessed of an inquiring mind which delighted in many studies including that of mathematics. His lodge at Rushton, Northants, has everything based in odd numbers, mostly threes. All the rooms are three or six sided and most of the external embellishments are triangular. There are three floors, three gables and the sides measure 33 ft. 3 ins.! Built in 1593/5 this is one of the earliest surviving examples.

Castles and towers were very popular and some, like that at Haldon, Belvedere, 1788, are complete and served as a genuine home. It stands 70 ft. high and dominates the country for miles around. Others like that of Ralph Allen at Bath, Somerset, are complete frauds being simply walls and facades. The tower, known as Old John, at Bradgate Park, Leicester, is a ruin which is alleged to have been built to mark the spot where the Earl of Stamford's son met an unfortunate death.

One unique castle folly is that of Clayton Tunnel near Hassocks in Sussex for here a small cottage situated over the mouth of the railway tunnel is lost between two turrets, complete with battlements, machicolations and the actual tunnel mouth lacks only a portcullis to complete the effect. This very non-functional railway masterpiece was erected during the 1840s.

Another impressive folly is the replica of the colosseum built by John Stuart McCaig in Oban, Argyll, in the 1890s. In this he combined his own interest in things Roman and a desire to help the unemployed of the district, and as a wealthy banker he could well afford to indulge both.

Alas, modern folly fabrication is not quite so carefree as it was and when, in 1935, Lord Berners sought to build a 140 ft. tower there was great opposition from many quarters and the Ministry of Health held an enquiry. However, Lord Berners won and the tall tower stands today.

These follies and many others like them might well be described as public, for they can be seen by anybody in the district. Another more private form of folly was the grotto and several of these survive in all their glory. Small streams were diverted or even created to provide tinkling waterfalls and small lakes. One grotto in the West Country even has a lion's den complete with marble lions. Some were decorated with shells or pebbles and there was an interesting survival of this British pre-occupation with caves in the, now largely extinct, childhood game of building miniature grottoes and displaying them for passers-by to admire and perhaps reward.

It is a little ironic that now, when man has more leisure than ever before, he also has less time, money, space and inclination to build follies than ever before.

Bibliography
F. Peacock and H. Pluckrose
Project through Craft (Buildings)
Macdonald and Co.

The Barbican Scheme, London. Note how the portions of older buildings have been preserved and made to blend with the new (Fox Photos)

The Circus and Pantomime

Circus Mural using life sized figures

As children grow older, they become more and more aware of their own deficiencies in ALL fields—consequently they become self-conscious. This self-consciousness is often reflected very strongly in their artwork—left to themselves they hunch lower and lower over their work, drawing smaller and smaller figures, getting more and more dissatisfied until finally, they give up the struggle completely.

Although it is difficult to jolt children (particularly older ones) out of this rut, especially if it has been going on for some time, it is not impossible.

First of all, lock away rubbers, pencils and small detail brushes and give them instead pastels, chalks, paints and fairly big brushes. Large sheets of strong wrapping paper are spread on the floor, the "models" remove their shoes and, if necessary, their socks and dresses, then they carefully lie down on the paper. Other children draw around the models. Our models in the photographs did none of these things and found themselves smothered in powder colour.

A certain amount of posing is possible—legs can be bent and arms can be raised. If the models lie face downwards on the paper and turn their faces to the side, a good profile can be drawn. The model will have to squirm about a bit in order that the part being drawn is flat against the paper.

When a satisfactory outline has been drawn, the children colour the figure, adding features and appropriate clothing. When the figures are finished, they are cut out and glued to a background.

Every conceivable subject can be tackled, using this method—footballers, underwater divers, dancers, soldiers etc.

As our topic is the circus, we asked a group of 9 year olds to make a huge circus picture using life sized figures, and as you see, it is a great success.

You will find that observant children discover many things for themselves when tackling these figures, i.e. the proper size of feet in relation to the body, how long arms really are, what happens to the shoulders when an arm is raised above the head and so on.

As a follow-up, children could be measured and full- or half-scale models made of them. The joints could be attached with split pins and this will enable the arms and legs to move. Circumferences of heads, lengths of noses, lengths of feet could be measured and interesting and amusing tables made of the results.

The initial stages

It's almost human!

A school letter box where the children can 'post' their Christmas cards can be made from boxes. It can be over life size and in the shape of a ringmaster, a clown, Father Christmas or even a postman.

Begin with the body, which is also the letter box. The teacher should cut out a 'mouth' at about the middle (diagram A). The box is mounted firmly on to two smaller boxes which will be the legs. Boxes or tins make the face and feet. Fix a piece of paper or card across the bottom of the box at the back to prevent the letters from falling on the floor. The arms of tubes or strips of card are added and hands cut out and attached.

To make his hat, cut out a brim shape and glue to the top of his head. The crown is a tube of paper or card – this can be attached to the brim with brown paper hinges (diagram B). Ears of paper, hair of wool, shoe laces of string, etc., are all added when he has been painted. A paper nose can be added as in diagram C.

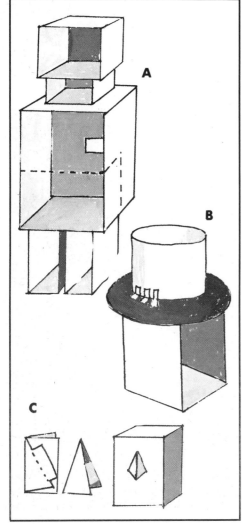

This ambitious frieze is made up from four sections

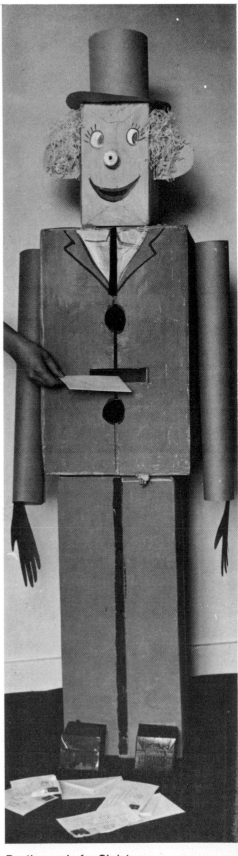

Posting early for Christmas

114

Prose, Poetry and Music

It is the function of this particular section to suggest poetry and music which can be included in the rich complex of interests aroused by such work.

To take an example, children making a study connected with the sea will not increase their factual knowledge from "The Rime of the Ancient Mariner" and the overture "Fingal's Cave", but teachers have found that Coleridge and Mendelssohn penetrate below the conscious, intellectual levels of the mind and release impulses which manifest themselves in creative work (including poetry and music).

It so happens that circuses and pantomimes make almost no appeal to poets and musicians, at least as far as I know. It may be that the "tamed and shabby tigers" of the circus repel them and while they may enjoy an annual visit to the uproarious farragos which open on Boxing Days, it would be understandable if they provided no inspiration.

Prose accounts of visits to these entertainments may be found in autobiographies and essays, but they are apt to be nostalgic in tone and nostalgia is a purely adult indulgence, not unnaturally. Moreover, grown-up recollections of childhood emotions are likely to embarrass children. For instance, little boys have a way of falling in love with fairy queens and suchlike (no doubt Miss Clark and Miss Black have many secret admirers of tender age) but they don't want anyone to refer to the fact.

Dickens' account, in "Hard Times", of the circus people has poetic intensity and sympathy and it is significant that, apart from the clown's dog, Merrilegs, there are no animals except horses in this particular outfit. Ninety-five per cent of the excitement of the performance is provided by the skill and courage of the acrobats and jugglers.

Any jolly, highly orchestrated music, almost, can suggest the activities of the ring and of Widow Twanky and Buttons. Dvořák's "Carnival Overture", Shostakovitch's "Barrel Organ Waltz", Strauss polkas, Offenbach, German, Sullivan and von Suppé, all have the right swagger, but it might be worth introducing children seriously to Sousa, provided care is taken to choose good performances, for Sousa wrote for virtuoso players.

Milhaud has a piece called "Le Boeuf sur le Toit" based on popular tunes of his day which I find dull, but it could appeal to children.

Wormser's "L'Enfant Prodigue" and Bartok's "Miraculous Mandarin" are both named "Pantomimes", presumably in the sense of being mimes, but more I cannot say.

Purists may wish to let their pupils know about the original pantomimes of Harlequin and Columbine. If so, it should be remembered that Schumann's "Carnival" includes "Pierrot", "Harlequin" and "Pantalon and Columbine" (Nos. 2, 3 and 15).

Hard on the last sentence came a record from EMI, most appositely, called "Pantalone's Pantomime", No. 3 of "Stories in Movement". Rachel Percival has devised a harlequinade as a basis for dramatic work for juniors (in the widest sense of mime, dance and the spoken word) and David Lord has written some attractive music in, I suppose, "Facade" style to describe it. Side 1 plays the music straight through and side 2 re-arranges it in seven sections to illustrate the characters and the finale so that children can rehearse separate sections. There are suggestions on the sleeve of how this might be done. This is a useful record and Lord's sparkling music is very well played. The scoring is for oboe, trumpet, trombone, guitar and percussion (7EG 8981).

Pantomime "Jack and the Beanstalk" at the London Palladium (Fox Photos)

The Origins of Circuses and Pantomimes

From the early part of the 19th century to the middle of the 20th century one of the traditional Christmas treats was a visit to the circus or the pantomime.

The origins of the circus lie back in the 4th century B.C. when it is recorded that a Roman ruler celebrated the capture of a town with some organised horse races which became traditional. Either because the horses went round in circles or because the spectators stood 'round', it became known as a circus. Later permanent sites were set up of which the largest was the Circus Maximus just outside Rome, capable of holding many thousands of spectators. It was shaped like a half ellipse and the straight side was occupied by stables and similar buildings whilst the spectators sat around the rest of the perimeter. Along the centre of the arena was a tall barrier surmounted by seven statues and seven large marble eggs, these were removed, one for each lap, until the full race of seven laps was completed. The races were run by chariots drawn, usually, by two or four horses. The charioteers belonged to one of four factions identified by the colours which were always red, green, white and blue.

Soon the races were considered too mundane and events such as trick riding were added to the programme. Later still, around 250 B.C., the first of the gladiatorial combats was staged and it was this form of public entertainment that gradually ousted the chariots from their pride of place. The permutation of combat was enormous; man against man; man against beast; beast against woman or woman against man. More and more blood flowed in the circuses as combats became more and more elaborate and the slaughter was ghastly.

The circus as an organised show seems to have disappeared with the Roman Empire and the only entertainment recorded during the Middle Ages was rather haphazard with individual performances such as jugglers and performing animals.

It was not until the 18th century that the circus once again appeared in England thanks to the ambition and enthusiasm of Philip Astley. Born in Newcastle-under-Lyme, son of a cabinet maker, he had a particular feeling for horses and so joined the cavalry, serving with distinction in Germany. At the age of 24 he was discharged from the army and set about creating his dream of a combined riding school and public exhibition of equestrian art. He acquired a small piece of land on the south bank of the River Thames near Westminster bridge and there he, his wife and son gave riding displays which were a very popular feature of entertainment at the time. He also trained performing horses such as the talking horse which spelt out its name, counted and performed similar incredible feats. After a very varied life he died in 1814 but his roofed-in amphitheatre continued in use for a variety of public shows and was not demolished until 1893.

Scenes from the pantomime of Jack and the Beanstalk at Covent Garden in 1888. 1. Climbing the Beanstalk. 2. Fight with the Giant. 3. Mrs. Giant. 4. The Magic Sword. 5. The Giant is Coming. 6. Converted. 7. A Sprightly Fairy.
Mansell Collection

Rivals sought to mount more splendid shows and extra items such as acrobats, dancers and other circus turns were added.

Travelling circuses apparently developed from the end of the Napoleonic wars and there are early references describing them at Bartholomew Fair, in London and on similar occasions throughout the country. From the middle of the 19th century onwards the famous names such as Sangers, Howes and Cushing begin to figure in the world of circus. Travelling menageries displaying exotic animals also date from the early part of the 19th century and by the 1820s there were two rivals who did their best to outsmart each other. George Wombwell founded his zoo in 1805 and his great competitor, Atkins, was not long after.

Pantomime is a great mixture and in Greek it means an imitator of everything and was acted in silence. It remained so until the 18th century when words and music first made their appearance. What is a pantomime? It is a very difficult thing to define but broadly speaking it is a combination of phantasy, drama, music hall and circus. It originated in Italy with the Commedia dell 'Arte which was apparently a form of local skit and dated back to the Middle Ages. It became stylised with certain characters among which were Clown, Pantaloon, Harlequin and Columbine. Harlequin gave his name to the type of sketch most popular in Britain, the harlequinade, and this form of comic entertainment is mentioned at various times during the 17th century but it is with the 18th century that it first figures prominently in the theatre. The name Pantomime occurs for the first time in a production of 1717 and in 1721 John Rich produced "The Magician or Harlequin A Director" and into this show he introduced the transformation scenes that were to become so much a characteristic of pantomime. From then on the popularity of this form of entertainment increased and Harlequin became the chief character with his magic bat which naturally enabled him to perform any amount of transformations! His traditional costume was of four colours each representing some abstract quality, yellow for jealousy, blue for truth, scarlet for love and black for invisibility. He was later supplanted by the clown when the part was taken by such great actors as Grimaldi who for 40 years was paramount in the country. In 1814 speech was introduced into the Harlequinade, for until then it was still mimed.

It was during the 19th century that the type of actor starring in pantomime began to change. Originally the leading parts had been taken by famous actors of the day, but now the music hall began to take over and some of the most famous names of music hall were also the stars of pantomime. Grandparents and great-grandparents will remember Dan Leno and Vesta Tilley, famous performers of their day! Pantomime's popularity began to decrease towards the end of the 19th century although it retained some of its hold until the outbreak of World War II. From then on it has declined gradually over the years until now the old traditional pantomime is practically dead along with the old tenting circus and for most people it survives only in the form of a flat picture on a glass screen!

Bibliography

Popular Entertainments through the Ages. S. McKechnie.
Christmas Pantomime. A. E. Wilson.
Clowns and Pantomimes. M. Willson Disher.
English Circus and Fairground. G. Tyrwhitt-Drake.

Craft notes on the Circus and Pantomime

That universal provider of experience—the television set—will have presented during the Christmas period entertainment featuring both the circus and the pantomime—the lucky few watching it in colour. For some there will be the very real thrill of a visit to the theatre and the big top and so from the children returning to school there should be a rich storehouse of memories on which to draw. Both of these subjects enjoy the advantage of being made up of many features which will allow for many individual assignments as well as group enterprises.

From the circus we can begin with the animals. The wild and fierce variety have a tremendous appeal for children, and using Plasticine, lions, tigers, and panthers can be modelled. Various platforms, bases and stands can be made from balsa wood or card, and after painting in bright colours be arranged in a semicircle around the animal trainer. A protective cage will be needed. Straws can be used for this purpose setting them at intervals in a neat roll of Plasticine. Small pieces of pipe cleaner can be used to join the roofing straws. Behind this, and other presentations, a long frieze of seated figures will set off the models very pleasingly. A simple plan is shown on page 118. The elephants, horses, dogs, seals and doves are all performers which will be taken up eagerly by children as their individual assignments. There will be, probably, keen competition for the chimpanzees task and the various impedimenta which is used during their act. For the monkeys, a hunt through the scrap box will often produce suitable material for the small stuffed fabric animals.

The skilful work of the acrobats will have appealed to some and the walkers of tightropes, swingers on trapezes, jugglers of balls will all have to be modelled with great care if they are going to appear to be the kind of persons who could carry out the delicate and daring manoeuvres. With many children—especially the younger ones—simple card cutouts will prove to be effective. A three dimensional effect can be obtained by the positioning of the figures on the apparatus which is made from balsa wood,

The Lion caged

wire and thread at different levels. The acrobats who perform their skills in the air will automatically suggest the idea of a mobile to some, while others will select a dramatic situation of a fingertip catch of the girl in mid-air who has just done two and a half somersaults from her platform. The clowns haven't been forgotten but reserved for those who cannot bear to think of any other part of the circus as being more important.

Here quite the most outrageous figures, faces and clothes can be encouraged. Materials can be fixed with Copydex around a simple card figure. For this simple figure, some articulation can be included by using a push through paper fastener at shoulder and hip joints. Where the figure is larger, 12 inches or more, then elbow, knee, even wrist and ankle joints can be included so that the clowns can be grouped in a life-like fashion.

The use of wire armatures and chicken wire figures can be included in the techniques the children are encouraged to try out in this section. Papier mâché heads will allow for some opportunities for wearing the things made. The basic shape of a head can be made from a length of chicken wire which is first of all made into a roll which is large enough to pass over the head. Secure the roll at one end with twists of wire. This will correspond to the neck. Next pull out the part of the roll above this to make a roundish shape. Now take smaller pieces of chicken wire and mould them into a nose, mouth and eyebrows to be attached, if it has been too difficult to "pull" them out of the coil.

Now cover with papier mâché and allow to dry for decoration. Outlandish costumes of paper or material can now be designed to go with the heads and the opportunity to wear and perform in their "heads" and clothes will be an obvious sequel. Recently in school a "car" was made up around 4 tables and chairs. From nearby dumps, tyres, wings, doors, and a steering wheel were acquired and added to the "chassis". Such a production has just the right kind of precarious quality which lends itself to the comic motor car sketch, and the clowns of the class would need very little by way of encouragement to embark on such a model! Within the pantomime theme there is scope for a large number of model theatre scenes. As well as those likely to have been seen in the local area and on television, there will be other firm favourites among the children. Books feature many of these classic stories with splendid illustrations to enhance them and supply further stimulus and information on which to draw. One might well ask for a stage scene to be created with a box with proscenium arch, curtains and backdrop. Once the story and the particular scenes have been decided upon then the figures can be produced, as with earlier suggestions trying something simple or sophisticated depending upon the age of the children. Background and other scenery provides tasks and opportunity for other members within the group and if time permits these can be made flexible enough to create quite quickly a number of scenes. If the efforts of a number of groups are concentrated upon one pantomime, then a story sequence can be developed in a number of stage settings. Simple dialogue can be tape-recorded and played back, with a spotlight being directed on the scene; with these synchronisation can be attempted. The further refinement of this is to produce these figures as puppets on sticks which will slide in and out to suitable music and dialogue.

Recently in school we were treated to this technique in yet another form when the figures used were simple cutouts. These were well prepared silhouettes attached to vertical or horizontal sticks and projected on to a white sheet by a powerful lamp. The way in which the audience became engrossed in the traditional tale presented in such an unsophisticated manner was something of an eye-opener to those who had been employing the hardware of the mid-twentieth century in an effort to improve the techniques of performance.

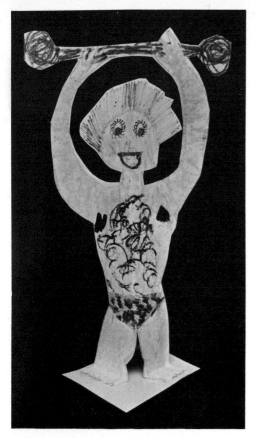

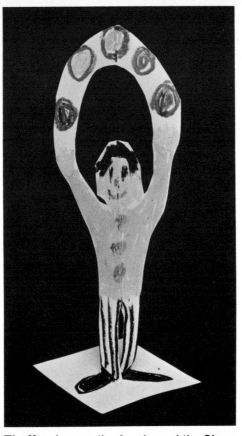

Simple folded cardboard figures   **The Muscle man, the Juggler and the Clown**

Foil Models and Group Modelling

Silver foil models can make very attractive groups for special occasions such as Christmas. Children will enjoy modelling Father Christmas with his sledge and reindeer. Father Christmas should be provided with a silver foil sack filled with sweets and the whole group placed under the Christmas tree.

Start with a rectangle of silver foil and make two tears at one end to make the arms and head and one tear at the other end to make the two legs. Model each limb by pressing and rolling the foil as if it was a piece of clay. Then cut out the shape of a cloak from a flat piece of foil with a pair of scissors. With practice the children will be able to press the cloak round the silver foil figure so that it keeps in place without the use of either adhesive or pins. These latter items can be used at first while the modeller is acquiring the necessary skills.

To model a reindeer the general process is similar except that pieces of foil will have to be left protruding from the head so that the antlers may be twined into place. Make two tears at each end of a rectangle of foil and model each section into legs, head and tail. Pull out two pieces on either side of the head and shape these pieces into ears. Roll out sticks of foil and then twist smaller pieces round the sticks and press and bend the whole into antlers. Twist the antlers round the pieces of foil that you should have left sticking out between the ears. Press very firmly to ensure the antlers stay in position.

A sledge for Father Christmas is made by joining two long strips of foil by smaller

118

strips which are folded round and squeezed very hard until secure. If it is needed to make Father Christmas suitably red his cloak can be painted with a non-toxic red paint which can be obtained for about a shilling. Father Christmas can also be made to look more realistic by the addition of a silver foil beard and silver foil boots.

Children can easily make a foil snowman as this model consists only of crumpled foil squeezed at a suitable spot to make a head. Improvements should be carried out by pinning a foil hat on the head and pressing foil stick shapes into the body to represent arms. Again a non-toxic paint can be used to make coloured buttons down the front of the silver foil snowman's body.

A silver foil circus gives scope for the making of all kinds of exciting models.

The clown is an obvious choice with large foil boots, a pointed hat pinned in place and a hoop for him to hold to give support. Horses, seals, elephants and other circus animals should all be attempted using a similar method to that used to make the reindeer. The elephant of course will require more foil for his long trunk and to provide padding for his body. All the models may be painted over with a non-toxic silver paint which hardens so that a permanent model is obtained.

The variety of models which can be made from silver paper is almost endless.

Editor's note

John Milsome's book *Modelling With Foil* (Queen Anne Press) gives further suggestions for group model making.

Design

If pattern work is to be fresh and creative, it is essential to dismiss any preconceived ideas and discover afresh by experiment just what pattern is. Pattern involves regularity and repetition. Natural growth in nature shows us this, so it is a good idea to use natural objects as a source of inspiration for pattern lessons. Leaves, tree-forms, shells, butterfly wings, tortoise shells—all show regularity and repetition in natural form (A).

Many man-made objects can also be used to show regularity and repetition. Windows, paving-stones, brick walls, fences—are all man-made examples of pattern (B).

If there is an element of experimentation in all pattern work, then stagnation of the work will be less likely. At first, it is not a good idea to use repeating pattern. The repeating pattern will probably appear as the result of various experiments, especially when using potato or lino blocks. Children should always apply brush to paper, making marks, before proceeding to picture-making. Pattern work will help the child to view the whole page and also give the child experience in breaking up and developing the shapes, using various marks. Pattern work has a direct bearing on picture-making, for the child is free to invent shapes and use textures and colours in any way. So an appreciation of colour, line, shape and texture will be developed through pattern work. It is best to allow the free use of available materials by all classes, and avoid, at first, patterns of "things"—otherwise the development of the child will be held up. When pattern has been basically understood, then suitable objects can be used as a source of inspiration. Pattern-making will develop a fine sense of colour.

One of our main concerns is to interest children in the surface forms and textures of natural and man-made objects. And after studying various objects and trying to render their surfaces, the children begin to appreciate the various aesthetic qualities that the objects possess. They begin to appreciate the beautiful colour harmonies, the interesting textures and the basic shape.

A

B

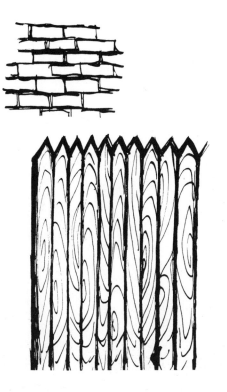

a. Mark with contrasting curved line.
b. Diagonal marks.
c. Using circles and squares or rectangles.
d. Starting near the centre.

e. Circles, rectangles, straight and curved lines.
f. Using vertical or horizontal lines as a basis for the superimposition of various marks.

g. Alternate lines of curves and marks.
h. Repetition of various lines and marks.

i. Repetition of the letter W.
j. Repetition of the letter E.

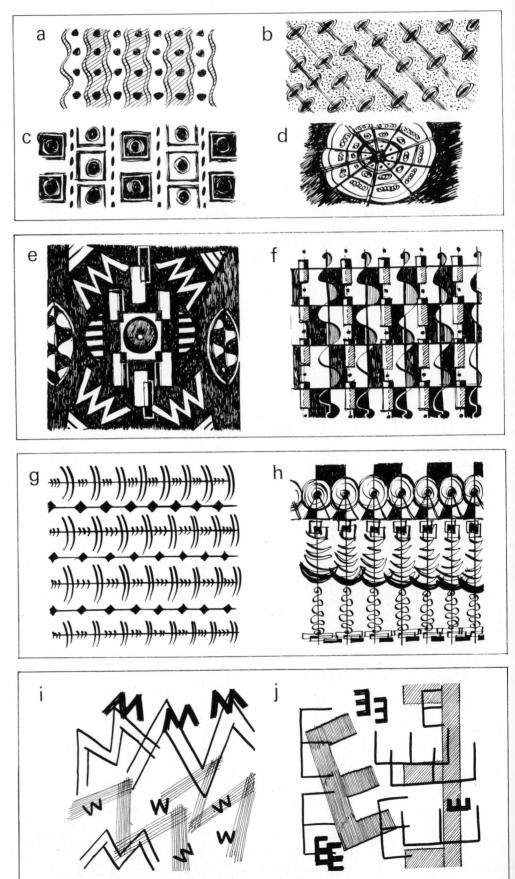

Growth Patterns

A start is made by drawing a simple shape on the base line (1). From any point on this shape another shape is drawn down to the base line on the right of the original shape. A point is selected on this second shape and a third shape drawn down to the base line on the left. A point is then selected on this third shape and a fourth shape

drawn to the base line on the right. This procedure is continued until the panel looks pleasantly filled. Some of the lines are then thickened and stripes and spot patterns are introduced to decorate some of the shapes. This does not restrict the use of colour. Poster colour may be used with great success.

The accompanying illustrations show how this design method can be applied to scraper board technique.

Patterns in Paper

Two pieces of paper are required. Quarter sheets of sugar paper are suitable for this.

One piece should be folded along its length, and with the fold at the bottom, the top edges should be folded back together, for about an inch, to leave a crease as shown in the diagram. Using scissors, cuts should be made up from the bottom fold to the crease at the top. Care must be taken to see that all the cuts reach the crease. About an inch should be left at each side as shown. The whole sheet of paper can then be opened out.

Using their second piece of paper, the children cut strips along its length. These should be about the same size as the strips cut on the first piece of paper, measuring about half an inch in width. These should be woven in and out to form a paper mat. It is essential to push the strips closely together, to make a tightly woven mat as a background upon which to work.

The pattern making may be done in two ways—the horse shown in the picture was made by pulling up the existing strips and pinching them between finger and thumb, where necessary. If the strips begin to pull out from the ends to leave gaps, new strips may be inserted from behind to complete the weaving again.

A running horse

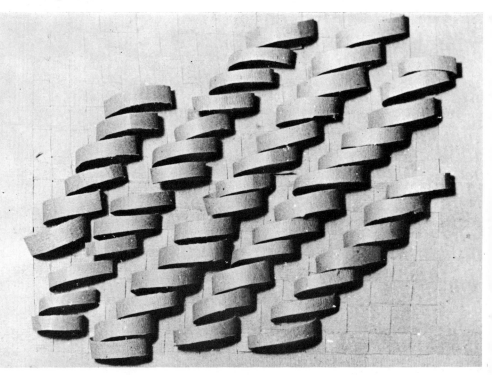

Coiled pattern

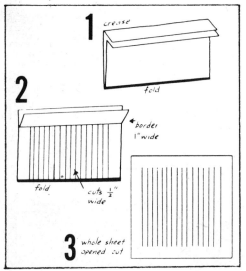

For the second method, pictured above, the mat is left flat, and new strips of paper are woven in and out on top of it to form the pattern. It will not be necessary to paste these into place if the mat has been tightly woven, as the criss-crossed strips on it will hold the ends firmly.

When the patterns have been completed, the strips sticking out at either side should be pushed under the inch wide strip which was left at the cutting stage, and pasted down with Copydex. The sides can be trimmed and the work will be framed in a neat border, ready for mounting.

Positive and Negative

I have found that children rarely have any idea of pattern. As pattern is a rather abstract subject to teach, and negative shape even more so, I used black and white paper to illustrate the subject.

All the children had was a rectangle of white paper and a basic shape, e.g. triangle, rectangle or circle in black paper. They had to cut out strips first of all, of varying widths and arrange them on the paper. The only stipulation was that no paper was to be thrown away. The pattern must include all the black paper.

In later lessons we went on to using any shape, cut out and stuck down opposite their negative shape. These led to work with many textures and colours of paper.

The mask was made using the same principle of not throwing any paper away.

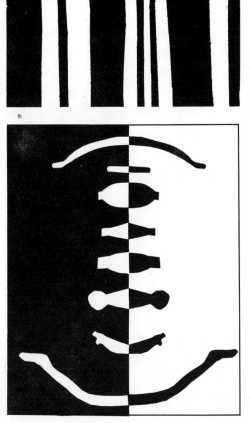

Patterns in Pen. . . .

Here is an interesting and satisfying idea which will be kindly accepted by forms of all ages. Seniors will recognise the familiar shapes of the accompanying contour design illustrations, whereas the younger children will appreciate the satisfying shapes and textures achieved by simple means.

The new felt pens are certainly the best medium for this type of work as there is a continuity of flow without the need for replenishing the ink. One wandering line across the paper is followed by another that draws close or wanders away a little and then back to follow the contour again. The teacher will easily illustrate the idea with a few bold chalk lines on the blackboard, and when given the word "go" each pupil will find this the subject for an interesting and unusual lesson.

This may at first appear to be another type of doodling but the best of these designs can be used for all manner of things, i.e. as book covers, mounts for notices, wrapping papers, etc.

. . . . And in Paint

It would be safe to assume the attraction of all abstract patterns lies in good arrangements of pleasant and unusual shapes, further enhanced by careful arrangements of light and dark areas, broken up with textures where necessary. The illustrations shown are of three purely abstract patterns and one that started as abstract but finally showed a flower bias. Two were commenced with shapes arranged at regular intervals and the true patterns placed over these shapes. The other two evolved from flattened circles. All are individual.

Patterns from Scraps

Using corrugated paper for printing

Our usual objective is to use whatever waste material comes to hand. Units from corrugated paper, used flattened or curled as illustrated above, must be used quickly and lightly as the tendency is to soften and disintegrate.

Using drinking straws

These paper decorations are made by drawing lines, loops or curves towards the limits formed by straight or bent straws. More vivid patterns could be achieved by using thicker points. But a delicate effect has its own place.

Joining the ends with Plasticine as illustrated is a device which children of seven years found for themselves.

Using flower shapes and acorns

Remembrance Day poppies were used here, though any artificial flower could be printed in the same way. The poppy is held by the stem at the back and surrounded by rays or brushed colour: then developed at will.

Acorn cups are ideal for small compact units as indeed any nut shell. A first pattern is shown far right.

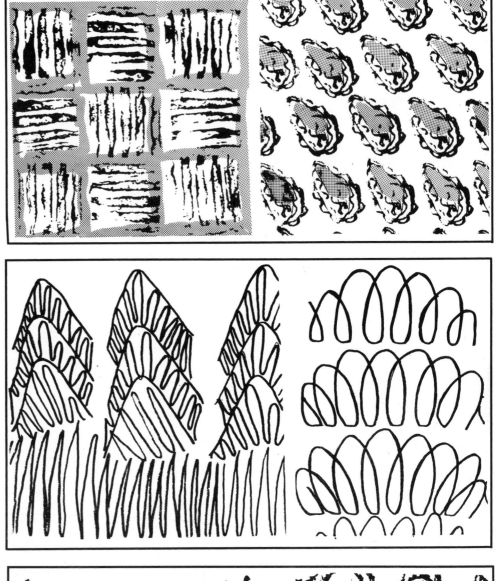

. . . . And from Cotton

It is said that there is nothing new under the sun and certainly this activity has been used in the realm of mathematics for many years.

In curve stitching one is really drawing a succession of tangents to a curve, thus making a replica of the curve at the points where they contact each other. Essentially simple in execution, appealing designs and colour blendings can be achieved by varying the use of materials and once the principle has been grasped, children can evolve new ideas and variants of the principle for themselves, striving for originality and self satisfaction both individually and in groups.

In mathematics the work is usually on a small scale using tinted card and embroidery cotton. In craft work the scale can be very much larger using strawboard, large sheets of card, newspaper, Polystyrene tiles, door and window frames, etc., and a similar variety of yarns from sewing cottons to rug wools toning or contrasting with the base material.

Two lines are drawn on the base to make a right angle or an acute angle with each other and equal distances are marked off on each line commencing at the angle made (see dia.).

Thread a needle and knot the length of yarn at one end. Insert the needle from the back to the front of the card at 1, and then from the front to the back of the card at a, giving the line 1a.

Bring the thread from the back to the front of the work at b and then from front to back at 2 (line b2).

Continue similarly until all points have been used, fastening off with another knot at i.

The nearer together the points are the smoother will be the parabolic curve obtained. When using heavy bases it will be found more convenient to loop the yarn round drawing pins or dressmaker's pins. If required these can be removed later after glueing the threads into place.

Patterns can be formed by using several intersecting lines or by using triangles, circles or curves instead of lines as a basic shape, and using a single colour or several for stitching.

If allowed a free rein the children may explore the possibilities of using their experimental work in picture making and 3D work as well as design.

If you wish to direct your children you can show them how to stitch the more complex cardioid, where the circle's circumference is divided into twenty-four equal parts and each point numbered twice round the circle so that 1 is also 25, and 6 also 30 and so on. One then sews from 1 to 2, 2 to 4, 3 to 6, 4 to 8, 5 to 10, 6 to 12, 7 to 14 and so on, to 46. If the circumference is marked into 48 equidistant points a kidney-shaped curve—the nephroid —can be stitched beginning 1 to 3, 2 to 6, 3 to 9, 4 to 12, 5 to 15, 6 to 18, etc.

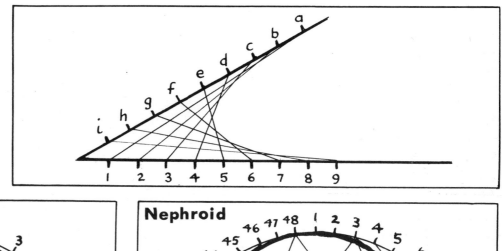

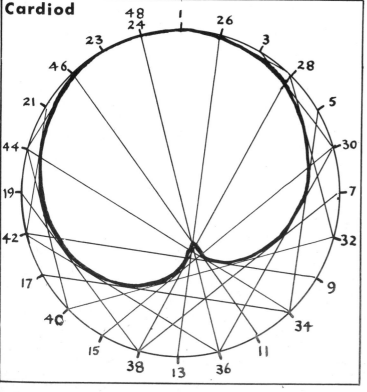

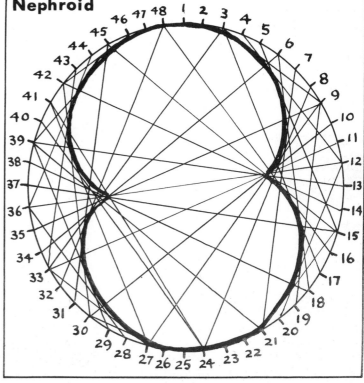

The Beginnings of Design

Introducing children to design can be one of the most rewarding aspects of teaching art and craft. Children have a natural feeling for pattern and like to give some order to their surroundings from a very early age.

The early stages of design work need not be complicated. Very simple shapes will often produce some of the most effective patterns, and endless variations can be developed from any basic shape. One of the simplest shapes, and one most familiar to children, is the circle. Round or circular shapes abound: pennies, wheels, hoops, balls, milk-bottle tops, ink-wells, plates, cups and saucers.

As a preliminary to pattern development based on the circle, the teacher should present the children with collections of various circular objects e.g. peas, drawing pins, coins, milk-bottle tops. The class should also be provided with a sheet of paper on which they should be encouraged to scatter their objects, so that they fall into a natural pattern. The coins in illustration 1 were simply dropped on to black paper. Several attempts can be made until a pleasing arrangement is achieved. The spacing between the objects will soon be seen to be as vital to the pattern as the objects themselves. Interesting shapes will arise through overlapping and grouping.

Where there is a concentration of objects more space around the group will seem desirable. At all costs geometric placing of the objects in rows or corners should be avoided. Attention should be paid to the groups as a whole and the balance between the clusters of shapes and the background.

Different materials may be used to record the pattern thus achieved: blue or black ink applied with a brush on white paper; white crayon or chalk on black or dark coloured paper; black crayon or charcoal on white or tinted paper will achieve the most direct results. It is not advisable to use pencils as these may produce a rather cramped interpretation. Great care should be taken to record shapes and spaces accurately. The shapes should be blocked in as they are drawn. The design may be further developed by high-lighting interesting background spaces with additional use of one colour.

This preliminary exploration could be followed up by a more planned piece of work using cut tissue paper as shown in illustration 2. Here we work with three different coloured tissue papers, pencils, scissors, paste and brush, white background paper (11 in. by 15 in.) and a series of different sized objects round which circles may be

Fig. 1

Fig. 2

drawn, e.g. paint palettes, saucers, lids of various sizes, ink bottles, water jars, etc.

The first stage should be to ask the child to cut as many different sized circles from the coloured tissue papers as possible. A number of these circles should then be arranged in a natural scatter pattern on the background. Once a pleasing arrangement has been achieved these may be pasted down. A further number of circles may be arranged on top of these to link and develop the pattern already achieved. Some of these may

be cut as rings or in a decorative manner. The design may be further embellished by decorating some plain circles with pen and coloured inks or wax crayons. This type of cut paper design is particularly valuable as it allows the children freedom to experiment with arrangements before committing themselves to a final design.

Experimenting with different materials will always prove stimulating to children and capture their interest. It is important to show them that there are many ways of approaching a subject and that the materials used will often dictate what form the finished work will take. The third illustration shows a further development using wax resist and coloured inks or dyes.* For this work a piece of white cartridge paper, an ordinary wax candle and wax crayons are required. The coloured wash may be either watered down coloured inks or weak dye solution.

First of all several large circles were drawn with the candle. At this stage the shapes drawn will hardly be apparent on the white paper, but this disadvantage can in itself be an asset as the work will of necessity be freely created. The paper was then washed with colour and allowed to dry. As the colour is applied the children will be able to see the pattern of shapes emerging on the paper as white areas, as the wax resists the dye. Additional intersecting circles may be drawn with the candle or more decoration added to the existing ones before a further colour is washed on. The areas thus waxed will remain the colour of the original wash. One of the pleasing qualities of this method is the textural effect achieved by the different pressures with which the wax is applied. The dye or ink will tend to seep into small areas of lightly waxed shapes and lines, giving a mottled texture to the pattern. After drying out once more, the design may be ornamented and emphasised by the judicious use of coloured wax crayons. This method of designing is of particular value in screen fabric printing.

A further experiment in design using cut paper can be based on a single large circle. The one in illustration four was produced by cutting a large circle out of white paper. Triangular shapes were then cut from the edge of the circle and turned outwards. Smaller shapes were cut from these and moved slightly inwards. The shapes were then pasted on to black paper. The design suggested a flower, so this was emphasised by the addition of cut black paper squares to form a centre. This is a very simple example of expanding a shape, but the method readily lends itself to more elaborate cutting. Other basic shapes, squares, rectangles, triangles will produce equally interesting and unusual designs. Although white and black paper are suggested, interesting effects can be obtained using strongly coloured poster paper.

*Any commercially produced dyes are suitable, e.g. Dylon, Drummer.

(above) Fig. 3   (below) Fig. 4

Three-dimensional work

Developing a single theme in design can be a means of introducing children to varied experience in the use of materials.

Certain children will feel more confident to express themselves in 3 dimensional work, others in fabric or collage. The child who lacks ability in the more conventional media of paint or pencil, may be adept in the manipulation of clay, lino, fabric or cut-paper.

After the preliminary work with circles it should be possible to introduce more complex circular forms. The workings of old watches and clocks are particularly interesting and varied in shape and form, producing a good source of design. A collection of these can be easily assembled with the aid of a class.

As the shapes are likely to be quite complex, a single piece will be sufficient for an initial study.

Parts are likely to be small, so it is important to emphasise the need for enlargement on the paper. The children should be asked to observe and record the shapes as accurately as possible. Compasses may be a useful aid for drawing the main circles; failing this, plates or other round objects at hand may be used.

Preliminary drawing may be done in pencil and followed up with black ink and pen. Brush and ink can be used for blocking in some areas. Alternatively a freer interpretation may be obtained by using charcoal or conte crayon and then the more precise detail of the workings can be added with pen and ink at a final stage.

Illustration 5 shows a group arrangement of watch parts. As a further development children may be asked to group a smaller number of parts in a like manner.

They may then be asked to make a choice of media for this design, based on their previous experience with differing materials. Coloured tissue paper, wax resistant materials, coloured inks, poster papers and paints should be made available.

The resulting designs could then be examined for their suitability for lino-printing or for three dimensional work. Illustration 6 shows a piece of fabric, lino-block printed from such a design.

Fig. 5

Fig. 6

Thus I would suggest that three-dimensional circular forms could be used to inspire decorative patterns for lino-block printing on fabric.

The pattern should be drawn on a piece of lino not less than 8 in. x 6 in. with chalk, biro or soft pencil. All lines drawn should then be cut with a number two lino-cutter. In cold weather it is advisable to warm the lino slightly to facilitate cutting (on a radiator, near a fire or even on the plate rack of a domestic cooker). Some areas of lino may be cut away with a number 7 or 8 blade, but great care should be taken not to remove too much from the design.

After cutting, the lino may be glued on to a wood block with an impact adhesive ($\frac{1}{4}$ in. plywood is suitable). This is not essential but does tend to produce a more even print, and prevents the lino from curling. It is also easier for the children to handle when printing begins.

The lino may be given a felt-like surface which will pick up the dye more easily and evenly. To accomplish this flocking mordant is rolled onto the lino with an ink-roller to form an even coverage. Flocking powder should then be generously sprinkled over the whole block to a depth of about half an inch.

Exerting a slight pressure with the palm of the hand will help the powder to grip. The block should be left covered for twenty-four hours before the surplus powder is shaken off. A soft brush should be used to ensure that all loose flock is removed, especially from the cut surfaces. Although desirable, flocking is by no means essential to producing a satisfactory print.

A piece of thin plastic foam sponge slightly larger than the block makes a suitable pad for spreading the dye. If the lino is mounted on wood, a mallet is useful; if not, an ink-printing roller is adequate for applying the required pressure.

The mixed dye should be brushed well into the foam-sponge pad until it is completely absorbed. If left on the surface, the dye will be picked up unevenly and produce smeared prints. Preliminary printing may be tried out on tempera or newsprint paper before work commences on the fabric. This will also enable the children to try out different repeating methods with the block. The lino should be dabbed onto the pad, rather than pressed, until it is sufficiently and evenly coated with dye. Too much pressure will

Fig. 7

force the dye into the cut sections, obliterating the design.

The block is then placed face down on the printing surface and tapped with the mallet in each corner and in the centre. If the lino is not mounted on wood, simply place it on paper and run the roller slowly over the back, exerting an even pressure. Particular attention should be paid to the edges of the lino.

After trying out the block on paper, work can begin on fabric. Best results will be obtained if the material is smooth, heavy creases having been previously ironed out. Fabric containing a lot of dressing, such as calico, should first be washed and ironed.

A piece of thick blanket placed on the table, under the fabric to be printed, will make for a better result.

Once completed, the fabric should be hung to dry out thoroughly. The dye may then be fixed by the application of heat. The simplest method is to iron on the wrong side with a medium hot iron for five minutes. If the fabric is washed subsequently, it is advisable to use very hot water as this continues the fixing process.

Suggested materials and sources:
Flocking powder ⎱ Dryad Handicrafts
Mordant ⎰ Ltd.
Fabrics—Calico, cotton, poplin.
Dyes—Printex dye stuff and binder.
Winsor and Newton,
Wealdstone, Harrow, Middlesex.

Other themes

A sustained study of a single theme not only lends a sense of continuity to the work, but encourages in the child a deeper awareness and understanding of his environment. The world around us is full of pattern, a stack of drainpipes in the builder's yard, rows of cars in a car-park, the pattern and rhythm of windows on a large building. These can all provide inspiration for design. Even scrap metal, the more rusted and corroded the better, will often give the most exciting shape, texture and colour, if properly observed.

Work of a more advanced nature may follow the basic work described in previous pages, which showed part of the workings of a clock. The relationship and movement of the cog wheels was the inspiration for the relief mobile in illustration 8. As described before, preliminary drawings and designs were made. The mobile was constructed from strawboard. Various sizes of circles were first cut and differing arrangements were tried with these, until a satisfying pattern was achieved. The circles were then painted in a decorative manner with powder colour and indian ink keeping to a limited range of white through greys to black. The shapes were then pinned with nails to a piece of white painted ply-wood in such a way that movement was possible. Connecting strips were added at this stage to link the sections of the design together.

One group of children chose to work together to make a large three-dimensional mobile on a similar theme. Illustration 9 shows one part of this mobile. The final product consisted of many wheels of varying size and design, which was eventually suspended as a group from the class-room ceiling, where it provided a conversation piece for many classes for weeks to come.

A reasonably stiff type of card was used to form the basic drum shape, which was stapled together. Previous experience of studying and drawing watch parts provided the inspiration for the design work within and outside the drum shape. Cross-pieces and additional decorative pieces were glued to the basic shape with rubber paste. The models were then painted black and white, and the children were encouraged to ornament their design in a fairly simple manner, taking care not to distract attention from the three-dimensional form and pattern already achieved.

A further piece of group work is shown in illustration 10, p. 133. This is a ceramic plaque

Fig. 8

in blue, green and white, which consists of a collection of tiles made by individual children. Red earthenware clay was rolled out to an even thickness of $\frac{5}{8}$ in. to make the tiles. For this part of the task the group were provided with two sheets of old sugar paper, two $\frac{5}{8}$ in. laths and a rolling pin. Before work begins the clay must be wedged well to eliminate any air-bubbles. This is best done in a fairly large piece which can then be cut with wire into suitably sized pieces for distribution. The clay is then placed on a piece of paper and the rolling guides placed either side of it. Rolling can now begin but the clay should be turned frequently, using the other piece of paper, to prevent sticking. Care should be taken to keep the rolling pin clean and free of lumps of clay, otherwise these will mar the surface of the tile.

When the correct thickness is achieved the clay will no longer stretch and the rolling pin will move freely across the surface of the clay.

The guides may then be removed, and a ruler, setsquare and sharp knife used to mark out and cut a 6 in. tile. Anything above this size will tend to warp badly in the drying out stage.

Decorative shapes were then cut from the

left over pieces of clay and trial arrangements of these made on the tile. Once a satisfactory design has been produced the pieces are ready for fixing to the tile, which at this stage should be carefully turned on to a modelling board. For fixing, a brush and water and modelling tools are required. The area of the tile to which a piece of clay is to be added should be roughened up with a knife and brushed with water until a layer of slip is produced. The piece may then be placed on this and the modelling tool used to seal around the edges. Great care is necessary to ensure that the two surfaces are really knitted together, otherwise the decorative shapes will tend to pull away from the tile as it dries out. Once all the shapes are in place, further decoration may be added by impressing the clay in a rhythmic manner with various shaped modelling tools, or by impressing with actual watch-wheels. The tiles should then be dried out slowly over several days, and turned frequently (twice a day) to prevent warping. Once dry the edges of the tiles should be sand-papered carefully. The clay is very brittle at this stage. They are now ready for biscuit-firing to a temperature of 950° centigrade.

The biscuit-fired tiles were then decorated with cobalt (blue) and copper (green) oxides. These were mixed thinly with water and applied with a brush. If the oxide is put on too thickly, the finished tile will have a metallic, rather than coloured appearance, and some bubbling will occur under the glaze. The tiles were then dipped in a white tin glaze and fired to a temperature of 1020° centigrade. The oxides break through the glaze to give a brilliant green and blue colour, while the unpainted surface of the tile remains matt white.

A suitable tin glaze can be prepared from the following ingredients: Zircon Fritt 78, Zinc Oxide 18, Tin Oxide 4, Podmores, Shelton Works, Stoke-on-Trent, or Wengers, Etruria, Stoke-on-Trent, are suppliers of these and other pottery requirements.

The tiles were finally glued on to a piece of $\frac{1}{4}$ in. thick plywood with tile cement. Marvin Medium supplied by Magros in gallon tins is a useful fixative for all types of tile and mosaic work. The tiles may be run with plaster to give a more permanent finish, and beading applied to the edges of the board.

Fig. 9

Fig. 10

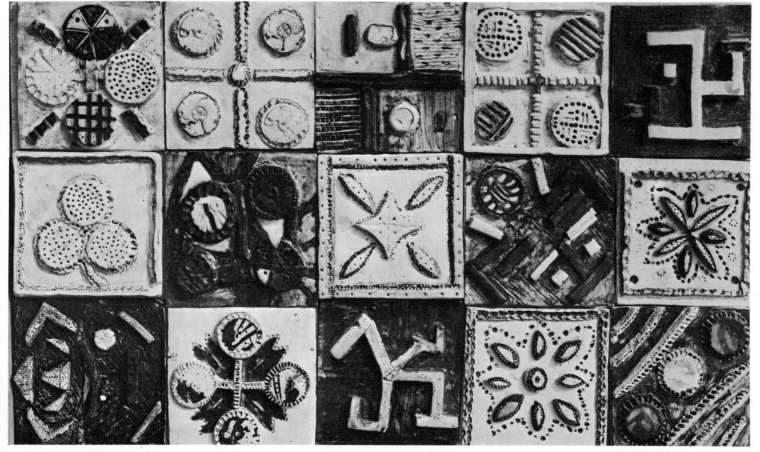

Fun with Mobiles

The Christmas Season can provide children with the opportunity of putting many of their design experiences into practice. A splendid opportunity for group work is provided, and children of less ability can successfully participate in some aspects of the work, especially where large scale decorations are required. Christmas decorations need not be complicated to look effective. Keeping to one basic scheme can give coherence to the work, while limitation of the choice of materials and subject matter will produce a feeling of order and continuity. Children will achieve better results if they are using the materials with which they are familiar. Coloured poster paper, gummed paper and card will generally prove more useful than laying in a stock of crepe paper which normally stretches, goes limp and lifeless, and is difficult to glue or paste.

Concentrating decorations into focal points is important. They will be far more effective this way, than spread out in a thin, even layer across the room being decorated. One good large arrangement of evergreen, strategically placed, is better than small pieces dotted about. Most of us have had the experience of

134

attempting to devise a scheme for a vast Hall, which can so easily swallow up any decoration, however imaginatively conceived. Any form of decorative design may be used to give light, colour and warmth to the darkest and coldest days of the year.

Mobiles can prove one of the simplest and most effective methods of enlivening a large area, as they bring colour, movement and a sense of lightness to their surroundings. They are an ideal group project to which children of all abilities can contribute effectively.

Designs based on the snowflake crystal, cut from coloured gummed paper, and pasted on white or contrast coloured card, can simply be strung with cotton and suspended in groups at different levels. Hoops or cross-pieces of wood or wire provide a suitable frame (Diagram 1).

To achieve a more three-dimensional effect, the cards can be scored diagonally and folded, then stapled together in pairs (Diagram 2). A six inch square is a reasonable size to work with, although some larger and smaller ones will create a more interest-

ing arrangement. Patterns not used in the mobile can be displayed in clusters on surrounding walls or windows.

Birds and fish also provide excellent subjects for mobiles. Simple bird shapes drawn and cut from card may have decorative wings and tails added with raffia or tissue paper. These can be very effectively hung from a coil of copper wire.

Fish shapes, drawn in duplicate on large sheets of white newsprint or tempera paper can be decorated boldly with wax crayons or cut coloured paper. The shapes are then gummed together round the edges, leaving the mouth open. A small ring of wire is then pasted into the mouth so that the "kite" becomes filled with air. Grouping a number of these together produced a large scale mobile. (See picture above).

Large areas of wall may be used to display friezes on a variety of themes: Christmas Carols of the narrative variety, "The Twelve Days of Christmas", "I saw three Ships", "Good King Wenceslas", "We Three Kings of Orient Are", "From out of the wood did a Cuckoo fly". Christmas stories and

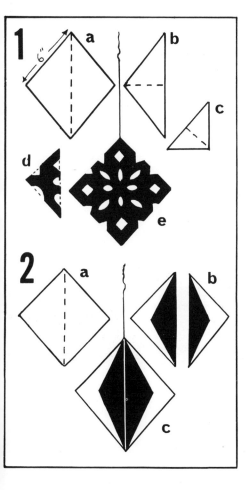

1. Method of folding paper for cutting snow flake patterns for mobile (right).
2. Method of folding card for three-dimensional snowflake mobile. snowflake cut-outs should first be pasted to 2 pieces of card which are then folded down the centre (A).
The folded cards are stapled together (B). Two more snowflake patterns are then pasted to the other 2 sides shaded in diagram (C). Contrasting colours can be used on the 4 sides.

legends readily lend themselves to interpretation in this way. To achieve a bold, direct effect the frieze is best built up out of cut paper shapes pasted on to a strongly coloured back-ground of poster paper. Before work commences, discussion should take place and different groups accept responsibility for various sections of the story. Parts of the narrative should be carefully selected for their pictorial potential. The completed pieces from each group can then be joined together and linking decoration added if required.

Mobiles from Balloons

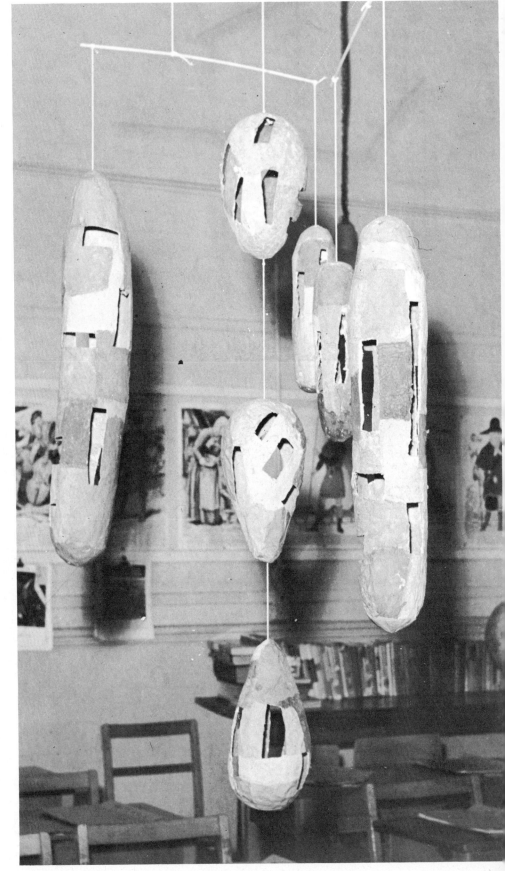

Unusual and colourful mobiles can be made by using balloons as modelling foundations.

The materials required are balloons of different sizes, newspaper, tissue paper, paste and tempera paints.

The balloon is blown up and tied. Paste a layer of tissue paper squares of convenient size—roughly four inches square for large balloons and smaller for smaller balloons—over the balloon. Follow this with a layer of newspaper squares. (Photographed above).

Cut or tear the newspaper squares beforehand and leave them to soak thoroughly in a bucket or bowl of water. Squeeze out the surplus water before pasting on the newspaper squares.

Do the pasting so that the paste penetrates the paper and the paper is pasted down evenly and securely, leaving no air bubbles or unpasted edges.

Alternating with a layer of tissue paper and a layer of newspaper will ensure that an even coverage is achieved. Eight or nine layers in all should be sufficient. But this can best be judged by the feel of the papier mâché when it dries out; it should be hard and firm.

When the layers are completed and the work dried out, cut rectangular holes in the papier mâché. A very sharp knife is needed for this. The outlines of holes of various sizes can first be drawn on the model as a guide.

The model is then painted in bright colours and a number of them hung as a mobile.

Do not hang the mobile in the centre of a room. The one in the photograph was hung centrally for photographing only. It should be hung for preference in a corner and low enough to be at eye-level.

Print and Dye

Tie dyeing and Potato cuts

We have based our experiment on a very ancient craft, that of Tie-dyeing. For this we need a needle and linen thread, potatoes and a packet of dark dye. Start by folding your material into three lengthwise and crease. Open out the fabric and fold into three across, crease and open out flat. You will now have a number of squares marked on your fabric. Draw a circle on a piece of cardboard, cut out and place in one square, draw round the circle with a pencil; do this in each square. Next take a needle and thread and run round each circle in small tacking stitches. Pull the thread up tightly and wind round and round the base of circle. Finish off thread firmly; the undone. Continue in the same way with each circle. Your fabric will now have a number of little bunches of gathered-up material and will look rather odd, however, this is quite in order. Next, mix and prepare the dye-bath, immerse the fabric and leave for a few minutes. Wearing rubber gloves lift fabric out of dye-bath and squeeze as dry as possible. Hang in the open air to drip-dry or hang over a sink or bucket. Drying is rather slow because the fabric is gathered up in pleats. When quite dry very carefully cut the linen thread and remove. Your circles will show up as white rings against a dark background. Now you must consider what shapes to add to your effect before cutting the pattern. Use poster colour when printing, you can keep to one shade or use two if you prefer. Illustrations A and B were started in the manner described but an oval shape was substituted for the circle in illustration B. The potato cuts in both cases were exceedingly simple but they have been carefully crossed to give certain effects. The small circle would appear insignificent unless a large, bold pattern was added to it. The much larger oval requires a smaller, more irregular shape as a finish. Many more interesting designs can be made by using different shapes to tack round and draw up. Size and placing too, will alter the effect and suggest various ways of developing new patterns.

A

B

Printing with a Match Box

Matchbox printing is a simple appealing craft especially suitable for young children because of its simplicity and economy of materials. The most inexperienced artist can make attractive patterns in a variety of colours simply by painting the edges of the cover of the matchbox (cardboard variety) with water-colour paint, and pressing carefully on a cheap unglazed art paper.

Fig. 1 shows the matchbox cover used in three ways, by bending, to produce simple "motifs". The paint used in the photograph is the opaque block variety, used straight from the block using a soft hair brush occasionally dipped in water.

Fig. 2

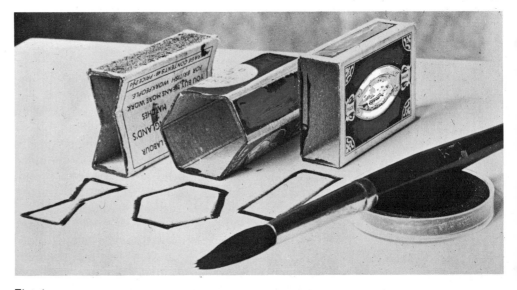

Fig. 1

Fig. 2 shows an example of an all-over pattern, based on a framework of pencilled squares, with additional brush work.

Fig. 3

Fig. 3 shows a circular pattern created in a similar way.

Fig. 4 shows two examples of a freer approach where one shape is repeated with some degree of overlapping.

It is the application of this type of work to other crafts which presents some problems.

Patterned papers produced by the methods described above are easily damaged by smudging, especially if used in bookcraft exercises where paste has to be used.

Fortunately there is a simple solution— the patterns must be printed with a waterproof ink. This is quite easy if the following method is adopted.

Take a small square of thick felt or flannelette (3 in. by 3 in.) and place in an old saucer or tin lid. Pour on it a small quantity of spirit ink. This intense liquid ink can be obtained in many colours (Fig. 5).

After a few minutes the pad can be used for printing, by pressing the matchbox cover first on the pad and then on paper. With a little practice, the printing is quicker than the brush and paint method (Fig. 1) as the cover will print several motifs one after the other, with one loading of ink.

Using this method the pattern dries extremely rapidly and is *positively waterproof*. Consequently the finished papers can be used with confidence where any pasting procedure is involved. Careless workers may even scrape off excess paste on the patterns without any ill effect.

In Fig. 6 are examples of patterned papers applied to (a) a circular spill holder made from a cardboard tube (as used for mailing posters, etc.), with a balsa wood base, (b) a simple booklet or stamp wallet, (c) a dinner mat, with cardboard interior.

The waterproof patterned papers could also be used for the following projects:

1. Printing on plain cotton fabrics, for dolls' dress material, doll's house curtains.
2. Printing on paper for doll's house wallpaper.
3. Coverings for portfolios, etc.

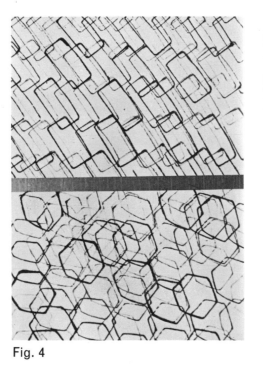

Fig. 4

Fig. 5

Fig. 6

Tie and Dye

Decorating fabric need not be confined to simple block printing and stencil work. Technological development in recent years has resulted in dyes being available which are easy for young children to handle successfully for tie and dye and batik work. These cold water dyes which are made by Dylon Ltd. in 18 colours are totally fast and will stand repeated laundering.

Tie and dye and batik are both resist processes. Parts of the fabric are tied, bound, knotted, sewn or waxed so that when the whole piece goes into the dye bath the colour does not penetrate these "protected areas"—so producing a pattern when the ties (or wax) are removed.

The cloth (which for initial exercises should be lawn or medium weight cotton fabric and washed before use) may be prepared in a variety of ways. The children will need to appreciate that pattern is produced by preventing some areas of the fabric from coming into contact with the dye. The simplest way of doing this is to gather the fabric to be patterned into a strip and tie it into a large tight knot. The knotted length of fabric is then soaked in cold water and plunged into a dye bath (see right). There are several ways of varying this technique. For example the fabric could be tied in knots along its length to give a repeat pattern, or a large knot tied in the centre of a square of material. To do this pick up a point of cloth in the centre of the square, twist it into a long strand and tie a knot.

Another simple method is to twist small objects (such as Infants' counting beads, pebbles or large buttons) into the fabric. This will give the typical snowflake pattern repeat. The beads are held in position with elastic bands. This stage is a vital one in the production of delicate patterns. The firmer the twist the greater the degree of patterning which will be achieved.

Making the Dye

To make a dye solution, soda and salt are required in addition to Dylon cold water dye. The following mixture will give two pints of strong dye:

2 level teaspoonsful of dye ($\frac{1}{3}$ oz.)

4 tablespoonsful of common salt (4 oz.)

1 tablespoonful of soda ($1\frac{1}{2}$ oz.)

Dissolve the dye in 1 pint of warm water. Stir. Dissolve the salt and the soda in 1 pint of hot water. Stir and cool. When the fabric is ready for dyeing mix the two solutions together. Once the soda has been added the dye is only effective for 2-3 hours.

140

Above. Dyeing. 9 year olds.

Right. Beads being twisted into a length of fabric

The length of time the fabric is left in the dye bath is best left to experiment. I have found that the work of young children (who find it difficult to tie tightly) is more successful if left in the dye bath for a short time. More complicated patterns (such as might be attempted by secondary pupils) will require up to one hours immersion in the solution. Rinse the fabric when dyeing has been completed and untie.

More advanced techniques

Once children have had some experience of handling dye and have grasped that tie and dye is basically a resist process, more advanced techniques may be introduced. Before describing some of these, however, I should point out that the success of the methods outlined here is largely dependant upon the tightness of the ties or bindings. Little children (8 years old and under) cannot manage this and their tie and dye experiments should therefore be restricted to those already outlined.

Cut the fabric (cotton lawn or soft synthetic material is most suitable) into the desired shape. This might be rectangular, triangular or round. The area which is to resist the dye —and therefore produce the pattern—is tightly bound with fine string or twine. During initial experiments these bindings should be quite haphazard for the accidental pattern so obtained is one of the most satisfying aspects of the craft. Thus the corners of a rectangle could be bound, or the fabric rolled along its length and then bound every four inches. Alternatively the centre point of a fabric square could be pulled up and bound, or the whole fabric length folded into a tight roll and bound across its centre.

When the fabric has been tied prepare the dye bath. Here it is important to follow the dye manufacturers instructions (e.g. on such things as dye, times, rinsing, washing).

However, it is worth remembering that bulky rolls will need longer in the dye solution than the knotted or beaded lengths. Indeed it is wiser to under dye the children's early experiments than to over dye them. There is little point in obtaining a deeper tone of blue, for example, if by doing so one all but obliterates the pattern.

The photographs illustrate the great variety of pattern which it is possible to obtain. The fact that these examples were all produced in less than a week by a group of nine year olds makes the process even more remarkable. These fabrics were only dyed once (although multicoloured patterns are obtainable by rebinding a previously dyed and patterned length and dyeing in another colour).

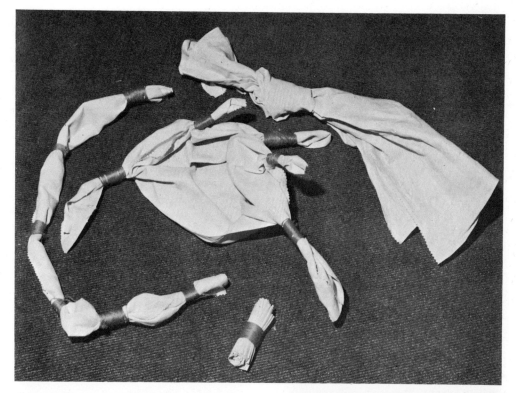

Some methods of binding fabric. This may be combined with knotting

Above. Pattern produced by centre binding and by binding each corner separately

Right. Rectangle patterned by pulling up and tying central point of fabric

141

Leading to Batik

"All art contains an element of the accidental." A sweeping statement, perhaps, but one which contains more than a mere germ of truth. Batik is a resist process which is always popular with young children because success does not depend solely upon skill with brush or graver. In any event effects achieved quite accidentally far surpass in colour and texture any which the typical primary school child could deliberately accomplish.

The purpose of this section has been to sow an idea and to let you, the reader, develop it with your children working within the limitations imposed by your classroom. Thus the batik process described here is meant to indicate a starting point for discovery—not an end in itself. The children will appreciate (if they have experimented with crayon resist and ebony stain) that wax repels water bound colours. Here they are extending their experience by applying their knowledge to fabric.

Wash and iron the cloth to remove dressing (cotton, spun rayon). Cut into suitable lengths (36 in. x 18 in.) for experimental dyeing. Lay a wad of newspaper on a flat working surface and pin or staple the fabric over this. Prepare the wax. A mixture of four parts candle wax to one part beeswax will give good results on almost any fabric. Melting the wax is a problem and an electric glue pot (see photograph) is the most satisfactory method of doing this with young children. These pots are heavy and so do not tip over easily. Moreover the heating element is well covered and control over temperature presents no difficulty even to a seven year old. When the wax is hot it is brushed into the fabric. Initially I let the child work the wax haphazardly encouraging almost total coverage of the fabric surface. (If a very heavy pattern is required wax should be worked into the reverse of the material.) When dry unpin the fabric and crumble it slightly. This will cause the wax to crack. Prepare a dyebath and dye the sample, following the manufacturers instructions for dyeing. Dylon Cold is equally suitable for batik. The dye will colour the areas unprotected by wax, flowing down any cracks in its surface to give a heavily crazed pattern. To remove the wax iron the fabric between two sheets of blotting paper using a moderately hot iron.

These designs could be followed by pictures painted in wax, regular patterns built up by applying wax in a stencil or round a leaf. Haphazard patterns made by dripping or

Brushing wax into fabric

Dyeing the waxed fabric

splashing hot wax on to the fabric are also worth attempting. All of this work provides ample preparation for batik pictures in which the process of waxing and dyeing is repeated to produce multicolour designs.

Suppliers of material
Dylon cold
Mayborn Products Ltd., Dylon works, Sydenham, London, S.E.26.
(This company also produces a series of teachers guides to dyeing. These are obtainable, free of charge, by writing to the company.)
Beeswax
Most branches of Boots the chemists.

Bibliography
Paper batik and resists
'Introducing crayon techniques' by
H. Pluckrose, Batsford
'Lets make pictures' by H. Pluckrose
Mills and Boon

Fabric dyeing and decoration
'Fabric Printing' by Lotti Lauterburg
Batsford
'Tie and Dye' by Anne Maile
Mills and Boon
'Book of Batik' by Ernst Muchling
Mills and Boon
'Simple Fabric Printing' by S. & P.
Robinson
Mills and Boon
'Fabric Printing by hand' by Stephen Russ
Studio Vista

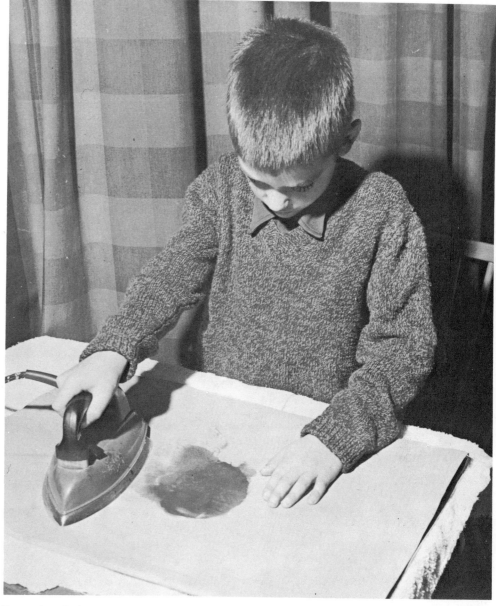

Removing the wax through blotting paper

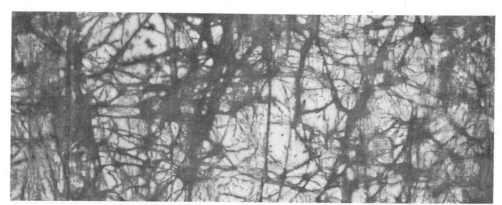

Batik designs. Showing wax applied on one side of fabric only. (Right) Wax applied on both sides.

Mono-printing

Mono-print is the term used to describe a method of printing where we take only one print from a prepared block. The advantages of mono-prints are speed, spontaneity and simplicity.

Materials required: smooth printing surface, rollers, printing colours, various sized hog hair brushes, scraper tools, printing papers, rags.

For your first mono-prints work small and keep your designs simple. Select your printing surface which may be a glass slab, lino block, sheet of plastic celluloid or formica. The size of the base is not important but remember to cut your printing paper accordingly. Have plenty of paper at hand as mono-prints are quickly done. Squeeze out the colour on to the slab; experience will tell you how much is required—too much will spread when the print is taken and too little will leave only a vague impression on the paper. To get thoroughly acquainted with the media I would suggest that at first you only do experimental prints. Start by putting one finger on to the inked slab, press firmly, then move your finger about, making a free spontaneous pattern. Select a paper giving a good colour contrast, place the paper over the inked area of the slab. Carefully lay it down and gently and evenly press all over the back of the paper. Another method is to roll the back of the paper with a dry clean roller; great care must be taken, however, not to apply too much pressure. Sometimes the weight of the roller in itself is sufficient. Now carefully lift and peel back a corner of the paper to check that enough pressure has been exerted to make a strong enough impression. If you want a stronger print replace the paper and re-press or roll the print again. Pick up a corner again to check if the ink impression is satisfactory; if so, peel the paper off the slab and lay it flat to dry.

Having now made one successful print using only a finger, ink the block again if necessary or just reroll it and try a pattern print using something hard and pointed: the end of a brush or pencil, a pottery modelling tool, paste spreader or try making a set of scrapers from slivers of wood. It is not advisable to use tools with too fine a point such as needles or knives as they make little or no impression in the ink. Print exactly in the way described for the finger print.

We have now experience of two methods of mono-print—soft smudged line as given by the fingers and the hard crisp line produced by a scraper. Further experiments can now

be conducted and the combination of line and texture is endless. Try dragging a hog hair brush through the ink or wrapping different types of materials around your finger and experiment with the impression. Further experiments can be tried by adding extra colours. These can be added while the block is being rolled either by sectioning the block into separate areas of colour and mixing the colours together with finger or pad or by carefully overlaying one colour on the other on the block and then incising the picture or pattern and print. Both colours will then show, to some degree, and will also blend together on the paper. Colour can also be added to the design or picture after all the scraping is finished. This can be applied to the block either straight from the tube in small blobs or painted on to selected areas with a brush.

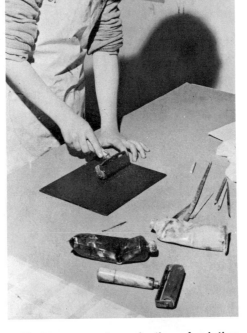

1. Having prepared a selection of printing papers and assembled together suitable tools to make the design, ink the block thoroughly. Experience will tell you the amount required

2. If the block has been inked thinly, a fine pointed tool such as a pencil can be used. If the ink is thick, use only tools with a broad edge

3. Different textures can be added with finger, cloth, stiff brush, etc

4. Having prepared a satisfactory design, gently lay the paper down on to the block. Take care not to let the paper slip sideways

5. The amount of pressure applied to the back of the printing paper depends on the amount of ink on the block. If sparsely applied use heavy pressure. If over inked use very light pressure

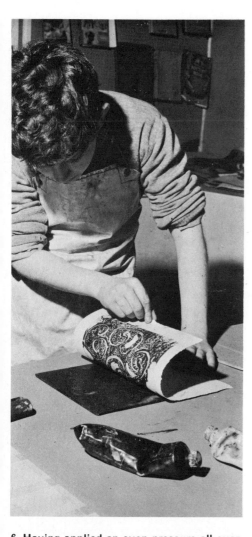

Finger Print
This can be done with the finger alone, or with finger wrapped in different textured cloths

6. Having applied an even pressure all over, peel back one side of print and check. If satisfactory remove paper carefully. If only a weak impression has been obtained replace paper carefully and exert more pressure

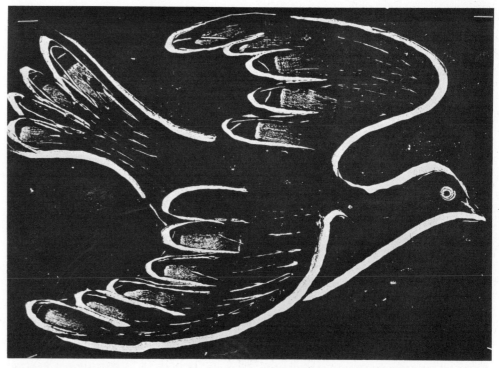

7. Checking the results

Stick and Brush Print
Outline of bird drawn in with shaped stick, other lines with pencil point

Slight textured surfaces of wings and tail done with stiff hog hair brush

Activities for the Under Eights

Young Children as Artists

There may be no recognisable 'end product' when this little boy has finished his hammering and his sawing, but at this stage of development, what he makes is of less importance than the experiences which are his during the making

These children are playing with clay. As they learn the limitations of the media, and as their powers of representation become more mature they will gradually produce objects which have a discernable shape

Seasonal themes are naturally of interest to children. At Christmas time particularly they become involved long before Christmas Day. The good school will be quick to utilise this natural interest

Helen and Paul were interested in giants. First they painted them, then they made them, not to somebody else's plan, but by exercising their own creative powers

This junior class is carving in salt. As they discover what can be done with a block of salt, and what cannot, it may be that something pleasant to look at will result. To tell them what do do and how to do it will deny them the experiences of finding out for themselves and will also stifle their creative impulses

Finger painting is a familiar enough occupation in any infant classroom. It is a good infant activity because all the senses are involved. Do we expect to judge the 'artistic merit' of these pictures? I think not, the activity is sufficient, we do not concern ourselves with results

Once a group have decided what they would like to make the teacher will have questions like 'How can I fix this bit to this bit?' The good teacher will ensure that her answer is not too comprehensive

Often in schools we find picture making restricted to one media so that children are able to develop a formula and thus become slick and gimmicky. Here children are using photographs and carpeting

It is important to encourage children to vary the scale of their operations and to stretch themselves to the limit and perhaps even beyond, for failure is as important to human development as success

When children are encouraged to use their own creative abilities it is incredible how ingenious and resourceful they can be. The teacher's task is to recognise when a child has come to the end of his resources and to suggest a new line of action

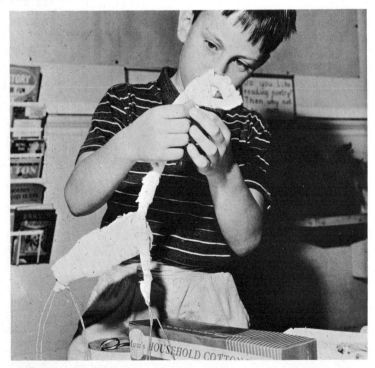

Skills develop in direct proportion to the degree of incentive. When we have learned the limitations of working with paper then the time is ripe to acquire a new skill, it may be building on wire. It will be most unlikely, however, if forty children develop the need to acquire this skill simultaneously

148

We are bedevilled, of course, by having to meet the needs of many children, not just one child. In many cases we try to organise our classroom so that we can treat forty children as one child. Forty children striving to assert their individuality will frustrate all our ploys in this direction

Models from Packing Tubes

Soldiers

One toilet roll centre makes the face and body of each soldier and a second toilet roll centre makes the legs and feet. (a) Cut the toilet roll in half, then cut away the shaded part. Now glue these two second pieces inside the body. Bend feet outwards. Cut out a hat brim from cartridge paper and glue to the top of the body. Now glue a third of a toilet roll on the top to make the hat. (See p. 150.)

If the children are very young, such things as epaulettes, shoulder straps, belts and collars can be painted on to the body, and the arms can be made from lolly sticks or strips of card. For the older, more able child, a realistic effect may be obtained by making the arms from rolls of paper. To make the arms bend, cut the roll in half, then join together with a hinge. (e) Each soldier has two epaulettes glued to the top sides of the arm. The shoulder flap is a strip of paper—tuck one end under the epaulette, then bend the other end down and glue to the body (d). Cut out a long narrow strip of paper for the collar and glue around the neck (b). Make the belt in a similar way, add the buckle and the scabbard (c). Cut out cuffs and glue around the wrists.

The trumpet is a cone of paper, coloured yellow or covered in gold foil. Push a long, thin piece of wire right through the head and let it emerge where the mouth will be. Now balance the trumpet on to it. Glue the soldiers hand to the trumpet, or fix with a pin.

The drum is a Sellotape centre, covered both sides with a circle of paper. The drum sticks are half of a drinking straw with a small circle on the end. To make the ears, cut out a small circle of paper, bend one edge back and glue to the sides of the head. The noses are small rolls of Plasticine glued to the face and the hair and moustaches are thick wool. The cockade is a bunch of wool, glued inside the hat. Now paint the soldiers and add shiny badges or buckles.

The cannon is a toilet roll centre mounted on half a large tooth-paste carton (g). Push the other half into the open end to help it stand. The wheels are two empty gift-type-ribbon-spools (saved from Christmas), but cellotape centres, covered on one side would do just as well. Complete by adding shafts made of card.

The horse's body is three-quarters of a large tooth-paste carton (f). Cut out four legs of equal size and length from stiff card and glue them to the body, making sure the horse is well balanced. Glue a piece of card, as wide as the body, to the front for his neck and curve it slightly with your finger. Add the head, now glue a smaller box inside the open end of the head to make the muzzle. Add ears, and when painted, glue on a mane and tail of wool. Thin string will make the bridle.

These soldiers are wearing the uniform of the Light Infantry Brigade of about 1858

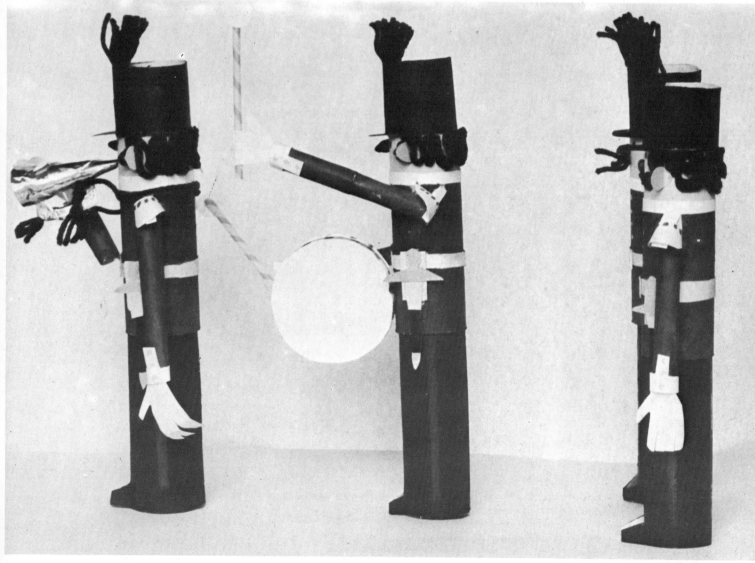

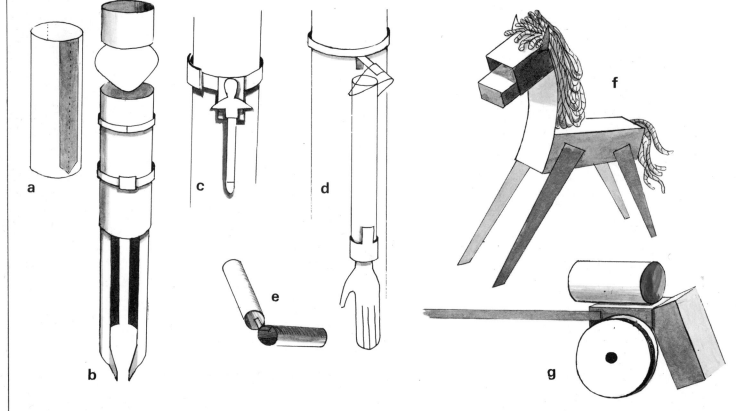

Ducks and Swans

A large box lid is painted blue with white waves.

The rock in one corner is made from an egg box section, turned upside down, glued to the water and then painted brown.

All the birds' heads are made from an egg-box section with the rough edges trimmed away.

The ducks' bodies are half to two-thirds of a toilet roll centre and their necks half a pipe cleaner. Glue one end into the body and the other end into the head (a).

Cutting the toilet roll centres may be difficult and help may be needed.

The beaks are cut from cartridge paper and and are also glued to the inside of the heads. The duck, taking things easy on the rock, has two yellow feet glued between its body and the rock (b). Glue the second duck to the water.

The swan's body is a cheese-spread box (c), the neck two pipe cleaners glued together and the head a trimmed egg-box section. The bill is made from cartridge paper coloured orange and is inserted into a small cut at the front of the head. Paint the ducks and swan.

The Pond

From green felt cut out lily pads and glue these to the water. The lilies are made from white tissue paper—each flower is three $1\frac{1}{4}$ in. squares; pinch the middle and glue to the water.

As a final touch, rushes can be made from any oddments of coloured paper and glued around the pond—a few bright flowers can be added here and there among the rushes.

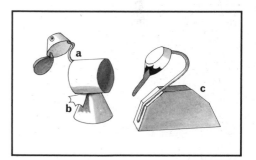

Faces from Paper Bags

These paper bag faces are quick and easy to make, and are effective when hung in large numbers at different levels.

Fill the bag with screwed up pieces of newspaper. Insert some wool or coloured paper strips into the neck and tie with a long thread.

Paint on a happy, sad or funny face.

Models from an Egg Box and Pipe Cleaners

The Spider

To make a spider like the one shown here you will need one section of an egg box and four pipe cleaners. The four pipe cleaners are twisted together in the middle (see diagram), and a large dob of glue put inside the body to hold the twist in place. Now shape the legs like a spider's. Finally, make a face from coils of Plasticine and glue these on to the body.

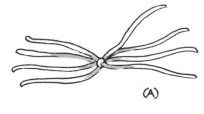

(A)

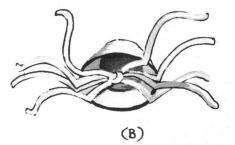

(B)

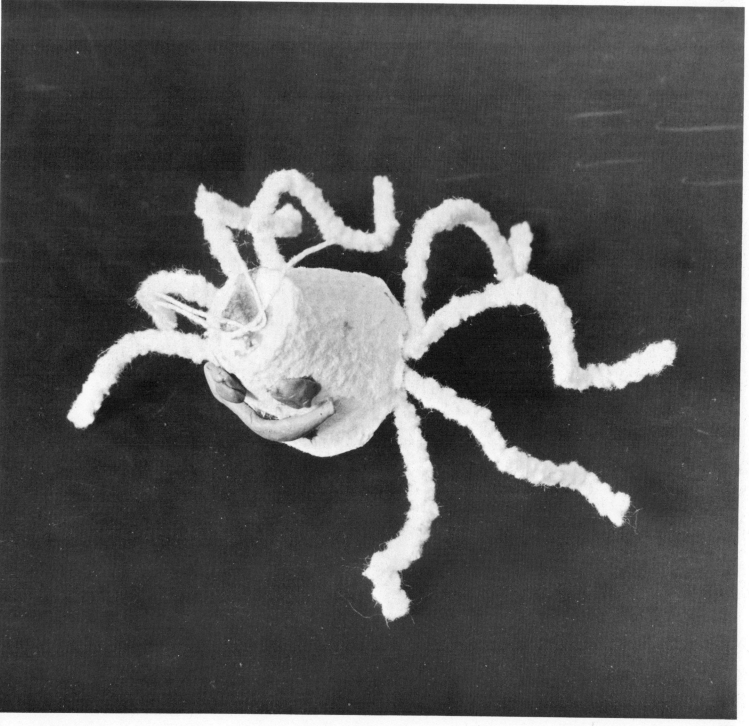

"From ghoulies . . ."

All Hallow E'en, or the Eve of All Saints Day (the 31st October), is the day which marked the end of the Celtic Year.

The apple harvest ends about this time of year and the many apple traditions, games and divinations practised at Hallowe'en were probably originally part of ancient thanksgiving rites—some of these survive as Hallowe'en party games (apple bobbing, snap-apple etc.).

The bonfire, once part of the Celtic religious ritual, has been stretched on to Guy Fawkes day—perhaps the effigy we burn today was originally a poor sacrificial victim. There is certainly evidence that the Celtic priests liked to see the old year out with lots of human sacrifices. And a pretty dreadful sight it was by all accounts—enough to give anyone nightmares! No wonder tradition has handed down the belief that on All Hallow E'en night the souls of the dead, ghosts, ghouls, witches and all manner of unwelcome supernatural beings are likely to make an unexpected appearance.

We have made a selection of these creatures from junk, based on models made by children of various ages.

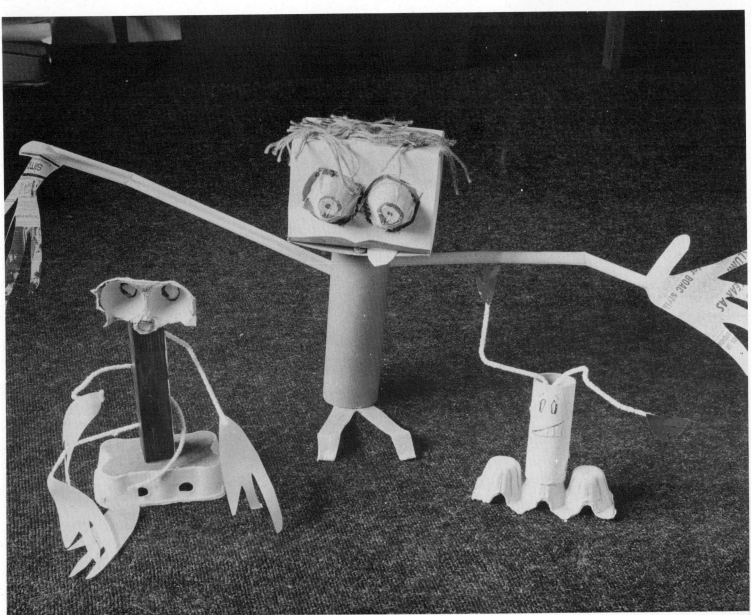

154

Four ghoulies are shown on page 154—one has a Vim tin body, a big box head, long feet cut from the lid of an egg box, horrid long arms and creepy paper fingers. To make the mouth, put a wedge of Plasticine into the closed flap of the box, then add a tongue and paint the lips (A). The eyes are each a section of an egg box.

To make the second ghoulie cut an egg box in half (B), then push a toilet roll tube over the centre "hump", the pipe cleaner arms sprout from the head.

The third ghoulie is made from a toothpaste box glued to an egg box lid. Two egg box sections are glued to the top to make eyes and he has four arms with huge floppy hands made from greaseproof paper.

The last ghoulie is very horrid—it has 14 eyes—all made from egg box sections glued to a big box. The arms are made from pipe cleaners.

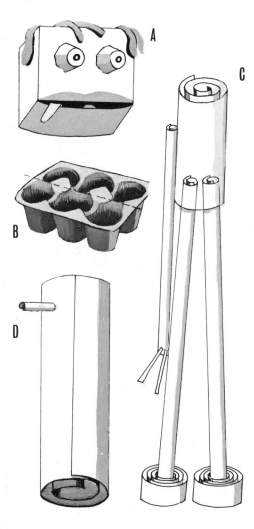

" . . . and ghosties . . ."

Ghostie is a Vim tin covered with white paper. He has no mouth or nose—just two huge eyes. His white hair stands straight up in the air—it is made from three pipe cleaners folded in half and pushed into the middle hole on the top of the tin. The hands should be long and spooky and white.

" . . . and long leggety beasties . . ."

We made two long leggety beasties. One has legs made from lots of toilet rolls joined together with gummed strip—each leg is pushed on to an egg box section which is then glued to an egg box lid (to help the model to stand). The face is a paper cup pushed on to the two legs, with pipe cleaner

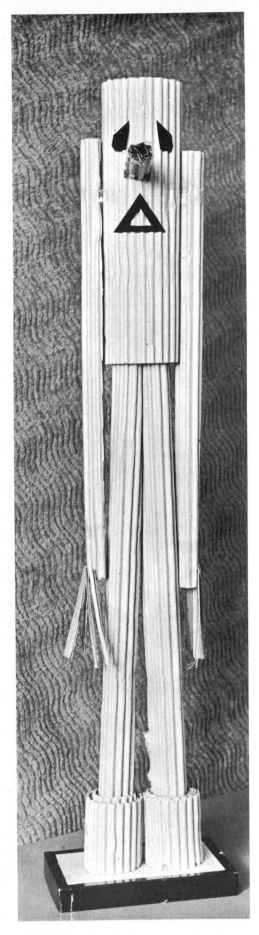

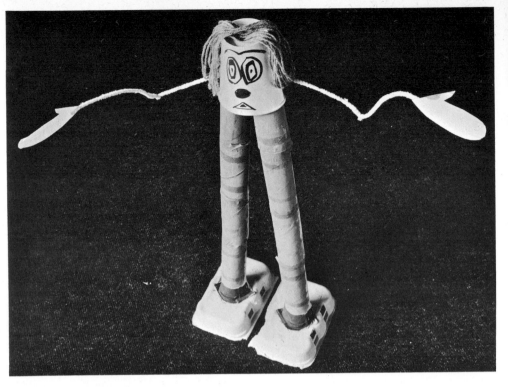

**Photographed below is the simplest
of all the models to make**

This weird "bumping thing" is a screwed-
up piece of paper with a face. It has five
elastic band legs, each with a Plasticine
foot. It slithers along the ground, banging
with its feet as it goes—something like an
octopus with boots!

arms coming out of the side. The other is
made from corrugated paper tubes. Begin
with the two long legs (C). Wrap long
narrow strips of corrugated paper around
the bottom of each leg, then glue the legs
to a box lid. The body is rolled around the
top of the legs (D). The long arms are fixed
to the sides and strips added for fingers.

Working with Clay

Children, Clay and Kilns

The firing of clay to an irreversible hardness is an ancient and fundamental discovery of man.

It seems somewhat more than a pity that the majority of our children can complete their primary education without having had the exciting experience of firing their clay forms. A pity because the process is relatively simple and the experience pregnant with opportunities capable of stimulating other forms of knowing. Some children have not even handled clay.

Most teachers are aware of and encourage the natural development of creativity, but because they lack know how are reticent to attempt an activity as "difficult" as building a kiln. I have written this article so that those who wish to participate may have some basic knowledge. It is not easy to produce a series of blue-prints guaranteeing success. Too little is known about these primitive kilns for the activity to be other than experimental, but I hope that what I have to say will encourage the more adventurous teacher to have a go.

Clay is a plastic responsive material the handling of which appears to give complete satisfaction to both children and adults. This material reflects spontaneously the mood, the conscious and unconscious intention of the maker, and it is this very quality that makes it such a valuable medium in the art programme.

It may be that young children are more concerned with the creative process than the completed artefact and that their interest does not extend beyond the completion. This could mean that firing is not within their immediate understanding. In fact they might not be able to link the making with the baking for unlike food it certainly does not taste better or even to some look better. Nevertheless children will enjoy the activity and will eventually begin to comprehend that this is a natural extension if not an integral part of the experience and procedure of working with clay.

Some primary schools may already possess an electric kiln. One cannot deny the convenience of twentieth century fuels but used without reference to other forms of firing it can dilute experience and retard understanding. At this stage of development it is no more necessary than the wheel and certainly does not involve children in such an intense activity.

Perhaps it is advisable at this point to reassure non potters that the construction of these kilns is comparatively simple, their firing with reasonable precaution safe and the cost with the exception of fire bricks very little.

I have arranged the sequence of kilns and accompanying processes so that there is growth and development from the simple to the more complex structures. It is intended that the children accept as much responsibility as they are capable of for the complete activity. It would be pointless for the teacher to assert sole rigid control.

These kilns must be thought of not as separate pieces of furniture into which pots are occasionally placed to receive the necessary treatment, but as structures that in their primitive simplicity require the ware whatever its nature to complement and sometimes support their construction. The first examples are not intended to be permanent but rather ephemeral happenings that can be discarded or rebuilt.

Sawdust Kilns

Young children are rarely concerned with making functional ware and so this simple kiln is ideal for making their clay forms more permanent. It is doubtful if they will immediately appreciate the quality of reduced carbon blackness and indeed many adults fail to do so. Some children often wish to paint them and I cannot discover any good reason to discourage this. Some children extrude their shapes from a lump and this form of construction usually withstands the thermal shock better than those figures made by adding the components, but this form of "synthetic" structuring ought not to be discouraged as this is their natural way of working. The children will become aware eventually of its inherent problems and seek means of rectifying them. The teacher can then suggest sticking the components on with slip (liquid clay).

The clay

For this type of firing it is essential to use a low firing clay usually red or yellowish grey in colour. Its resistance to thermal shock can be increased by adding as much builders' sand as the body will take and yet remain sufficiently plastic to use (approximately 20 per cent but some experiment by the children will be necessary to get the best local results). The sand also opens up the body allowing it to breathe and dry more easily. The educative value of digging and preparing clay should not be ignored and it ought not to be too difficult to locate good beds just below the surface. Good clays can often be found in the washing pools of sand and gravel pits. These clays being close to the surface have already been weathered and except for the removal of foreign bodies are ready to be used. Naturally the excess moisture must be drained off and this is best accomplished by spreading a layer of the clay over an absorbent material such as plaster, sacking or newspaper. If this proves impossible the local brick works will usually supply an excellent low firing body.

Children who become aware of surface textures can be encouraged to burnish some areas of the clay smooth, using a pebble, glass marble or spoon. Careful burnishing can produce a beautiful finish. Others may wish to scratch marks on its surface or press textured objects into its receptive skin. The permutations of this kind of experience are innumerable and the children have sufficient imagination to develop its possibilities with a minimum of teacher motivation.

When the ware is dry, preparation for the firing can begin. Care must be taken at this stage as dried clay is very brittle.

Requirements:

One oil drum for the chamber, lid removed and pierced like a roadman's brazier but with smaller holes.
One metal lid similarly pierced.
Three bricks.
A quantity of dry sawdust.
Two firelighters.
Time early morning.

The metal container is placed upon the bricks so that some air can circulate through the sawdust during the firing.

Approximately six inches of sawdust is placed in the bottom of the chamber and the first layer of ware is placed upon this (largest pieces at the bottom). Plenty of room must be allotted to each piece so that it can be surrounded by sufficient fuel. Be careful not to place too close to the perimeter. A second layer of sawdust is placed on top of and around the ware with a clearance depth of at least three inches.
The next layer of ware is placed and the procedure repeated.
After the final layer of lightest ware has been placed the chamber is topped off to a depth of at least six inches.

The firelighters are broken up and distributed evenly on and just below the surface of the sawdust.

On no account must paraffin be used in the presence of children.

The kiln is now ready for lighting. A ceremony that excites even the oldest child. At first the flames will burn merrily but eventually they die down and the sawdust smoulders gently like a well lit pipe. If the sawdust is damp combustion will be difficult and it may be necessary to relight the fuel.

During the day the sawdust will burn away revealing the work. It is necessary to prevent this by adding more sawdust as and when necessary. At the end of the day the container is topped up and the lid fitted. The kiln is allowed to burn out over night in a safe corner of the playground. It may be opportune to warn the caretaker of its value, as in my experience it is possible that a bucket of water will douse its contents.

The kiln when cool, may be emptied. Do not attempt to fish out pots while they are still hot as this can cause them to crack. There will be some breakages and disappointments. This is the lot of even professional potters, but I do not believe children are adversely affected by these experiences, and in fact they accept this challenge with greater fortitude than many adults.

The quality of this low fired clay is at first perhaps so strange as to prove unacceptable to some adults and even some children may wish to paint their terra-cottas and so hide the reduced blackness or mottled redness. There are several ways of complementing these burnt terra-cottas, whose strange quiet beauty probably demand long contemplation. Burnished surfaces can be further polished with wax. Scratched or engraved surfaces filled with powdered chalk mixed with liquid gum or paint.

This soft biscuit ware is obviously fragile and as children grow they will expect "better" results. In my next article I shall describe how it is possible to extend the sawdust kiln into a bonfire and simple tunnel kiln capable of slightly higher temperatures.

The sawdust kiln I have just described can and has been safely used with six to seven year olds, and whilst the activity and results are ephemeral, the process of preparation, organisation, knowledge gained through experience and the joy of controlling the element of fire in a creative operation make this a significant educative activity.

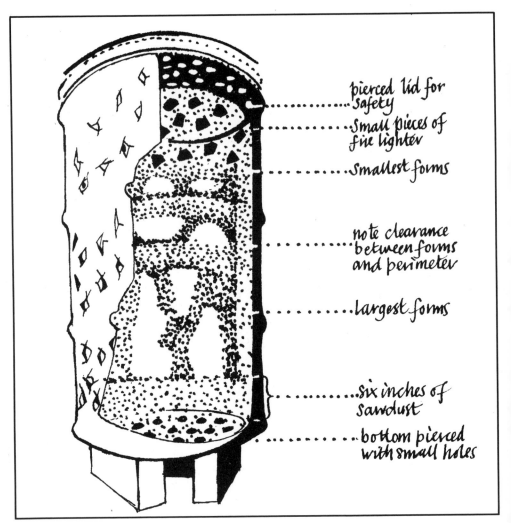

pierced lid for safety

small pieces of fire lighter

smallest forms

note clearance between forms and perimeter

largest forms

six inches of sawdust

bottom pierced with small holes

Oil drum sawdust kiln

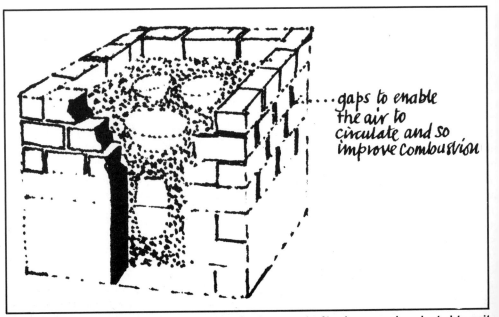

gaps to enable the air to circulate and so improve combustion

An alternative design for those who wish to fire larger pots. Its shape can be adapted to suit any size of terra-cotta

The naked flame

After the relatively prosaic experience of the sawdust kiln there comes a desire even a compulsion to master the magical properties of the naked flame. Perhaps those of you who do not share my particular craving need to be convinced that there are other more worthwhile reasons for lighting a fire, and of course there are.

From the potter's point of view there is a real need to produce ware that is slightly harder and naturally the intensity of a bonfire is greater than the smouldering embers of sawdust. Not that much greater it is true and it is necessary to experiment with more advanced kilns to produce temperatures capable of melting non-poisonous chemicals to glass (lead compounds will melt at 750 degrees centigrade but these are very poisonous in unfritted forms and ought not to be used in schools).

I have previously mentioned other forms of knowledge motivated by a study of kilns. Already a simple study of local geology has been necessary. The kilns I am to talk about can include the complementary study of both geography and history.

I am indebted to Messrs Michael Cardew and John Newick for my knowledge of African potters and their kilns. For the African the bonfire is a totally adequate kiln. The pots produced are soft in comparison to European earthenware but their nature is perfectly adapted to their function. (Cool storage for liquids and cooking vessels capable of withstanding sudden changes in temperature.) Children building and firing a modified version of such a kiln will begin to learn something of this remarkable culture: knowledge gained through meaningful participation.

Obviously this type of kiln is more easily constructed in a rural setting for it will be necessary to gather brushwood, grasses, ferns, etc., to make the firing successful. It is wise to gather too much rather than too little but I am sure that most children will enjoy such an operation.

Again it is advisable to use a low firing clay with an addition of sand (about 20 per cent). It is probably more advisable than it was with the sawdust kiln as the change in temperature is likely to be more dramatic.

A circular hollow about nine inches deep is dug and filled with dry sawdust. The rim of the hollow also helps to support and contain the blazing wood. The size naturally depends upon the amount and size of the work. It is advisable not to be too ambitious for the

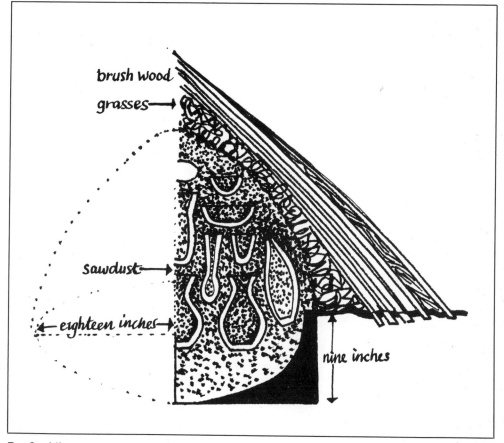

Bonfire kiln
A modified version can be used for firing glazes. The glazed ware is placed in a saggar and covered with a kiln shelf. This muffled chamber is then placed on to some bricks and encircled at a distance of about six inches with fire. As the muffle gradually becomes warmer the fire is eased towards and eventually completely surrounds it

larger the area the more difficult it is to obtain an even temperature throughout the fire. A three feet diameter is sufficient.

The largest pots or terra-cottas are placed on to the sawdust and arranged with the same care and attention to detail as the previous kiln.

Another layer of sawdust is then placed in and around the pots to a depth of at least six inches.

The second layer of pots are then nestled gently into position and the process repeated so that the resultant shape is a cone like mound of sawdust.

Some of the dry brushwood, etc., is placed carefully around the mound to a depth of at least six inches.

The fire can then be lit around the base. A slow burning flame is ideal. The sawdust helps to protect the ware from the initial thermal shock, but it also means that more

fuel will have to be added during the firing.

This must be done carefully and evenly and on no account must large logs be thrown haphazardly on to the fire. Eventually the sawdust will burn away and the perimeter pots will be visible. It is the critical period of the operation and certain precautions should be taken. I have known pots shatter, missiling their broken bodies among scattering spectators. This can be prevented by careful observation and at the right moment adding greener wood and grasses to the fire. This helps to protect the naked clay from cold draughts. More fuel is added and one may see the beginnings of faint glowing pot amidst the embers. When this stage is reached greener brush wood is added and the now settling mound is covered with damp leaves or sods. This helps to contain the heat and protects the ware from cold draughts.

In the morning the site is inspected and if

cool the ashes may be investigated and encouraged to release the "jewels". With luck 75 per cent of the terra-cottas will have survived.

African potters of course get better results but then they are artist craftsmen with considerable experience. They will probably have completed their firing cycle in less than an hour. A bonfire kiln in this climate may take at least two to three hours. The longer the firing the harder the pot. They also preheat their pots before subjecting them to the intense flame. This preparatory procedure I have attempted but rejected, largely because of our climate, and the delicacy required in the handling of warm brittle ware which is beyond my inexpert ability.

Romano-British type kiln

Be forewarned this is a more difficult kiln to build or fire. It has a rudimentary firebox, flue, chamber and an embryonic suggestion of a chimney. In the diagram I have attempted to illustrate two ways of building this type of kiln. The left-hand side is nearer in kind to its ancestors and is built almost entirely from natural materials. The right-hand side is built largely from manufactured materials and is more likely to prove satisfactory, especially if the ware is placed in a saggar slightly raised from the floor with lumps of clay.

The greatest problem with this type of kiln is that the flames are not easily encouraged to penetrate evenly throughout the chamber. They so easily pass up and over the ware escaping without work through the chimney hole. It may prove necessary to fit a baffle tile at the entrance to the chamber. It can also be solved by making the flues at the rear larger than those at the front. This is best done by building a checker floor. At all times it is necessary to keep these flues free from obstruction.

If you decide to make a clay roof remember that the ware must be so placed as to support it. The theory is that the clay eventually fires hard and that this provides a temporary but adequate roof. Unfortu-nately my ancestors were not Romans and my first kilns looked more like abandoned dug-outs on the western front. However others may be more fortunate in their first attempts. The ciment fondu dome certainly works and it is not difficult to make.

Some detailed care is necessary with the stoking. Having split your fuel into pieces about one inch in diameter and stacked it in a convenient but safe place, start the fire slowly. It is important not to allow the ash pit to become clogged for it is better if the air passes through the fire and not only over the top. Little and often is the secret of stoking.

It usually takes about nine hours to complete the firing cycle. When finished all entry and exit flues must be sealed.

The kilns I have so far described must be primarily considered as experimental experiences, and those of you who wish to develop a real continuous interest in terra-cotta and pottery will wish to possess a more reliable kiln.

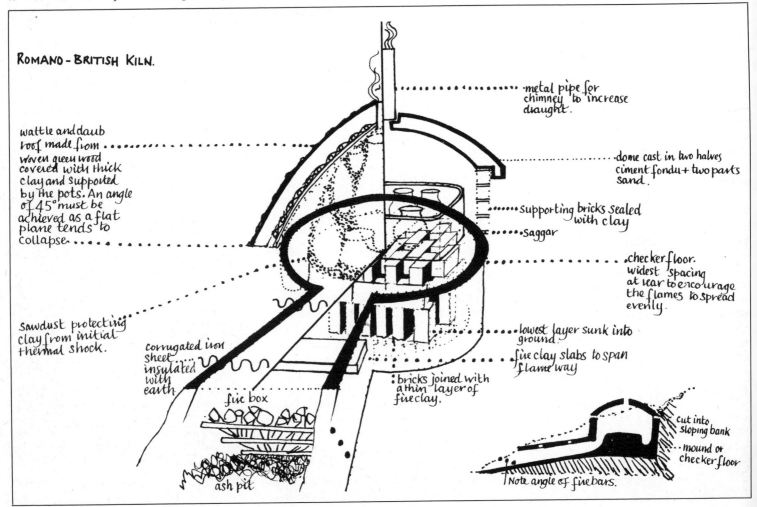

ROMANO-BRITISH KILN.

metal pipe for chimney to increase draught.

wattle and daub roof made from woven green wood covered with thick clay and supported by the pots. An angle of 45° must be achieved as a flat plane tends to collapse.

dome cast in two halves ciment fondu + two parts sand.

supporting bricks sealed with clay

Saggar

checker floor. widest spacing at rear to encourage the flames to spread evenly.

sawdust protecting clay from initial thermal shock.

lowest layer sunk into ground

fire clay slabs to span flame way

corrugated iron sheet insulated with earth

bricks joined with a thin layer of fireclay.

fire box

cut into sloping bank

mound or checker floor

Note angle of firebars.

ash pit

Modelling with Synthetic Clays

Newclay Products

This article is the first of a short section about a new modelling material that has recently become available; a material that the writer thinks has many considerable implications for the teacher. It is an improved modelling clay, and is called Newclay, but before going on to describe its advantages over what is presently available, it will serve a useful purpose if we first consider the shortcomings of normal clays.

Unquestionably, the chief source of complaint stems from the brittleness that clay develops on drying. Any model made by the children that is more ambitious than an ash tray, is unlikely to arrive home intact. The frustration for teachers as well as for pupils that arises from this, often results in the abandonment of the material in the classroom. Other faults, such as the tendency of the limbs to part company with the body, and the inability of the thinner sections to take weight, are perhaps not so important. But clay crumbles and powders so readily, and is, in consequence, walked about the school. This condemns it in the eyes of many people; in particular caretakers.

Advantages

By contrast, this new material is a non-brittle clay, and therefore solves to a large extent many of these problems. But more than this, it allows many quite new and original techniques to be adopted.

You may now, using Newclay, encourage the children to make more complicated, and quite delicate shapes, and expect them to survive normal handling, and some impact. A dropped model is not necessarily a broken model.

But apart from the toughness that this clay develops, the finished pieces can be treated with the Hardener that the firm supply. The degree of hardness that is obtained depends upon the number of applications, but it is possible for work to acquire a stonelike feel, with great resistance to wear.

One incidental side effect of this treatment is that the clay becomes almost impervious to water—although the makers would not go so far as to say that you could drink your morning cup of tea from it.

On the point of room cleanliness; the compactness of Newclay resists the tendency to crumble and dust, and is therefore very much easier to contain, so that users can probably look forward to better relations with the cleaners.

But as I said earlier, Newclay does more than overcome the shortcomings of conventional clays. The amount that it shrinks on drying is very small indeed, which proves to be very important. This fact, allied with its toughness, makes many new practices possible. I have made—and fired, too, incidentally—tiles of more than three square feet, and little more than a quarter inch thick. With no special attention they remained quite flat—almost glass flat. A comparable tile in normal clay would be difficult even to lift from the table on which it was made. It would probably break from its own weight. This must be good news for tile makers, and will give fresh impetus to the many who use this art form. I foresee the making of large coffee tables covered by just a single tile. What a tremendous challenge to the artist that would be.

3 dimension

Small four by four tiles can be produced so thin and flat as to look almost commercial. For sculpture too, both light and serious, Newclay will cause some changes in techniques. For the first time it is now possible to make and allow to dry a model formed about an armature or wire frame. Previously, using normal clay, the modelling would break up into rows of beads along the wire as it dried. But now cracks are very unlikely, and even if the odd one does develop, it can be easily and completely mended.

And more spectacular even than that, the whole thing can be fired in a kiln—clay, armature, the lot. That, I think, is a real break through.

There are a few other bonuses of rather less import, but these we can discuss later. Let us, in finishing this first article, consider how to make use of the material at an elementary level by going through the complete process of making an uncomplicated model; right through to the take home stage.

Processes

Newclay comes in 28 lb. bags, so that if you chop it up into forty pieces, each piece will be about the size of a tennis ball. Now our subject has a ball of clay in his hot hands, and this he squeezes into his version of Yogi Bear. He digs in holes for the eyes because he says that he is "going to stick some beads in there later".

The model is stood near a source of heat (oven, radiator, fire) to dry, but no distortion or cracks develop because warping and cracking are the result of uneven shrinkage, and there is no shrinkage—or hardly any. After a short while, Yogi is "white dry", so you take it and immerse it for a minute or two in a bowl of Hardener. (You keep a quart bottle of Hardener already made up in the cupboard.) The model goes back to dry for a moment while the colours are mixed, and then, it can be painted.

Surface finishers

Painting complete, and just before he gets a chance to cover it with red spots, you take it from him, and once again dunk it in the Hardener. This helps to fix the colours, and give a scratch-resistant surface. Dipping in a stronger mix of Hardener would in fact produce a very hard gloss.

The beady eyes are glued in with a P.V.A., and for better or for worse, this little model could last a very long time. Always a chastening thought.

A chunky and strong little model of a baker nears completion

Synthetic Clay on Supports

It is a contradiction in terms to talk of unfired pottery, but that, nevertheless, is the description that best fits the work I am about to describe. This is a method of making claywork that results in the finished piece being hard, tough, and colourful, with a high gloss glaze that in appearance is indistinguishable from its pottery counterpart.

The process is based on Newclay, and must have a great deal to offer any teacher who is keen to teach claywork, but is without the specialist knowledge to make "pot", and also for those that teach in a kilnless school.

I described on page 161 the nature of this clay, and how to take advantage of its special properties for making just a simple basic model. On this page we can take the subject to an advanced stage; to the level that might be reached by any serious student of sculpture.

In terms of handling and modelling techniques, Newclay differs little from conventional clays in that it permits the normal coiling, pinching, and slab processes. Indeed, it is quite splendid for these last two. Those learners who remember struggling with their first introductory pinched pot might now find that they suffered unnecessarily. And do all the slab pots that your children make look as if they have suffered from an implosion? A slab box out of Newclay will retain its flat sides, and consequently the lids will still fit when the work is finished.

The small bird in the picture is a typical model that we can expect from upper juniors or young secondaries after a little practice. This was made by joining two small pinched pots together to form the body. A touch of moisture to weld the seam and smeared over to seal it off. Gently, the whole is whacked with a ruler into an egg—a pleasant task. Head, wings, and tail, were all joined on with a little smearing and a touch of water. Smearing is important as it bonds the clay, and in this instance it is more important because it is not to be fired. So far, all more or less normal clay modelling practice.

The surface can be smooth or textured, and once it is dry it is painted. Actually we use temperapaste or poster colour, but any water mixed colour would serve, including powder colour. This bird was painted a gentle shade of green, and after the paint had dried, it was immersed for about five minutes in the "standard mix" of Newclay Hardener. We keep a quart of this already made up in a bottle in the cupboard because the powder takes a little time to dissolve.

The reaction of raw clay to this liquid is unexpected to say the least. Looking for all the world like slightly tinted water, one expects the clay to soften on immersion. In fact, an increase in hardness is immediate, and when this model was extracted, and dried off, it became a very great deal harder still. Had immersion been extended to about an hour, the dried model would have taken on a little of the cold hardness of stone. But it is no use trying to reconstitute any clay that has endured this petrifying process.

As in pottery, the last stage is glazing. The same Hardener is used, but this time a small quantity at far greater concentration—4 oz. to half a pint of hot water. Once it has gone clear it is ready for use, and is applied with a brush. The effect is to heighten the colours and produce a gloss that well resembles a pottery glaze. Opaque and coloured glazes are available too by the simple addition of white and coloured paints. With some practice you will soon find that the children are producing a non-pottery that would fool the experts.

The final satisfaction comes when you find that pots and models so made can be "washed up". They are almost waterproof. Not enough to contain water of course, or enough to eat the Sunday dinner from, but that is about the extent of its limitations.

But to return to the modelling, a not very much used form is that executed about a wire frame or armature. The potter would not normally regard this in his province; it is a technique reserved for the student of sculpture. But not any more. Metal and wooden frames become necessary when any particular feature of a model cannot be expected to stand its own weight in clay. Obvious examples are giraffes, birds with long legs or necks, some insects possibly, and of course the human figure once it stands over a foot or so high. The composition illustrated here is an example of the class of work that is within the capacity of secondary pupils. The figures were built up over copper covered iron wire, "pin" men that were bent into position, and then locked together with fuse wire, thereby gaining stability from all four legs. A little clay was pinched over the joints to stiffen them, and the modelling begun.

Now this would have been a useless exercise using normal clay. Taking a plaster cast would be out of the question for young people with such a complicated figure and as the clay dried there would be the inevitable series of cracks along the whole length of the model. But using this new clay the cracks do not occur, or at least if the odd one does show itself you wait until it is bone dry, and then mend it. This is easy, just a few drops of water around the fissure, the sides are tooled together, and the modelling made good.

If you have a kiln, all this could be popped in and fired. Now that I think is quite an original technique, and one that should recommend itself to any student of sculpture. Yet if this is just a sketch model, a maquette for a more serious piece, or again, if it is just one of twenty such models, the output of your fourth year group, then out with the hardener. Soak the whole thing for a quarter of an hour, and then once it is dry, finish it with any of the normal mediums. Even bronze it with resins; it is substantial enough to make it worth while.

This relatively simple process as described can be adapted with some minor modifications to the whole field that is normally reserved for the potter.

Newclay may be obtained from Newclay Products Ltd., Overston House, Sunnyfield Road, Chislehurst, Kent.

Below. An unfired bird made on the basis of pinched pots

Right. A lively example of the use of Newclay over iron wire

Synthetic Clay for Tiles and Mosaics

The word "tile" according to the Oxford Concise, means a slab of fired clay, but this definition will prove far too narrow for the purposes of this article. For the sake of these notes you must accept that a tile is anything that is flat, and ranges in size from a quarter inch, to three feet square, both sculpted and flat, fired and unfired. In this, the last of the three sections on the Newclay process, many of the rules will have to be changed to make provision for the expanded possibilities.

Starting with the smallest, tessera. The pieces have never been initially difficult to make from the thin slabs of clay, but for the pottery teacher the process gets progressively more nightmarish as the clay dries out and the thousands of little pieces steadily accumulate. Now, here is a complete alternative.

Roll out the Newclay to the thickness of a school ruler, and when it has stiffened up a little cut it into pieces. This little job has been enormously simplified by using the tessera cutter that Newclay Products supply. Now let it all dry, and the big surprise is that you can still pick up the whole sheet again. Each of the pieces is still attached to its neighbour as if adhered to a piece of backing cloth. Indeed, they look remarkably like those ready-made mosaics that you can buy in sheets.

Paint the areas of tessera with water-colour paints, and when this has dried paint it with the instant glaze now available from the same Newclay company. Let this too dry, and you are then ready to start the really pleasant part of the exercise. I know of no more convenient way of making up mosaic. Simply snip off the pieces as and when you want them, and the surplus is stored flat and in layers in a box for future use.

And now for the conventional four inch square tile. The special advantage offered here is that commercial flatness need no longer be the prerogative of the trade. Make your tiles as always by rolling out the clay between batons—on cloth of course—and then cut the tiles to size. Leave them out to dry, but this time without any special stacking; leave them on a wooden surface for preference, and under normal conditions they will dry quite flat. If you do have a mind to fire them, they will fire quite flat too. No need now to pretend that you prefer your tiles to be curled up a little at the corners because it shows that they are hand-made. A very real challenge to the tile decorator is the very large tile. And of course you can

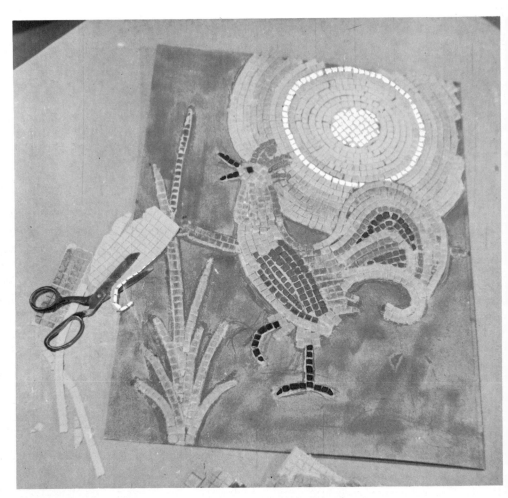

Sheets of "mosaic" being cut up in readiness for fixing into place

make these in Newclay too. I would guess that there is no limit to the size that is possible except that you must be able to get them into the kiln and with some room to spare. Large tiles are dry, strong and safe to handle regardless of their thinness. And here again they will remain quite flat.

Panels made up from several tiles are easier for young children to make. An excellent seven foot "Rocket" engine was made by some infants in a S.E. London school, and then fixed to the playground wall. It looked splendidly impressive. Panels made for outside walls must of course be fired and glazed to withstand the weather. But on a well protected site, and if the school is without the means to fire the work, you can still achieve completely satisfactory results. Let me suggest a way of going about it.

The selected group choose a subject and each draws an interpretation of it. A concensus settles on the best one, and this is scaled up on to a large sheet of paper. The

shape, or shapes, is covered with a thin layer of clay made up from lots of little pats all pumelled together. Run a rolling pin over all this to compact it and to achieve some sort of flatness, and then cut it up into the shapes befitting the design.

These separated tiles can be decorated with modelling, and then still further with powder colour or tempera—anything so long as it is not a waterproof paint—and then clear glaze it. The colour will be tremendously heightened by this glaze, and the quality of the colour so improved that the children get an immediate satisfaction from the finished look of the work.

Glue it, pin it, or screw it to the wall, and that's it finished. A far cry from the long drawn out pottery process. Not so durable of course—and that is not always such a bad thing—and perhaps it can never give the deep satisfaction of well fired pottery, but at least it is all over and finished with in two or three days instead of as many weeks.

Theory and Practice

An Attitude to Design

We include here some extracts from an article published recently in the journal of the Royal Institute of British Architects by kind permission of the editor. David Medd, the writer, is employed by the Architects and Building branch of the Department of Education and Science and has been concerned with many exciting school designs including the Eveline Lowe School, Marlborough Grove, London, S.E.1 (photographs of which are included here).

"I have been sacrificed on the altar of aesthetics, and the colour hurts me more than the noise." So said the headmaster about his new school. "A building is not a beautiful shell, and neither is it a functional shed. A building is the coherent solution of a problem of living." So said Professor Bronowski. Here are the two starting points open to the architect, succinctly expressed: to start with precept or to start with people. But this is about experience in schools, and there are two reasons why school building over the last 20 years has become important. First, the seminal influence has been those schools that have been inspired by education (the influence of the others has fallen by the wayside), and second, it is through the school building programme that the most concerted and continuous effort has been made to get the building industry into the 20th century.

Modern techniques for the provision of heat, ventilation and light are removing some of the constraints in design. This is good in that the architect can gain more command in the deployment of space, but bad if it leads to ignoring some of the important attributes of a school's environment. It requires wisdom to use a newly won freedom, but none to take liberties. It is only just now being realized by the public that architecture can be bent towards their needs and is not something over which they have no control, like the weather. However, the starting point remains the great tussle in the architect's mind. Do you have a concept of what looks good, what formal devices and proportions make for good architecture, and hope they do not conflict with or compromise the life and opportunity the building is intended to provide for? Or do you, on the other hand, let your imagination become inspired and guided by the activities and aspirations of people and organize the spatial implications in a way that probably has no formal precedent?

Learning is an active process. Is this play or drama? Outside raised area, Eveline Lowe School, London (Photograph I.L.E.A.)

Making education the starting point has two main implications, one for the architect, and the other for the educator. It raises the question of where and how the architect works in order to become emotionally, intellectually and professionally involved in education (rather than a building jack-of-all-trades). For the educator it raises the question of how he makes his contribution to design. To do this creatively, I am convinced the current idea of the brief has to be abandoned. These, however, are subjects which cannot be expanded here.

The days have passed in education when teachers were regarded as having a set quantity of information which they poured into the pupil, like filling a vessel with water. The discoveries that educators made over half a century ago about how children learn, and their application in state primary schools

over the last 20 years, have been some of this country's greatest inventions. Earlier methods did not recognize that learning is an active process, or that each individual is different. Teachers are not therefore concerned with a class of 20, 30, or 40, or whatever; for a class is an abstract unit. Teachers are concerned with 20, 30, or 40 individual pupils, each of whose ambitions and needs will be different. Children are no longer regarded as Wordsworth observed cattle in "Written in March" in 1802:

"The oldest and youngest
Are at work with the strongest;
The cattle are grazing,
Their heads never raising;
They are forty, feeding as one!"

It is now clearly understood that it is not only from the teacher that children learn, but from each other. There is no doubt

Education is becoming less impersonal
Mrs. Eva Phipps involved in children's learning

(Photograph I.L.E.A.)

therefore in my mind that the most revolutionary influence in school life on school design is the different relationship between teachers and children, and between children and children. To use a mechanical analogy, each child is like an engine, and each engine requires a different starting technique. The teacher has to learn the techniques, and then cope with a situation in which each engine will run at a different speed and in a different direction, and for different distances. A teacher is like a conjurer having to keep all the balls moving in the air.

Education is becoming less impersonal and a more personal process. We are not therefore designing for clearly defined processes in clearly defined rooms in clearly predictable group sizes to the same extent, but more for a variety of interconnected

activities that used to be considered separate. For example, books and study opportunities are not exclusive to the library, but are wanted all over the place. Similarly water, hammers, and wire are not the preserve of the workshops but are wanted all over the place. Similarly one may need to be noisy near where someone else needs to be quiet. The need for immediate access to a book, a large sheet of paper, a film strip, or a hammer, not only puts an end to the day when furnishing a classroom meant providing 15 or 20 dual locker desks, or a laboratory three or four rows of parallel benches, but probably puts an end to the classroom and laboratory as we have known them as well. Teachers have physically and metaphorically descended from their platforms. They are now amongst children, not in front of them, in a joint adventure.

Another influence is the increasing use of audio-visual and electronic equipment in teaching. These are with us fundamentally to enrich pupils' experiences and to provide further means for individual practice, rather than to impose a new order of their own on how teachers work or how children are grouped. With their increasing availability will come the increasing diversity of the grouping of pupils and the consequent need for more variety of spaces.

What I have described implies changes in every aspect of design, acoustics, lighting, floor finishes, partitions and so on. But they are not changes that merely swing the pendulum from one side to the other, from black to white, but changes that add to the complexity and variety needed in the school.

The School Environment

We must see the school environment as a framework in space, and not a framework in time. In other words the building is not there to permit children to be efficiently conducted through the maze of a timetable. The building and its relation to the surroundings are there to speak and be articulate to children, and by "the building" I mean everybody and everything in it as well. By "speaking to children", I mean nothing less than providing inspiration for children of all ages by means of first-hand experiences of all kinds.

So many children come from feckless or impoverished homes, and so many more have backgrounds that are boring and provide no creative mental or practical outlet that advertisements, "pop" and "the box", instead of being occasional stimulants we can take in our stride, become the chewing gum of the ears and eyes, and finally the mind. Eventually the gum hardens, and forms over the mind a protective covering like slates on the roof of a house, which forever resist the absorption of life-giving material and direct it along the gutters and finally to the drains. The school environment has nothing less than the responsibility of preventing the gum from hardening. By "speaking to children" I mean that the school must attempt to do nothing less than instil a sense of wonder at the works of nature and man. To a child a school can provide the adventure of an unexplored country; it can be like a market round which you can browse—there it all is, take in what you want; it can be like, in fact it can actually be an exhibition in which the raw materials, the tools, the machines, and the things that

Learning or playing or just living?   **A quiet moment at the Eveline Lowe School**   **(Photograph I.L.E.A.)**

children, teachers, scientists, artists and craftsmen make are there to touch, to feel, to study, to read, to play with, to inspire and to wonder at.

Educationally a school building is not something separate from its surroundings. The building and its surroundings, whether they be in the city, in the suburb, in the valleys or the mountains, together form an educational opportunity. In fact environmental studies are the process of extracting every opportunity you can from your surroundings. Doors, windows with views large and small, verandas, covered work areas, sheltered extensions of the interior to the outside, are all important devices for breaking the hermetic edge of the buildings and making psychological and physical links between the inside and the outside which together enrich and widen the scope of the work people can do, and which together, not separately, make in fact the educational opportunity of the school. Modern building construction, and modern educational psychology of learning have dissolved the hermetic edge of the building which used to be monastic in its thickness and height. The burst of light, space and colour with which our new schools have illuminated education has been our single most effective contribution in capturing the spirit in building of modern education itself.

The aim is "to channel and widen the scope of the work people do."   **(Photograph I.L.E.A.)**

167

Creative thinking

It is rather unfortunate that the words "creative" and "creativity" have become so over-used that they are beginning to lose something of their force—unfortunate because it is difficult to express the ideas they convey in any other way. To be creative is to look at life in a certain way, seeing many possibilities in a situation. Some people have greater ability to think creatively than others, but we all have this ability in some measure. Although the creative process holds difficulties and problems, it also gives us some of the most satisfying and stimulating of our experiences.

Creative thinking involves letting the mind wander over a wide range of experience, selecting and relating and structuring, seeing and examining many possibilities before reaching a conclusion. The final stage of this process is communication or expression. At this point creative thinking takes form according to the discipline of the way in which it is being expressed. This may be a dance, a poem, a mathematical formula, a picture or many other things.

This discipline is learnt through the need to communicate. Once we thought that children should learn skills and techniques first and when these were developed, then expression could begin. This frequently took so long that by the time a child had enough skill to express, he had nothing he wanted to say. Now we realise that skill is more easily developed in the context of a strong desire to express, and that the teacher's job is to evoke the desire to express and to help the pupil to find an appropriate form.

Torrance, in his book "Guiding Creative Talent", lists many of the characteristics of the highly creative person. He is adventurous, accepts and is sometimes attracted by disorder, attempts difficult jobs—sometimes too difficult, desires to excel, is determined, does not fear being thought different, is full of curiosity, is independent and confident in his own thinking, is intuitive, sensitive, receptive to external stimuli, is visionary, versatile. He is likely to have some traits more commonly found in the opposite sex. He is also non-conformist and is likely to disturb organisation.

If we endeavour to educate people so that they become more creative, we must accept that what we do may create its own problems. Although Torrance is here speaking of the highly creative person, it is likely that more creative education will produce more creative people who disturb organisation. I think this will be worth it, but we must recognise that to educate people to be creative is to

educate people who do their own thinking and this is far from peaceful.

Why is creative thinking important? In the first place it is important in the development of personality. The better our ability to think creatively and to express our thinking, the more satisfying and mentally healthy life can become. Creative expression is a deep human need and education has a duty to help children to satisfy it. Even at a fairly low level, we are seen as people by others through the way we move, speak, dress. These are forms of expression of what we are and we are happier when we feel that they represent us adequately.

When creative learning is given its proper place, other learning is better. By creative learning, I mean learning in which children are given genuine opportunities for first-hand experience and encouraged to draw, test and express their own conclusions from it, instead of taking on trust the findings of others from books and from teachers. These have a place too, but in the primary school, learning at first hand is more important. It should come first on many occasions. The opportunity for creative expression also appears to give children a confidence which carries over into other learning.

Some of the American researches show that highly creative children are often over-achievers, performing at a higher level of attainment than is suggested by their measured I.Q. This too suggests that creative learning is likely to be better learning. We should also include in this summary the simple fact that the person who works creatively enjoys life more. He is too busy and involved to be bored, and through his own activity develops standards of judgment which enable him to enjoy other peoples' creative efforts too. Happiness would seem to be a very sound aim for education, but one which is often rejected.

Changes in education usually come about when good educational and moral reasons for change coincide with good economic reasons. Many of us would agree that the education in many of our schools, particularly that in our grammar schools, is not nearly creative enough. Some highly intelligent boys and girls, in fact, do very little which can be called creative from the time G.C.E. casts its shadow until post graduate level. It may be that a good economic reason for changing this will be found in society's need for people with ideas. It is this which has inspired much of the American research. What needs to be established is what produces creative thinkers.

Teachers vary a great deal in their ability to get creative work from children. Some appear to create an atmosphere in which there is a constant outpouring of ideas from the children. Other teachers find this much more difficult. The teacher who gets creative ideas from children is not necessarily a good practitioner in any particular creative discipline himself. It could be that the teacher who gets good work from others is one who can work best through other people.

Thinking creatively—or just doing what she is told?

If we examine further the qualities in a teacher which draw creative work from children, we can see that the teacher who wishes to enable others to work creatively must first develop the openness of mind characteristic of the creative person. This means a readiness to accept what children offer along a very wide front.

Such a teacher must really enjoy other people's creative work. Work in which one reveals one's personal ideas and inner self, is very sensitive indeed and withers easily. The teacher's reception of the children's work and confidences is of vital importance. It must be genuine. It must be real. And it must reward real creative effort. One must respect children and believe in them. If you do this, they continually delight and astonish you with the inventiveness and originality and freshness of their ideas.

Teachers who complain that their children have "no ideas" have usually created this situation by their non-acceptance or even non-recognition of the ideas which the children have produced. All children have ideas. This must be an act of faith for all teachers who hope to see evidence of it.

The good teacher needs to be able to see from another person's view point. This is why creative artists sometimes fail as teachers. Their own vision is so strong that they can only help those who see in a similar way. The work of an individual must be personal to him. It may still reflect the personality of the teacher, because he is

Why Art Teachers should start teaching Poetry

The great majority of really talented sixth form poets in my school have been art specialists. The youngest pupils automatically illustrate their writings, and do so elaborately and without being asked. It is obvious that our own students already integrate much of their art and writing work, and perhaps their teachers should follow them.

Many of the methods of "free writing" and a good deal of the art "teaching" are common—not only in some shared methods of stimulating creative work, but, more importantly, in the evaluation of that work. The justification for doing what we do—something to do with education of the emotions—is similar, whatever different techniques may be mastered in the process.

I believe we should deliberately mingle our subjects more—to revert in many cases to the situation our children knew in the primary schools—and we might begin by asking art teachers to become teachers of poetry.

Poetry "teaching" in fact is very easy, and should be especially so for an enlightened art teacher, even if he neither writes nor reads it at the moment. Basically, it is a question of providing a context in which the work can flow forth.

Much child writing is in the form of "free verse", and pupils of all ages and abilities can write this, without any previous experience. They need to see some—and many teachers find D. H. Lawrence a useful start. Holub and Prevert might be particularly interesting in the art room; some of the Liverpool poetry appeals to senior pupils especially. All these books are easily available as Penguins. Better, if the art teacher has some favourite free verse, this would do. The basic point to be made to the pupil is what free verse is—or rather what it is not. It does not rhyme. It has no particular length, either in beats to a line, or lines to a verse, or poem. "If you say it *is* a poem, it *is* a poem."

Provided that you insist that they cannot write in verse—and there are always some children who seek the security offered by writing rhyming doggerel instead of something personally felt—they master it quickly.

The verse will flow easily, although it may be left to the art/poetry teacher to find the stimulus for the poems, which may be hurriedly written off, perhaps without revision in a matter of minutes. There are infinite variations of the stimuli available in the art studio. The pupils can each write from a piece of their own art work. They can all write from one particular piece by one of the group. They can write from "real" pictures. They can write on the top of duplicated drawings—which especially appeals to younger children. They can write—and paint—to musical stimuli. Each of these suggestions is reversible. And so on.

This work can proceed valuably for some time. It may be, however, that there is a craving for more "form" in their poems, and this might be especially so in the adolescent years.

One possible approach is through "posters"; Christopher Logue and others have made a popular art form here, and pupils welcome the chance to produce large wall versions of poems and paintings.

Similarly, other verse forms—haikus, acrostics, alliterative verse—are not beyond average children in the way that formal rhymed verse usually is. But above all, the art/poetry teacher is able to *display* the work produced in a way that the English teacher cannot, with typed poems on classroom pinboards. Exhibitions of poems and paintings are exciting—and the four-dimensional display produced at Eltham Green School for their 6th Form Conference was particularly impressive in this way. A class exhibition of this sort, perhaps four-dimensional, perhaps with tape recorders hidden in the middle, playing relevant music would be a valuable project.

I write as an English teacher struck by the similarity of much of our approach and worried by the forces of anti-education in our schools. In so far as we are engaged in a common attempt at education through art, we should more often teach across subjects. This is not to say that there are not whole parts of our separate crafts that should not remain separate. It is absurd, however, to limit out joint endeavours to sending pictures up to be illustrated, and paintings down to be written about, and closing our classroom doors. The best approach might well be team-teaching, with the art and English specialist working together. The next best thing might be for the art teacher occasionally to be a poetry teacher. It will help our task, to prove that poetry writing and reading is of very great value, and not something either hated, done because he makes us do it, or done in the privacy of one classroom every so often and unrelated to anything else anywhere. The case for poetry as part of education—and life—is precisely the same as that for Art.

(continued from p. 168)

providing an atmosphere and the stimulus for work, but it must first reflect the personality of the child.

The teacher who wishes children to work creatively must provide an atmosphere which leaves them feeling free to experiment. This kind of permissiveness and acceptance is not easy to define, and very difficult indeed for the young and inexperienced teacher to achieve, for one needs to be able to sense the difference between the necessary freedom and licence. This poem, for example, could only have been written in a school where children were able to express themselves in less orthodox ways if they wished to do so.

The Crucifixion

Pontius said, "What shall we do with him?"
"Crucify him! Crucify him!"
"Well he's all yours,
Do what you like."
So they took him away
And did what they said they would.
They crucified him.

"We're off to crucify Jesus,
Hooray! Hooray!"
They took him to Golgotha,
That was a hill.
They sang all the way,
"We're off to crucify Jesus
Hooray! Hooray!"
They nailed him to the cross,
And made sure he was dead

And stuck a spear in his side.

On the third morning
In the garden of Gethsemane
"He's gone," cried a voice,
It was Mary Magdalene's.
Suddenly a gardener appeared,
Well Mary thought it was, but
It was Jesus. Mary wept,
"Where is he?"
"You've taken him!"
Jesus answered, "I am your Saviour,
Go and tell the Disciples."
Mary ran as fast as her legs could carry her.
One by one they came and peered in the tomb.
They saw only two angels
Glittering
"He's risen, he's risen,"
They yelled.

Relating Art to Life in Leeds Schools

During recent years the special Arts Department of Leeds Education Committee has done tremendous work to revolutionise art in schools in an endeavour to bring it into line with life.

The enterprise based at Spring Bank Teachers' Centre, is intended to awaken a more appreciative conception of art and life in the minds of pupils. Similar departments exist in other areas, but probably none have a more enlightened and enthusiastic approach.

The original idea followed a nation-wide campaign relating to art in schools. An Art Specialist employed by the Department would take a selection of pictures to various schools. Some were reproductions; others originals depending on suitability and money available. Half his time was spent in an advisory capacity; half in working for teacher training.

Then, five years ago Mr. Alan Gummerson, a former teacher, was appointed full time. His job consists of getting out into the schools, trying to relate art to life and to make pupils think about a certain object or material (concrete for example) and experiment with it.

Having worked with children for nine years he states: "You never know what children are going to remember, but all adds to their experience of life."

Now he, Lecturer Paul Walker and Mr. John Oxley are kept fully engaged. Their headquarters, a former large house, is at Headingley, Leeds and from its attic floor come many ambitious schemes to set children thinking for themselves and relating their thoughts to activities. The work does not merely consist of supplying pictures and crafts to schools but to convey the true meaning of art to pupils and sometimes even to their teachers. However the main concern is to awaken a creative and thoughtful response in the minds of children so that they will gain a wider experience and not regard art in its many forms as divorced from life. This often works out in diverse ways in schools. What Mr. Gummerson calls "cross fertilisation" occurs. "If we can formulate something from students' work and send it around the schools, it often awakens a surprising and gratifying response."

One new project is the making of an entirely new set of films about Art and Artists. These are of artists talking and demonstrating their own work. Included are Kenneth and Mary Martin and Robert Welsh, the designer. In his case pupils will see a film of him at work and then handle the

Murals at the Primrose Hill County Secondary School, Leeds

various stages of a completed article; in one instance a pepper mill. The children will handle the objects—get the feel of their texture and shape in various stages and from the film will see how the work is built up, how it is marketed and how he arranges his office work.

Apart from this aspect Spring Bank runs Teacher Courses—an obvious feature of such an establishment. These have included Print-making and allied subjects. In the case of a recent Fabric Course the intention was to awaken the awareness and enjoyment of fabrics, finding new forms for old materials and new materials for old forms.

The function of the department is both concrete and abstract, displaying the changed attitude towards the former conception of arts and crafts. Both Mr. Gummerson and Mr. Oxley believe it is no longer

advisable to give a child a book of explicit instructions and tell him to make an object in a certain way. Instead he should be left to find his own methods and interpretations so that art becomes part of his life. The creative section of a child's make-up must be cultivated.

One of Mr. Gummerson's planned future projects relates to Noise. In this tape-recorders—the children's own—will be taken into the streets to record noise—any noise —and then the sounds will be put together with others—some from old pianos.

"Children have such things as tape-recorders—let them be encouraged to use them creatively", he states. Because of this individualistic approach it is no surprise to hear him declare: "Everything and everybody should be valued for themselves and not manipulated."

Art and Craft in Schools Today

Here we set out a selection of provocative articles on teaching methods and approaches to young children's learning. Although of particular interest to teachers, the pages which follow also provide much to interest parents and others whose work brings them into close contact with young people

The outcome of conferences held to discuss the place of craft in secondary schools has been the idea that craft and science can work together for their mutual benefit. While this policy is aimed, in short term, at producing the technologists that we are told we need, and in this sense may be expedient, it is certainly true that liaison between craft and science could make a valuable contribution to a boy or girl's general education not only from the vocational aspect.

The general principle of breaking down subject barriers throughout the school curriculum is surely a sound one. The primary schools have already shown that this method of working is viable, and art and craft subjects have formed an important foundation for this approach. In the secondary school things are more difficult. Most teachers are specialists, and tend to think of their pupils as specialists too. Where does one begin with a teacher who talked in the staff-room of "Our scientists in the second form"?

While liaison between craft and science is at last gaining momentum in the schools, it is strange that the "heavy" crafts of wood and metalwork have not made much progress towards integration with their corresponding art departments, where often constructions in various materials including wood and metal are made with no reference to the craft-shops at all.

It has been evident for a long time that a new approach to craftwork in school was needed, partly because of increasing affluence and also because of the development of plastics during the nineteen-fifties.

The craft lesson was usually a sort of thrift club, where boys could make various pieces of equipment for themselves or their homes, that were serviceable, and cost only a few pence. Starting with the immortal teapot stand, boys tackled gardening tools, fishing gear, toys, and a whole sequence of racks: egg, pipe, magazine, soap, toothbrush, toast and towel. While these were excellent material for fostering one of the most important aims of a craft course—the development of a sense of design—it became clear that the cheap plastic articles obtain-

able were far more satisfactory than those made in school. The woodwork course was particularly hard hit by these events and even boys who had benefited little from the design course could see that "Correct use of materials" excluded wood from many of these articles and hundreds of toothbrushes are more hygienic because of it.

This void that has existed at the core of the craft course is being filled by craft/science liaison, but while metalwork and science can forge strong links, the case for woodwork appears to be somewhat weaker. The integration of crafts in general, and woodwork in particular, with art would seem therefore to be a problem worth studying.

Of course it is universally true that combined courses are always difficult to organise, usually because of lack of communication and understanding between staff. Specialisation is always going to provide the easiest approach to education, for while a teacher may enjoy the exploration of a partly-known field of study with his pupils, he naturally feels that where time is at a premium, most of his teaching should be done where his own experience can be used most efficiently. Whether efficient compartmentalised education is ultimately better than less efficient, though broader education where links between subjects are more thoroughly forged is, of course, another question.

Added to this general argument, the desire for craft teachers to specialise is heightened by emotional attitudes that are the outcome of the place of craftwork in the curriculum. It must not be forgotten that craftwork has only quite recently become an acceptable part of the school curriculum; in fact it is true to say that there is plenty of evidence to show that it is still considered a Cinderella subject. Many craft teachers have spent a deal of energy making the subject respectable by insisting that craft must be a subject in its own right. It must be "pure"; it must never be handmaiden to other subjects in the curriculum. Above all it must have its academic side. Metalwork, with its obvious links with engineering has fared rather better than woodwork which seems to have achieved its respectability by a too narrow specialisation; with cabinet-making as the core of the practical work coupled with a demand for lengthy History of Furniture essays and a too detailed technology course as the academic boost.

The root cause, therefore, of the emotional outbursts from craft-teachers when they are asked to co-operate with other subjects, is

Design and manufacture of small electric motor—Bristol Comprehensive School

usually a lack of confidence in their subject's status. Of course, it is also true that queries of this sort are sometimes prefixed by unfortunate phrases such as "If you have a boy who is doing nothing" or "Bill Bones has never been very good academically, so I thought he might be good with his hands".

Ignoring the poor craftsman's emotional problems, if we can, in what direction can bonds most easily be made between art room and craft shop? At the most mundane, there are all the problems of fixing and framing that occur in the art room, which can be dealt with in the craft shop. This is the least useful approach, as the pupil can still think in two separate compartments about the "art" and the "craft"; and the craft-teacher will certainly feel that he has been called in to do the hack work.

The approach that is needed is the one which allows craft to be looked on as another way of tackling a problem, not a question of mere manual dexterity in solving it. Skill is basically more a pattern of thought than a manual facility.

Pupils in the artroom should look at new materials introduced from the craft shop. Not only should they look at the basic properties of these materials, but also at the shapes of traditional wood and metal joining processes, and the shape and pattern left on materials by the craft techniques used in the workshops. A close look, helped by lens or microscope, of wood and metal surfaces, especially when exposed by sharp tools (not always insisted on when used in the art room) can be the starting point for painting, sculpture, fabric and pottery design. In the craft shop the design of an article, and the value the pupil can get from making it can be transformed by the consideration of problems usually related only to art; conversely, the techniques of the craftroom can often be the means of realizing an idea in art that cannot be expressed in terms of the materials and processes normally associated with the art room.

How thin these ideas sound on paper! Generalisations seldom sound meaningful, yet too detailed exposition often prevents imaginative development. Later in this article specific examples will be given of students who have found useful links between art and craft in the hope that they will stimulate co-operative thought between the subjects without crystallising out any set attitudes that will prevent further exploration.

Even the closely related heavy crafts and art often make only intermittent contact, yet genuine co-operation between these two subjects would help to expand pupils' vision in a way that can only be educationally advantageous.

If we first look at some of the similarities and differences between art and the crafts, some of the obstacles preventing mutual understanding of their underlying tenets may become clearer and therefore solutions more easily discovered.

In the art room we wish to help the child to discover and express himself by the use of many different materials. The course will probably include the collection and recording of the shape, colour and texture of unusual, beautiful and interesting objects, the discovery of other artists' work, and the examination of many materials to understand their nature. The nature of a material is coupled inseparably with the nature of the techniques used upon or with it, and in order to allow aesthetic judgments free rein we keep these techniques as unsophisticated or even as primitive as possible, hence the use of such painting techniques as dripping, splashing, pouring, blowing and daubing with the fingers. We could say that in its exploration of the materials, art is searching for modes of visual expression from which a general or universal language can develop.

The craftsman too is concerned with the nature of materials, but he, on the other hand, examines them with a specific purpose in mind. His exploration is often carried out with sophisticated techniques using tools that have been developed to produce only particular shapes or states in the material. It follows that certain aspects of the material's nature are more significant to the craftsman than others. Thus the language of craft is a specific one.

It is not surprising then, that the craftsman often confuses brilliant technique with

"The discovery of aesthetic qualities in shapes that he originally considered failures profoundly changed his outlook" (see page 174)

artistic achievement. He feels that art produced with manifestly little technique must be worthless, or worse still that the time taken in production is in direct proportion to artistic merit.

Where in fact does the true value of technique lie? It would seem that good technique becomes important when it offers the *only* way to achieve a specific aesthetic or utilitarian goal. Hence the sound educational maxim that a technique should only be taught when the pupil feels the need of its services, and not for its own sake. The aesthetic field is just as restricted when only the specific skilled techniques of a particular craft are allowed, as when only unskilled exploration of a material is possible.

If we remove the educationally unsound basic craft course that seeks to teach technique for its own sake, what are we to put in its place?

Surely it is possible to plan a basic course, say in woodwork, around a series of exercises designed to expose the nature of the wood, which could then be recorded for artistic, or for that matter utilitarian or scientific purposes.

For example:

1. A basic planing exercise whose object is to produce long curling aesthetically pleasing shavings.

2. A chiselling and sawing exercise aimed at exposing different patterns on the wood surface, that can be recorded and developed for designs in painting, prints, weaving and pottery.

3. More specifically than above, exercises with blocks of wood that can be planed, chiselled, sawn and abraded to make blocks for printing. A check on the quality of a child's planing is just as valid if a print is taken from the surface as when a straight-edge is used.

4. Exercises with different saws that produce different shapes. Some will be strong, others weak depending on the direction of grain. Broken pieces may reveal new patterns and textures.

5. Exploration in a scientific way can easily lead from the exploration of shape in an artistic sense. Simple tests on the strengths

173

of certain shapes could be made, "What is the best shape for a tenon?" Broken pieces may be glued and rebroken to discover the relative strengths of different glues.

6. The introduction of new tools could often be in the form of an artistic exercise. Surfaces could be altered by the use of:
(a) A rough plane; (b) A router; (c) A mortice chisel.

One requirement the craftsman will probably wish to make in such a scheme would be that only correct techniques would be allowed. The list can of course be extended, and similar lists developed for the metalwork course.

Experience in a College of Education brings many instances to mind, where liaison between art and craft helped to give the student broader vision. Three rather unusual examples are given.

A student was particularly interested in forgework. He discovered that his techniques were quite inadequate to produce his immediate goal, a wrought iron gate. He embarked on a course of practice to develop forging skills. All failures, in the craft sense, were saved, in the first place so that he could see his progress which must have seemed painfully slow. As his skill grew so did a large pile of worked pieces of iron. From these pieces he was persuaded to make a selection from which a piece of abstract sculpture was made. The discovery of aesthetic qualities in shapes that he originally considered failures profoundly changed his outlook. His obsession with skill disappeared and he concentrated on sculpture. All his work developed quite remarkably in its aesthetic content.

The second example concerns an art student who found it particularly difficult to work freely with a material. However, he was a sound craftsman with an interest in mathematics which led him to experiment with proportions based on the Fibonacci Series and the Golden Section. These experiments prompted a series of paintings which helped him to develop a freer approach to his work.

The third example shows the result of a few moments' work with shavings picked from the workshop floor.

If the craftsman can introduce artistic ideas into his workshop, can the artist offer a reciprocal service, and further the development of sound workmanship in the artroom?

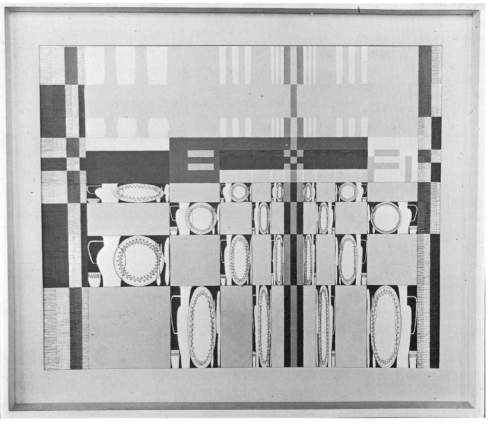

The Refectory. A painting based on the centimetre square and the Fibonacci Series

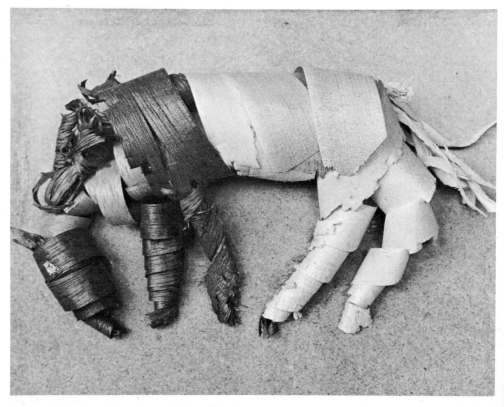

Grazing horse found on the workshop floor

174

Can then, the woodwork course benefit from an approach that linked it more closely with art, by including in the basic course a scheme that used craft techniques to expose the aesthetic qualities of wood? Whether the scheme was put into practice solely by an enlightened craft teacher, or whether the art teacher joined the woodwork class for part of a lesson were questions left unanswered. Close proximity of the two rooms could help such a scheme, while of course the development of team teaching could make it redundant.

Many organisational problems present themselves when co-operative schemes are attempted, but one simple way of solving timetable and staffing difficulties might be to make the basic art course take place in the craftrooms for the first few weeks while the crafts use the art room only. Perhaps not such a crazy idea as it sounds given a broad-minded attitude from the teachers concerned.

If one questions the use of specialist rooms for basic courses, it is only a short step to question the value of the basic course in art itself. Certainly many basic courses, cast as a sort of catalyst for aesthetic activity, often degenerate into an inhibiting medium, especially for the less artistic pupil.

There is, in fact, an unconscious deception practised in art courses that seldom affects the corresponding craft course. In the last article it was mentioned that craft techniques were often sophisticated, whereas in the basic course at least, art techniques were repressed so that aesthetic expression was unhampered. The danger of teaching craft skills for their own sake can be made clear because the skills themselves can be easily recognised. However when the techniques of say controlling paint are reduced to a very insignificant level they never disappear entirely, and therefore the danger of teaching them for their own sake is doubled, insomuch that the teacher may be quite unaware that he is doing so. Many individuals who state quite categorically that they never teach techniques are happy to show pupils how to splash, blow, and drip paint. Instead of unhampered aesthetic response, the children have become blinkered in just the same way that craftsmen become blinded by their techniques.

The universal nature of the language of art hinders our teaching here too. If we verbalise then we tend to do so in general terms only. We talk of shape, space, relationships,

volume, pressures, movements and so on, which often confuse and bemuse our pupils. We may wisely refuse to lead them verbally but we may inadvertently influence them strongly in other ways. Recently a colleague was at a loss to explain the similarity both in content and size of paper constructions produced by a group of students that he had been at great pains not to influence, other than by presenting them with attractive materials. Later he remembered that as they collected these materials he had stood in the room idly wrapping a strip of paper round his fingers!

Whether we like it or not we cannot give children knowledge of a material without giving them some minutiae of technique and without a little of our own personality rubbing off on them.

While it is true that if an art course works perfectly, that aesthetic problem-solving and exploration of material for its own sake is sufficient, we know that in practice some pupils may never be aware of the problem they are supposed to be trying to solve, and exploration of a material often becomes obscuration. Pupils soon become depressed when pleasant materials grow ugly under their manipulations. Since aesthetic pleasure by-passes them they feel the whole thing is a waste of time. The only movement in the class is that of materials passing from stock-room to waste-bin. The child's education is at a standstill.

The influence of crafts on the art course can help prevent this stagnation. The blunt chisel, the distressed saw and the unsharpened knife so often found in the art room, and the lack of oil-stone, cramps and suitable glues give evidence of just one mundane field where craft knowledge can bring enlightenment. But all the crafts offer avenues for the development of ideas either from a basic course concerned with the recording of natural objects, or a course concerned with exploration of materials. The metamorphosis of discoveries to comply with the materials and available techniques of the various crafts can bring about a development that is aesthetically desirable, and give definite form and specific purpose to a half-formed idea.

Examples of this sort of development spring to mind

A student found some fossil-bearing pieces of rock and brought them back to the art

room. Although recorded in various media, the patterns remained uninteresting until translated into three different toned veneers. The idea of using these for a coffee table top meant that further modification of the design was needed. It seemed that the modification required for the specific craft purpose gave it a quality that it had not possessed in its original form (see Fig. 1).

The toast rack illustrated was designed by an art student, not to solve problems of construction, but to solve problems of relationships. The rack was to be "at rest", and tapers, chamfers and volumes of various mock-ups had to be adjusted to meet this requirement. Work on this simple utilitarian article gave insight into problems of space and volume which a basic art course had failed to provide (Fig. 2).

Fig. 1

Fig. 2

So far I have made no mention of the liaison between crafts and art in the obvious areas of co-operation between the subjects where the craft shops may produce articles for the art room (easels, picture-frames, armatures, etc.) and the art room design posters and diagrams for the craft shop. This was deliberate insomuch that co-operation of this kind can degenerate so easily into a situation where one room is "getting something on the cheap" and hack work results. In these cases the problems tend to be solved by the teachers and not the pupils, the educational value to the pupil is lost and hostility and resentment at being "used" replace goodwill and co-operation.

If the two departments *can* manage to come together on equal terms then genuine co-operation produces excellent results. The problem of designing a woven cover for the upholstered stool illustrated was simplified by thinking of the material and stool as a single unit. Colour of timber, type of construction, the proportion of legs and rails, nature and extent of decoration must influence the final shape, size and colour of the upholstery pattern. The co-operation of art and craft department *from the beginning* of the project is essential. It is no use calling in the other department as an afterthought.

Another student decided to make a case to carry his family of recorders. The handle became a sculptural problem, solved with the help of Malay Jelutong, such an excellent timber for carving trial shapes. Holding the recorders within the box was a difficulty. The recorders were beautiful forms in themselves and were to be displayed. Their various parts needed to be arranged logically as well as aesthetically. On no account could the recorders be allowed to fall against one another when being carried, but they must be easily available when the case was opened. The interaction of both aesthetic and utilitarian demands, sparked off ideas that enabled the problem to be satisfactorily solved.

Some materials too, seem to offer avenues of co-operation where both art and crafts can come together on an equal footing. The use of Polystyrene as a modelling material that is subsequently used as a pattern for direct casting in aluminium, and the many applications of glass reinforced polyester resins spring to mind.

Heavy crafts and science are moving together, co-operation with the art department is beginning. Can other subjects too, make real contributions to each other's disciplines

by sensible liaison? Can the huge gulf that still exists between the practical and academic subjects of the curriculum be bridged? Is it possible to help the integration of subjects without incurring opposition from many specialist teachers?

It would seem that the process may well be speeded if, in the larger schools at least, we could appoint Directors of Practical Studies, whose job would be to act as liaison officer between the aesthetic, practical and academic work of the pupil. This person must be a teacher well versed in workshop practice, knowledgeable about modern and

traditional materials, sound in aesthetic judgment, who at the same time is capable of understanding the basic ideas brought to him by pupils from their academic subjects. The traffic he would have to deal with would travel in three directions. Ideas from a child's academic course could be developed into feasible models and apparatus that could be made in the craft rooms. Crafts would be looked at from a mathematical and scientific view-point that could give new emphasis and sense of purpose to the work, and both movements watched to ensure that a sound aesthetic standard was maintained and a

The co-operation of the art and craft departments from the beginning are essential

The handle became a sculptural problem

The recorders were beautiful forms in themselves for display

third channel provided to take suitable work into the artistic field where experiment and exploration of ideas and materials could continue on aesthetic lines.

Fundamentally, the ability to see possibilities in an academic, practical and aesthetic sense is required, and it would seem reasonable that a person broad enough in his approach to have these abilities would be able to develop a pupil's ideas and tidy up his designs so that the transition between these subjects was made smoothly, and moreover, without causing the specialist teacher to move far from his field of study.

Unfortunately, we are so conditioned to the idea of specialisation that it is easy to believe that Directors of Practical Studies with this breadth of vision must of necessity be supermen. This surely is a fallacy.

Many teachers have interests that weld together several subjects, and given training for this sort of work, it would be reasonable to suppose that positions of this nature could be adequately filled. Even so, it would be unreasonable to suppose that every school would be able to create new posts of this type. A move in this direction could be

made, however, by re-orientating the technical drawing course that many schools have already established.

Drawing in its fullest sense should be made the basis of the technical drawing course. The working drawing, the language of craft, must be broadened to include drawing and sketching as a method of recording at present associated with the art room. Linked to them must be opportunity and apparatus for the development, recording and communication of ideas by mock-ups, model-making, and photography. Facilities for mathematical analysis and space for observing apparatus and experiments in progress would also be required. To afford time for this approach it would seem reasonable to cut down on some of the specialist work that at present forms part of the technical drawing course. For example, problems in solid geometry often have very little relevance to anything other than examination passing.

Facilities of this sort could mean that ideas and problems from every part of the school can be sifted, assessed and then directed to the appropriate department

where the final development and realisation can take place.

Liaison between subjects will undoubtably develop in the next decade. If a reorganised technical drawing course, perhaps re-named the Practical Studies Course, could stimulate co-operation, then it might be possible to convince teachers generally that a broad approach, unhampered by arbitrary subject boundaries, can not only provide a sound general education, but can so develop insight that specialist subjects gain significantly in spite of some reduction in the time allocated to them on the timetable.

The primary schools are already reaping the rewards of this type of approach, and it would be a pity if the emotional problems of the craft teacher, the delicate sensibilities of the artist or indeed the myopic vision of their academic colleagues prevented sensible courses from developing in secondary schools.

Photographs of work by: P. Marshall, D. Lannon.

177

Learning Situations and the School Environment

Let us now look in some detail at the children's environment which we create within our schools. In fact, this environment over which we have considerable and direct control does, of course, begin at the entrance to the school grounds, but at this moment we are concerned with the environment of the child within the school building. The main entrance space to the school is of importance for a number of reasons. It is the place which for all those who enter by it, first sets the tone and atmosphere of the school. Is it welcoming, light, colourful and orderly or is it foreboding, dark, drab, cheerless and untidy? We have possibly walked through the main entrance so many times we no longer see it. Perhaps we should, the next time, look again, consciously, with our eyes open, asking ourselves what standards have been unconsciously accepted.

Main entrance spaces will vary architecturally from school to school. A lot will depend upon the type of school and the time it was built. If the school is an old one and a "Grammar" it's entrance space may well have been designed to impress upon those who enter that here is a place of learning, to be properly respected, even venerated. It will probably be solid and severe in style. If the school is a new one and a "Primary" it's entrance space will almost certainly be light, colourful, and designed to create a happy and welcoming atmosphere. It is with these widely different situations we find ourselves today. Yet in whichever we are, it is possible and most necessary to create an environment which states clearly that here is a school which believes beauty, order, light and happiness are important, and that those who enter are welcome as friends. When considering or re-considering the use and layout of the entrance space, it is easiest to do when the space is clear of furniture and with the walls bare. When the canvas is clean as it were, one can make a start. Various questions now need to be dealt with carefully. Is the space to be used by staff and visitors only or is it to be used by children also? Is it a circulation space? Could the space be a display and reference area? Could small groups of children work in the area, undertaking the arrangement of small exhibitions of interest to the school as a whole, and of interest to visitors and parents who might also wish to use the entrance space when waiting to see the Head or a member of staff? The answers to these questions will largely control the disposition of furniture, display stands, pin-up board and lighting. It may well be possible to arrange

Main entrance to a Hertfordshire school

things so that the space can fulfil a variety of useful functions. If a display-frame of the room-divider type, e.g. Versiform, Versatile Fittings, Marler Haley or Speedframe, is used, combining shelving and panels of pin-up board, small exhibitions on a theme chosen by the children can be arranged. The exhibition is a modern form of communication and children under the guidance of their teacher can prepare and set up such an exhibition. The planning, research and preparation of the material is exciting and stimulating work, and the results can be shared by everyone else in the school. This idea can be used at all levels of education. Five-year-olds in the Infants' School, as everyone knows, love to collect things and if asked to bring in things along a certain theme, an attractive display can result. The height of shelving and pin-up panels in a display-frame needs to be considered in relationship to the eye-level of the children.

It is very unpleasant to have to try to look at things which are high up, partly hidden by a shelf. Pictures too should be hung at or even below eye-level of the children. So often one sees in schools pictures hung at or even above the adult's eye-level. It is thought perhaps that they need to be high to be out of harm's way, but surely if the whole of the school environment is a happy and pleasant one, the pictures at the children's level will be enjoyed and appreciated as part of the whole and remain safe. Certainly in places such as a main entrance space and where large numbers of children are not moving, pictures can be hung at a low level. The lighting of entrance spaces too is important. If it is a dark space it may well be best to use small concentrated areas of light instead of attempting to light up the whole space. With two or three spot lights on a display-frame exhibition, a small table and low standard lamp, an attractive grotto-like effect can be achieved. Such pools of light in the general darker space can be very exciting. If the space is large enough to divide up into a few small spaces, the grotto effect can be emphasised. Books, articles the children can collect or borrow themselves, such as natural history material, articles borrowed from the local School Museum Service or Museum, can be displayed in an exciting way creating a rich and rewarding reference area. Some of the smaller spaces might be provided with a rug so that younger children can sit or lie on the floor as they so often enjoy doing at home. Thermoplastic tiles are not very pleasant to sit or lie on! To divide up the larger space, simple display screens made of medium-hardboard and covered with felt on both sides can be used, e.g. Marler Haley Multi-screens, Versatile Fittings. In the Secondary School the handicraft room would probably be able to provide suitable screens with medium-hardboard on each side internally framed with softwood and edged with hardwood. Such screens can be used for displaying graphic work and textiles. It is important however to surface the medium-hardboard with a fabric. Felt is excellent for the purpose, and although initially expensive, lasts for many years and is, therefore, economical in the long run. If no surfacing material is used the medium-hardboard quickly becomes unsightly with pin-holes. It is best to use a neutral quiet colour felt, such as grey, for this will not clash with the colours in paintings or other objects displayed. The use of grey also avoids problems when the school is being re-decorated for felt, looked after by a regular brushing with a stiff clothes brush, will outlast the paintwork in a school.

If space permits, adjustable shelves up to about 8 inches in depth can be fitted to display screens. Slotted strips are screwed through the medium-hardboard to the internal frame of the screen. Into the strip brackets are fitted at suitable heights, supporting the shelves, (Tebrax Shelving, Versatile Fittings). These are best constructed of three-quarter inch veneered clipboard edged with hardwood strip. The veneer can be a laminated plastic or wood. If the latter is used, and this can be extremely pleasant, three coats of egg-shell finish polyurethane varnish give a very durable surface.

The use of graphic and three dimensional materials together in a display is very much more interesting than the use of one or the other on their own. Photographs, drawings,

real natural history specimens, museum specimens, models and books together provide a rich stimulating display in which children can become actively involved in the ways mentioned previously. An entrance containing such a display is not only meaningful to the children who have made it but is also of value and interest to the other children and staff in the school. Visitors too will be favourably impressed and become immediately interested and involved in the work of the school. This can frequently lead to offers of help in a

variety of ways. An exhibition on the theme "The Last Hundred Years" containing examples of Victoriana, picture postcards, articles of dress and personal ornament was known to arouse such interest that members of staff and visiting parents lent other relevant items, such as a phonograph, rag rug and a large picture of Great-Great Grandad in his Sunday-best.

In such ways the gap between home and school can be bridged: perhaps the most important and urgent thing we need to do today.

Collection of bottles made by infants in a Lincoln Primary School

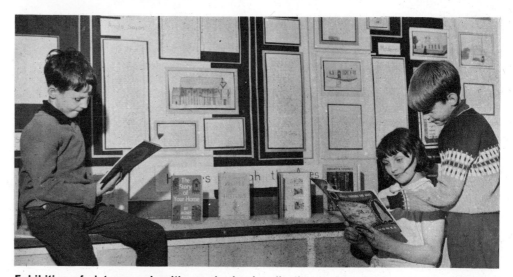

Exhibition of pictures and writing and a book collection to describe a project on "Homes" Hyde, Cheshire Primary School

All photographs by kind permission of "Teachers World"

Simple, straightforward display techniques are invariably the most effective. It is when an attempt to be "artistic" is made that things so often go wrong. Paintings arranged in diagonal, échelon patterns place emphasis upon the artistic efforts of the person who hung or pinned them up, rather than emphasise the individual qualities of the paintings themselves. Remembering to avoid placing the paintings too high, the top edges of the mounts can be lined up horizontally. This gives a visual stability to the displays even when the mounts and pictures are of different sizes. A thin string pinned and stretched horizontally across the display board on the wall will serve as a guide line.

Transparent adhesive tape is not suitable for fixing pictures on a wall. It is so tempting to tear a piece off the roll rather than to use scissors that when used it so often looks messy and untidy. When used on a wall it also frequently leaves a mark when removed.

Medium-hardboard display boarding for the pinning up of paintings and drawings is best. Ordinary hardboard is not suitable as pins cannot be pushed into it. As mentioned on page 179, such boarding should be covered with felt, hessian or other suitable fabric to prevent the boarding becoming unsightly with pin-holes. When pinning things to display boards, drawing pins are best not used as their heads are large and prominent. Dressmakers' steel or brass pins, especially if used with a pin-pusher ("Woden" Pushpin No. 170 from Do-It-Yourself shops), are very good for everyday use. "Lills", a short pin, is very inconspicuous.

Another unobtrusive pin is the map-tack (Velos Map Tacks—from stationers). These are excellent as the colour of the pin can be matched with the colour behind it. For general use, on white mounts, the white map tack is best of course.

When pinning up paintings in a horizontal row, the space between their mounts should be equal. If more than one row is necessary, a new horizontal line for the top edge of the mounts, using the guide string again, can be used for the other rows (see Fig. 1).

Where it is possible it helps to line up the verticals too. A margin between the outside lines formed by the rectangles and the edges of the display board should also be left. The top and sides should be equal and the bottom margin slightly larger (Fig. 1).

Such a system results in an orderly straight-forward arrangement and saves a lot of time

as one knows exactly what one is aiming at. An interesting variation on this system, if one is fortunate enough to have the space, is to line up the top edges as before but to leave blanks to form a chequer-board pattern. The spaces between the mounts on the top row control the positions of those on the bottom row (see Fig. 2).

Lettering which accompanies such displays can be done on small rectangular cards and integrated with the paintings, drawings or photographs (see Fig. 1). A type transfer letter—Letraset, from Letraset Ltd., Valentine Place, Webber Street, S.E.1—is excellent where a crisp type finish is needed. Type transfer lettering is technically extremely simple and requires no special tools. The letter is transferred from a semi-transparent sheet by rubbing over it with a smooth round surface such as the cap of a ball-point pen. Neatness and care are necessary, as in all lettering, but very long practice is unnecessary. Spacing and layout are important, but here again the skill and vision can be gained by a little practice and interested observation of lettering in the world around us. It is wise to stick to one style of lettering. The style used on motorways for its clarity and legibility is available in a

variety of sizes. Capitals and lower case letters are used on motorways because together they contribute towards legibility and for the same reason are best used in displays. Having chosen the style however, as soon as one is satisfied with it, stick to it. Different sizes will be needed, but to have numerous styles is not only visually confusing but also complicates the maintainance of a stock. Incidentally, after use one should keep the labels and lettering prepared for displays in a safe, clean place, as one may find one needs them again at a later date. It is also useful to take a photograph of any special exhibition, before dismantling it, for reference purposes.

The setting-up of small exhibitions in schools, whether carried out by the teacher or the children should be an enjoyable creative activity. For it to be a creative activity the suggestions made in this series of articles should not be thoughtlessly adopted. The suggestions are made in the hope that they will be starting points. As one's interest and skill in display and exhibition work develops, an increasing understanding and enjoyment of others efforts in this field will develop too. The work of the professional in shop window display, in

Fig. 1

Fig. 2

sufficient space to carry a small wire hook can be used. Two hooks should be used with clear nylon cord to hang the picture. In this way pictures can be easily changed or moved about the school without having to knock picture hooks into the wall at different places. The moving and changing of pictures at fairly frequent intervals, a month is probably about right, is important, for pictures hung in the one place for a long time go unnoticed. It is a good idea to run a picture-exchange scheme with neighbouring schools especially for small schools where no School Museum Service or Art Gallery Picture Loan Scheme exists.

Paintings, drawings and photographs can often be improved by mounting, although this should not become a thoughtless habit. White cartridge paper is very suitable for mounting drawings and powder colour paintings, but photographs seem better on card. Clear rubber gum is a very good clean adhesive, (Cow Gum from P. B. Cow (Li-Lo) Ltd., Slough, also Stationers', Artists and Draughtsmen's Materials Shops). Any surplus which gets on the mount is easily rubbed off with a clean finger. Brightly coloured mounts, when used in quantity, will always cause a serious distraction from the paintings themselves. The mount should enhance the painting not dominate it, and to have a variety of coloured mounts may well create an overall colourful effect but it is very likely to be gaudy, destroying the beauty of the individual child's work.

Not all displays are concerned with paintings or designs of flat surfaces. Fig 3 is a good example of extreme differences of style in three dimensional form.

the more progressive Museums and Art Galleries, large offices, Travel Agencies, and exhibitions such as those at the Design Centre, The Haymarket, in London will be of considerable interest. The designer will not have intended the ordinary onlooker to have noticed his design techniques, he will have been directing attention to the articles displayed. As you will be interested in his display techniques you will be looking at his work in a special way. Through this careful looking your own vision will develop. It must always be remembered that the objects being displayed are of paramount importance and the display techniques must be quiet, subtle and unobtrusive. Good display, like good architecture, is, I believe, quiet and well-mannered.

Particular attention has been paid to the use of entrance space for exhibitions. There well may be of course other centres in the

school where small exhibitions and displays can be arranged. The library is an obvious one. Corridors are not so easily used for the display of solid objects, as the danger of accidental damage is present. Pictures however can be used, both those created by the children, bought by the school and borrowed from the School Museum Service, or Art Gallery Pictures Loan Scheme. Pictures with deep frames need to be placed where they will not be caught by passers-by, but this should not mean placing them high up out of harm's way, above eye-level. Such paintings hung in a corner where a corridor changes direction are safe and create a pleasant effect at the end of each corridor as one walks towards them. Framed pictures are best hung from a strip of "J" satin finished aluminium guttering obtainable from Builders Merchants or Caravan Manufacturers; alternatively a hardwood strip fixed on the wall close to the ceiling with just

Fig. 3

Almost any corner of a classroom provides space for exhibitions. The theme here was "Knights and Armour"

Creativity in the Lower Primary Range

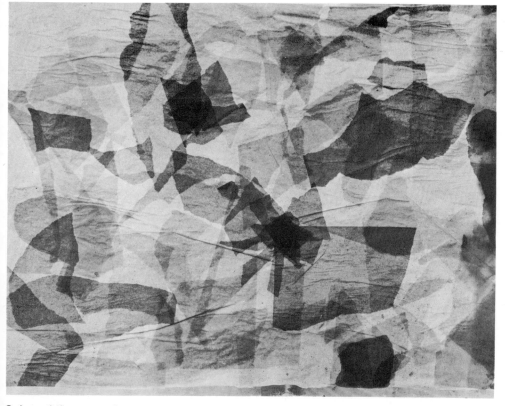

Coloured tissue overlays

It is an accepted fact that children are strongly influenced by their environment. Obviously then, the more we can do to put the children into an exciting and colourful world with opportunities for exploration and experiment, for discrimination and for making decisions the more rich, vital and alive will their Art and Craft work become.

We are a vital influence in the creation of this environment and we, and all about us, have a great responsibility to provide an atmosphere of mutual sharing and co-operation and to encourage an experimental approach whereby the children find things out for themselves.

It must be remembered that though there are many branches of art activities, they are all interrelated and overlap, therefore no attempt should be made to keep them in watertight compartments.

As colour is implicit in the child's life, great joy is derived from activities simple in themselves, yet allowing the children to explore the world of colour and learn something of new media.

Much freedom can be allowed in this, as by the very nature of the materials used, few inroads need be made into the sacred school stock! Collections of cellophane, coloured tissue, sweet papers, newsprint, magazines, gift wrapping paper, fabrics etc., can be usefully employed and most children will contribute to such collections if encouraged to do so.

A useful beginning to colour exploration might be the collecting together of articles of one colour but different shades. If these are grouped on a table or desk the children will become increasingly aware of how many blues, greens etc., exist. Arguments will arise over those colours which are borderline—the green which is almost blue or the orange that is nearly a red, a lively discussion among the children will follow. In these days of overcrowded classrooms it may be impossible to allocate valuable space for this purpose. Perhaps there is room in the corridor—then other classes can share the colour table and contribute to the activity. Again, this may be impracticable, then colours may be collected from magazines or posters and mounted collage fashion on large sheets of paper. These can either be mounted immediately they are found or alternatively stored in a box until a large number of cuttings are available for mounting. If the colour sheets are put on the wall or door, they will look most attractive.

One or both of these activities, though perhaps spread over some time, will gradually cause the children to show a "built in" awareness of colour and cause them to be continually on the alert for materials displaying new and exciting colour groupings. They should not be confined to Art time but should be constantly added to from day to day.

From the use of opaque colours found in pictures, cuttings and colour table objects, one can move into the world of colour mixing using cellophane and tissue papers on a variety of backgrounds.

Many of the children will have already become familiar with weaving and darning. If transparent papers are used for warp and weft, some very pleasing effects will be obtained and the children can discuss what happens as the strips of paper interweave. A better effect is sometimes achieved if the resulting paper cloth is mounted and hung so that the light shines through it.

An exercise which invariably gives interesting effects and yet can be managed by children having minimum dexterity, is the covering of a piece of paper with torn coloured tissue well pasted down. The children can discuss together, and perhaps

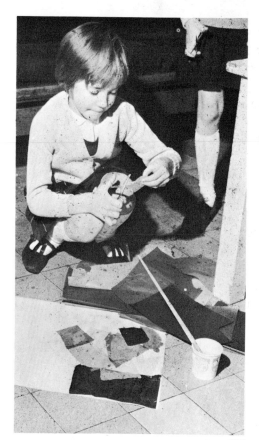

Colour experiments on damp paper

record, what happens where one colour of tissue overlaps another. At first a free choice of colour can be given and later the number of colours limited to two—the choice being left to the individual—and further observation of what happens where overlap occurs.

Other variants of this exercise are to use differently coloured nets and laces over either paper or materials, and by using the tissue paper on greaseproof paper or directly on to the windows of the classroom.

One can combine classroom decoration with colour study by folding a number of pieces of card in half and colouring the right-hand face with one colour and the left with another. String several of these units together and suspend them. It will be interesting to note

that the reflected light from one face will alter the hue of the other.

Let the children look at their colour experiments through cellophane or observe the changes that appear when the light passes through a prism on to their work.

The children could now begin to carry out their experiments with brush and colour. By placing two wet colours next to each other and watching the result, let them now see, for example, that blue and yellow will result in green where the two colours have run. Some of the children might find it helpful to work on wet paper which offers many possibilities of colour blending and some may like to paint on coloured tissue.

The children can further experiment by painting areas of varying density. Density

of colour can also be shown by folding pieces of cellophane, tissue or net, and mounting them on white paper.

Much useful enjoyment can be obtained by collecting the findings of the class into a chart or book compiled by themselves showing by overlapping that, for example, red and yellow make orange, and blue and yellow make green. It can also be shown that by adding a layer of blue the green darkens and so on.

Surrounded by the results of their experiments they will have a heightened awareness of colour and texture which will enrich the whole of their day to day environment and thus give a new meaning to their Art and Craft work.

Experiments with colour

As has already been shown, some things are distinctive through colour, others are distinctive through their texture. People tend to think of texture in relation to needlework materials and paper, but this is a very restricted viewpoint, for all surfaces have a texture of some sort, some well defined, others barely distinguishable. A stone wall may present a bold texture while a planed piece of wood is smooth to the touch, and between the two is an infinite variety.

However, the children are already familiar with the feel of many cloths, so it may be opportune to start inculcating a "texture awareness" by making collages of various hues of material—all the blues, reds, etc., together, thus introducing a new concept, but linking it with work which will by now be familiar. They will become cognizant of the different textures and how tonal values are affected by broken or smooth surfaces, and should be encouraged to examine not only with their eyes but with their fingertips. From here one could continue experimenting by collaging say, dull and shiny fabrics rough and smooth, those with a pile and those without, or even "thick and thin". Collection of fibres can widen their interest and include strings, wools, cottons, hair, fur etc., in fact anything from which cloth is made. Texture here will vary from the fine, shiny, lurex thread to heavy rope and hairy sisal, and from raffia to fillis.

Children of this age usually enjoy puzzles and competitive games, and this quality can be exploited by putting pieces of material possessing well defined textures into a bag. The pieces of material should be about four inches square and it is sometimes an advantage if the bag has a drawstring neck. Let the children put their hand into the bag, select a square without looking and say which one they are holding, then take it from the bag to see if they were right. Corduroy, velvet, net, lace, carpet, fur, towelling, and brocade lend themselves to this and later, perhaps, wool, cotton or silk could be added. As their tactile awareness develops other articles can be added to the puzzle bag, wood, stone, sandstone, plastic, Polystyrene, steel wool, cotton wool, sponge, corrugated card, a marble, a penny, a screw, a nail to name only a few. Care should be taken to ensure practice with both right and left hands and if the texture collection can be hung within the children's reach, perhaps beside the colour table, they can play and experiment whenever they have time.

Cuttings of hair from illustrations in women's journals

The children would now probably enjoy making textures of their own. Units could be formed "tile-fashion" each child devising his own textured tile and the whole brought together as a composite panel. The tiles may be constructed in a variety of ways using drinking straws, Polystyrene chips, rice, seeds, foam rubber, match sticks, chopped string, hair, sand, undiluted Marvin in blobs and trails, iron filings, sawdust, etc. One can even get rid of all those horrible little ends of chalk! The successful use of these articles demands a reliable adhesive. Experience has shown that Marvin (by Margros Ltd.,) diluted with a small amount of water is admirably suited to this work. Alternatively, a layer of tissue pasted over the whole tile will hold smaller items securely, and this has the advantage of adding colour to an otherwise monochromatic piece of work.

After some time spent on exercises similar to these, the children will have begun to develop very definite optical and tactile senses, while the preparation for the exercises and the collection of a large and varied selection of materials will help them to form the useful habits of collecting, orderly storage and sharing.

Studies of this kind will after a while show that surface textures are often as distinctive as colours and will stand us in good stead if printing is subsequently attempted.

A varied collection of wrapping papers

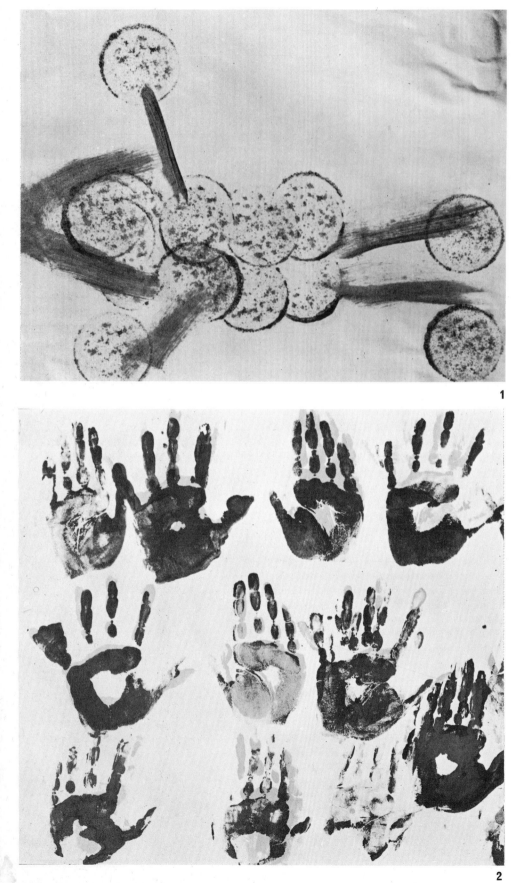

1

2

How readily children appreciate a world of colour, how enthusiastically they set out to explore its wonders, and how necessary for them to be given scope to express this feeling in their collage work and to extend it to constructions, (thus introducing a third dimension to their work).

Throughout our consideration of creativity we have stressed the vital part played by exploration and experiment, and the exciting finds it was possible to make.

Now comes the problem of recording the textures that they have discovered or made. Collections of interesting surfaces can be made, but they tend to become bulky, take up more room than can be spared and apart from this many things are immovable or too large to collect.

Rubbing presents children with a new and interesting activity and a further opportunity for discovering surface texture.

By using wax crayon and paper it is possible to make an almost photographic reproduction of a host of designs, shapes and surfaces in a matter of moments. Some children may be already aware of the principle of rubbing so that after a few trial runs to re-establish their technique, they will be ready to experiment and progress, moving paper or surface and making more than one rubbing. Rotation and overlapping, either in a controlled or random way, enable the child to make some very interesting and satisfying all-over designs.

Progress will probably be rapid and the children (who have already developed a tactile sense) will soon become "rubconscious" and will be seen running the tips of their fingers over the surface of objects seeking new subjects. Even the woodgrain in their desk lids will not be immune.

Interesting experiments may be carried out using chalk, charcoal, blacklead pencil, pencil crayons, wax crayons, heelball or even scraping lead pencil dust on to the paper and then rubbing with the fingertip.

Pleasing results are often obtained by placing the object under a sheet of paper and rubbing the paper with a wax candle or crayon and then giving the whole surface a powder or water colour wash. The children will by now have become keen and competent and will want to extend their activities and to seek further afield for new subjects.

Various types of leaves will interest them, street name plates, car number plates, wall surfaces, brass plates, in fact almost any surface that is not smooth will respond to rubbing. In addition children will continue to invent their own surface prints by sticking down various objects—old envelopes, pieces of string, washers, bottle tops, wire straps etc., and then rubbing the resultant design.

Experience will soon show that a wax crayon used on its side gives the best result and that thick objects are more difficult to rub. Kitchen, brushwork, cartridge, typing or any paper that is not too thick will serve for this work.

Our rubbing work can now lead on naturally to printing; indeed, some of the texture sheets we made for rubbing may now be used again. For example, pieces of string glued down and inked over will give an excellent print when a sheet of paper is placed on to it and smoothed over. Making prints has been instinctive with children from a very early age. Fingerprints from dirty hands, so often the cause for reprimand, would be a good place to start. The hand comes next, placed on an inked surface and then pressed on to paper. Several handprints carefully arranged would form an attractive pattern. An inked or painted sole, a step on to paper and a real footprint is made.

There are a great many "ready made" blocks around us. Fingers, hands and feet we have already mentioned. All that had to be done was cover with ink and press on to paper. This technique—if it can be called such—can be applied to things like shoe soles, match boxes, jar tops, cotton reels, nail brushes, blocks of wood, stick prints, sponge etc., and no cutting or mounting problems need hinder the child in his mastery of new media.

The idea of gluing several objects on to strawboard or wood can be introduced when the children wish to use small objects such as coins, sequins or matchsticks, which are too difficult to use individually, or when a group of objects of similar thickness is to be formed into a pattern. The children should be encouraged to think of this idea for themselves—it should not be difficult for them if they have already made texture units and rubbing sheets. Once made, delightful variations of spacing, direction and overlapping in one or more colours can be achieved.

Printing methods can be further varied by the use of cut prints. Here the choice of materials is wider than the ubiquitous potato! All

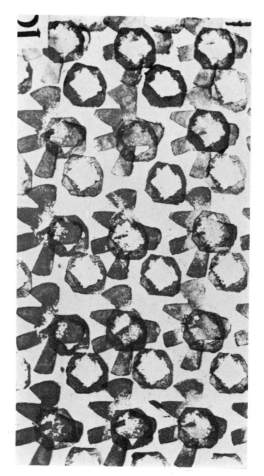

root vegetables, brussel sprouts, some fruit, cork, rubber, plaster, etc., may be used. The children will find more if urged to do so. The thought of cutting their own "stamp" never fails to interest and amuse them.

At this stage it is sometimes interesting to impose a restriction upon them, making them work with another child and telling them to make a pattern together, each being responsible for one block, the two blocks to make a pleasing whole. Many will find this difficult but the extra thought required, coupled with the necessity to be aware of, and have respect for, another child's work make it a worthwhile task for the more adept.

From abstract design they often progress to cutting shapes of flowers, ships, fish etc., and their skill increases.

Group printings can then be started. If these are put low on the wall they can be added to a little at a time until a satisfactory conclusion has been reached. Our children thoroughly enjoyed making a group printing of a football crowd—all the faces being potato prints—and a road scene being made

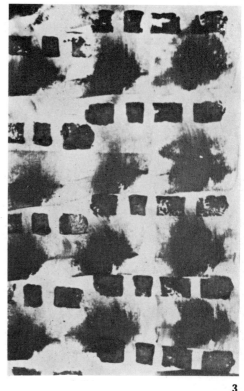

3

1. **A Pad-a-wax resist**
2. **A "ready made" block. Hands**
3. **Two patterns from root vegetables and chips**

from chips (uncooked!), string glued to wood, and strawboard shapes.

A word on materials might be helpful. Papers we have already mentioned. Painting media are oil bound inks, water bound inks, a powder colour mixed with paste, glycerine or even eggwhite. In early stages experience whispers that oil bound inks are best left alone as they present difficulties when it is time to clear up. We have found that young children manage best with powder colour mixed with 1 part water, 1 part glycerine to a fairly thick paste. This can be spread and applied with a thick paint brush and does not dry out rapidly in warm classrooms. It is easily washed away at the end of lessons and keeps reasonably well in small screw-topped jars. Rollers, although useful, are not vital for printing at this level.

Having had the thrill of reproducing by rubbing, when the "picture" appears almost magically, the children have moved on to an activity which gives them exciting results and where they can create the materials and control the results, thus opening for themselves a limitless field for experiment.

Suppliers of art and craft materials

General (paint, paper, ink, etc.)

Arnold & Co., Butterley Street, Leeds

A. Brown, Perth Street West, Hull

Dryad Ltd., Northgates, Leicester

Educational Supply Association, Pinnacles, Harlow, Essex

Keep & Sons Ltd., 15 Theobalds Road, London, W.C.1

Margros Ltd., Monument Way West, Woking, Surrey

Reeves & Sons Ltd., Lincoln Road, Enfield, Middlesex

Rowney & Co. Ltd., 10-11 Percy Street, London, W.1

Winsor & Newton Ltd., Wealdstone, Harrow, Middlesex

Adhesives

Copydex Ltd., 1 Torquay Street, London, W.2

Evostik Evode Ltd., Stafford

Marvin, Margros Ltd., Monument Way West, Woking, Surrey

Dyes

Mayborn Products Ltd., 139 Sydenham Road, London, S.E.26

Skillbeck Bros. Ltd., Bagnall House, Glengall Road, London, S.E.15

Handicraft material (including fabric scraps)

Nottingham Handcraft Co., Edwalton Hill, Nottingham

Paints (acrylic)

Cryla/PVA, G. Rowney Co., 10-11 Percy Street, London, W.1

Marvin, Margros Ltd., Monument Way West, Woking, Surrey

Polymer, Reeves & Sons Ltd., Lincoln Road, Enfield, Middlesex

Paper (sticky)

S. Jones & Co. Ltd., 252 Southampton Way, Peckham, London, S.E.5

Pencils

F. Chambers, Stapleford, Notts.

Eagle Pencil Co., Ashley Road, London, N.17

Royal Sovereign Pencil Co., Pontyclun, Glamorgan

Venus Pencil Co., 169 Lower Clapton Road, London, E.5

Pens (felt-tipped)

Mentmore Manufacturing Co., Six Hills Way, Stevengage, Herts.

Speedy Products Ltd., Copers Cope Road, Beckenham, Kent

Plaster

Superfine Dental Plaster, Boots Pure Drug Co., Nottingham

Plasticine and modelling clay

Modeline, Cosmic Crayon Co., Ampthill Road, Bedford

Plasticine, Harbutts Ltd., Bathampton, Bath

New Clay, Overstone House, Sunnyfield Road, Chislehurst, Kent

Polystyrene blocks

Mardel, Margros Ltd., Monument Way West, Woking, Surrey
(also market electric modelling tools)

Rampin (for panel pins)

Dryad Ltd., Northgates, Leicester

Sheeting (plastic)

Colortone, E.S.A., Pinnacles, Harlow, Essex

Takibak, G. Blunt & Sons, North Acton Road, London, N.W.10

Stain (ebony)

Dryad Ltd., Northgates, Leicester

Wax crayons and chalk

Freart and Finart, Cosmic Crayon Co., Ampthill Road, Bedford

Index